Post-Bellum, Pre-Harlem

Post-Bellum, Pre-Harlem

African American Literature and Culture,

1877 – 1919

EDITED BY

Barbara McCaskill and Caroline Gebhard

New York University Press

NEW YORK AND LONDON

NEW YORK UNIVERSITY PRESS
New York and London
www.nyupress.org

Library of Congress Cataloging-in-Publication Data
Post-bellum, pre-Harlem : African American literature and culture, 1877–
1919 / edited by Barbara McCaskill and Caroline Gebhard.
p. cm.
Includes bibliographical references and index.
ISBN–13: 978–0–8147–3167–3 (cloth : alk. paper)
ISBN–10: 0–8147–3167–8 (cloth : alk. paper)
ISBN–13: 978–0–8147–3168–0 (pbk. : alk. paper)
ISBN–10: 0–8147–3168–6 (pbk. : alk. paper)
1. African American arts—19th century. 2. African American arts—20th
century. I. McCaskill, Barbara. II. Gebhard, Caroline.
NX512.3.A35P65   2006
306.4'708996073—dc22   2005037589

New York University Press books are printed on acid-free paper,
and their binding materials are chosen for strength and durability.

Manufactured in the United States of America

c 10 9 8 7 6 5 4 3 2 1
p 10 9 8 7 6 5 4 3 2 1

For Our Students

Contents

Acknowledgments

Like so many books, this one has been long in the making, the subject of countless electronic-mail, telephone, and face-to-face conversations between us since the late 1990s. We now have the pleasure of thanking many institutions, colleagues, staff, students, family, and friends for their crucial aid and support. At the 2002 Modern Language Association (MLA) Convention in New York City, we chaired a special session on the post-bellum–pre-Harlem era that provided an opportunity to air prospective themes and questions publicly before a very large audience of students and scholars. We are tremendously grateful to the MLA for accepting our proposal, and we extend warm thanks to the panelists who joined us in presenting their research: Richard A. Yarborough, Robert M. Dowling, and Margaret Crumpton Winter, who shared an essay jointly written with Rhonda L. Reymond. At earlier stages our project benefited from the contributions and suggestions of William L. Andrews, Keith E. Byerman, M. Giulia Fabi, Stephanie L. Gordon, and Cherene Sherrard-Johnson. We especially express heartfelt appreciation for the support and feedback of Richard A. Yarborough, who greeted our project with enthusiasm, guided us to New York University Press, and remains an advocate and friend.

At New York University Press, our editors Eric Zinner and Emily Park have eased the rigors of the composition process. We are indebted to them for their patience, encouragement, sensitivity, and constructive criticism. And we thank the three anonymous experts who reviewed our book for carving time from extremely busy schedules to read our manuscript carefully and direct us to additional sources and models.

Barbara: Caroline is the best coeditor anyone could ever have, much deserving of an award for her patience in phoning and emailing me, a formidable scholar and critic, and a rock-solid friend. I also owe a world of thanks to many people who have inspired this volume in ways they may not even know. I convey much respect and gratitude to my former teaching assistants from the ENGL 2400L lecture sections: Billie Bennett, Tiffany Boyd-Adams, Jeanine Casler, Nancy L. Chick, Bradley Edwards, Valerie Frazier, Stephanie L. Gordon, Jurgen Grandt, Sandra Hughes, Nicholyn Hutchinson, Sharon Lynette Jones, Valerie Levy, Angela Mitchell Miss, Leslie Petty, Monica Smith, Fara Sneddon, Michael Wilson, and Margaret Crumpton Winter.

During intensive stages of this project I benefited from the laughter and wisdom of colleagues on the MLA Committee on the Status of Women in the Profession, especially Julie Abraham, Kimberly Blockett, Dana Dragunoiu, Rosemary Feal, Karen Shimakawa, Karen Swann, and Kimberly Wallace Sanders. I am also very blessed to have friends and colleagues near and far who model excellence and good fellowship: Marlene Allen, Valerie Babb, Joyce Backus, Jane Barroso, Fenice Boyd, Mary Carruth, Julia Erhardt, Arlene and Cesar Escalante, Lesley Feracho, Roberta Fernández, Freda and LeRoy Scott Giles, Michelle Y. Gordon, Michael Hendrick, Janell Coreen Hobson, Dolan Hubbard, Sylvia Hutchinson, John Inscoe, Sujata Iyengar, Tayari Jones, Doris Kadish, Sonja and Paul Lanehart, Christine Levecq, R. Baxter Miller, Sharon L. Moore, Diane and John Morrow, Lioba Moshi, Timothy B. and Eve Troutt Powell, Kirsten Rambo, Sarah Robbins, Cecilia and Jorge Rodríguez Milanes, Mandy and Jason Salensky, Elena Shakhovtseva, Nikki Smith, Greg Timmons, Elizabete Vasconcelos, Seretha Williams, Stacy Wright, and Weihua Zhang.

My final work on this manuscript was supported in part by the Radcliffe Institute for Advanced Study at Harvard University. I salute Radcliffe Institute staff members Lindy Hess, Jeff Potts, and Paula Soares for enduring the clankety-clank of Building 34's second-floor printer as I edited yet another version of this manuscript, and my Radcliffe research partner, Christine DeLucia, for amiably working around my pressing deadlines. I also acknowledge the partial support of the University of Georgia during my year as an Augustus Anson Whitney Scholar at Radcliffe, especially the advocacy of Hugh Ruppersburg, senior associate dean of the College of Arts and Sciences, and Nelson Hilton, head of the Department of English. Without the confidence and self-direction of particular students at the University of Georgia, this year would not have been so very productive. My hat is off to Keely Byars-Nichols, Lauren Chambers, Jessie Dunbar, Candace Hill, Lauren Jones, Megan Leroy, Sherietta Murrell, Charles Earl Pitts, Ondra Thomas-Krouse, Leslie Wolcott, and Rafael Young.

And last but never least, I cannot ever thank enough my family—Mom (Mrs. Inez Owens McCaskill); Sandra, Mark, Chris, and Samantha Hill; and Brenda and David McCaskill—for their unwavering positivity, and for shrugging off my crankiest writing moods. Okay, it's done!

Caroline: I thank the National Endowment for the Humanities (NEH) for sponsoring two seminars for college teachers—one directed by John Brenkman at C.U.N.Y., where seeds of my essay on Paul Laurence Dunbar germinated, and the other by Mary Jacobus at Cornell University, where that work began to take shape. I am also grateful to the NEH for a faculty research grant enabling a sustained period of work and reflection that allowed me to embark upon the larger project of coediting a volume of original essays.

I must here acknowledge my coeditor, Barbara McCaskill, who at every step has shared the pains and joy of this project and proved an exemplar of scholarship, good counsel, and friendship. I am thankful, too, for my home institution, Tuskegee University, especially my friends and colleagues in the Department of English and the Bioethics Center, for providing an inspiring and challenging place in which to think and work. This project is informed at many levels by the more than a decade that I have taught there. I would be remiss if I did not mention Tawia Ankumah, Barbara Baker, Loretta Burns, Vivian Carter, Fannie Cooley, Frances Krouse, Connie Price, Muhjah Shakir, John Stone, and Frank Toland in particular for all they have taught me. I would also like to thank the dean of the College of Liberal Arts and Education, Benjamin L. Benford, for his steady support, and former English Department secretary, Dorothy Wilson, and secretaries in the dean's office, Mary Parmer and Marie Hunter, for all their help. Most of all, however, I must thank my students: their questions have helped to remind me always of my overriding purpose in undertaking this book.

For their assistance in my research, I gratefully acknowledge the staffs of the Ohio Historical Society in Columbus, Ohio; the Paul Laurence Dunbar historical site in Dayton, Ohio; the Auburn University Library, Auburn, Alabama; and the Tuskegee University Library and Archives, Tuskegee, Alabama—especially Deborah Haile, Cynthia B. Wilson, and the late Sandra G. Peck.

I also owe a long-standing debt of gratitude to mentors and friends, most of whom live far from Alabama. They include Sharon L. Davie, Peggy Howland, Donna Landry, Heidi Nicholas, Alan and Jill Schrift,

Kathryn R. Stafford and Jeff Crespi, Rosemarie Garland Thomson, and Cheryl B. Torsney. Since 1994, the Constance Fenimore Woolson Society has combined scholarly exchange with spirited camaraderie, and I thank them all for their warm encouragement. I am very glad to acknowledge as well my Auburn Sangha for their practical as well as moral support: John Clifton, Steve Dobson, Michael Gray, Peter Harzem, Julia Kjelgaard, Jolly Roberts, Conrad and Janice Ross, and Garth Stauffer. My greatest debt, though, is to those friends and family whose material and emotional backing I have needed the most and who have given me more than I can ever repay, especially during the last difficult year of this project: Judy Troy and Miller Solomon, Leonard Ortmann and Rebecca Davis, Barb Baker, Eve Stalker, and Gwendolyn Jones—and my family, especially my brothers, Jim and Bob Gebhard, my sister, Elaine Gebhard, and my parents, Jim and Joan Gebhard.

Introduction

Caroline Gebhard and Barbara McCaskill

Charles Waddell Chesnutt (1858–1932) recognized the peculiar "in-between" status of the years 1877 to 1919.[1] Flanked by the end of Reconstruction and the end of World War I, this period bore witness simultaneously to some of the brightest creations in African American culture and one of the darkest periods in its history. He christened this time "Post-Bellum–Pre-Harlem," since it looked back to antebellum years and forward to a future glimpsed but not yet codified by the term "Harlem Renaissance." Chesnutt wrote that he had lived to see the flourishing of Harlem and a public much more receptive to serious Negro fiction than when he published his first book, *The Conjure Woman* (1899), some thirty years earlier; yet its reissue in 1929 belies the conception of the Harlem Renaissance as a sudden development with little relationship to the era that preceded it. Moreover, from Chesnutt's discussion with his mentors, the *Atlantic Monthly* editors Walter Hines Page and William Dean Howells, we know that there were crossover African American writers who achieved recognition and fame among both white and black readers before Langston Hughes (b. 1891), Zora Neale Hurston (b. 1902), and the other "New Negro" literati.

The thirty years or so between the collapse of Radical Reconstruction in 1877 and the close of World War I were once simply labeled "The Dark Ages of Recent American History"[2] or "The Decades of Disappointment," for the increased violence and de facto racial segregation that has come to define them.[3] This negative judgment of the period has persisted, even though in these years a striking number of black Americans riveted national attention for their creativity and vision: most famously, Booker T. Washington (1856–1915) and W. E. B. Du Bois (1868–1963) but also writers such as Paul Laurence Dunbar (1872–1906) and Frances Ellen Watkins Harper (1825–1911), artists such as Henry Ossawa Tanner (1859–1937) and Edmonia Lewis (1845–1911), and crusaders like Ida Wells-Barnett (1862–1931), who spent most of her adult life agitating against lynching. No less influential were authors such as Pauline Elizabeth Hopkins (1859–1930), James D. Corrothers (1869–1917), and James Weldon Johnson (1871–1938), who were far better known in black circles and largely invisible to white audiences. Nevertheless, because Radical Reconstruction failed to create a truly "democratic, interracial order,"[4] this era has often been seen as the "nadir" for African Americans in the United States. Historian Rayford W. Logan's oft-quoted 1954 book, *The Negro in American Life and Thought: The Nadir, 1877–1901,* has given the post-bellum–pre-Harlem period its most enduring and misleading name.[5]

There is no denying that the court-backed establishment of segregation in the South and the withdrawal of federal troops led to crippling disenfranchisement of a newly freed people in this region, and to widespread discrimination everywhere in the nation. It also unleashed a national epidemic of racial violence: by most historians' reckoning, rituals of "lynching and sadistic torture" with "black men and women as the principal victims" peaked in the United States during the 1890s.[6]

Yet focusing exclusively on black victimization and de facto slavery gives us an incomplete picture of these critical years in America's history. In these decades, African Americans sustained and strengthened the vocal press and bedrock spiritual institutions they had organized during slavery, built new educational institutions, and created networks of political and social leadership to resist both the illegal and legal violence aimed at keeping them from full and equal participation in the nation's life.

Post-Bellum, Pre-Harlem offers an overdue reappraisal of this age, reestablishing it as a crucial stage in African American cultural and literary history and a period of high aesthetic experimentation and political dynamism.

Renaming "The Nadir"

The very difficulty in naming this era, that it has not one but many names, suggests the intensity of competing agendas, visions, and histories. In addition to the Nadir or the Age of Lynching and Jim Crow, it has also been termed, derisively, the Age of Accommodation. The burst of black women's writing that distinguished the period has led some to call it the Woman's Era, while others refer to it as the Age of Du Bois or the Age of Washington, after its most prominent spokesmen. Should it be called the Age of Uplift, in reference to the economic, educational, and political policies that the race's men and women promoted? Or, for its place on the timeline, is it more accurate to see it as post-Reconstruction or pre-Harlem?

The negative evaluation of this epoch begins with the architects of the Harlem Renaissance. In *The New Negro* (1925), the book that helped launch the Renaissance, Alain Locke declares, "the Negro too, for his part, has idols of the tribe to smash."[7] Responding to Locke's imperative, the critic William Stanley Braithwaite calls the celebrated post-bellum–pre-Harlem poet Paul Laurence Dunbar "the end of a régime, and not the beginning." Dunbar, he insists, embodies "the limited experience of a transitional period, the rather helpless and still subservient era of testing freedom."[8] According to Braithwaite, it is the generation of Harlem Renaissance writers, "the brilliant succession and maturing powers of Fenton Johnson, Leslie Pinckney Hill, Everett Hawkins, Lucien Watkins, Charles Bertram Johnson, Joseph [Seamon] Cotter, Georgia Douglas Johnson, Roscoe Jameson and Anne Spencer [that] bring us at last to Claude McKay and [younger] poets" who mark "the first real masterful accent in Negro poetry."[9]

Literary historians and critics have long followed Locke and Braithwaite in formulating negative judgments of the post-bellum–pre-Harlem epoch as a whole. For example, in *A History of Afro-American Literature*, Volume 1, *1746–1895*, Blyden Jackson echoes Rayford W. Logan: between "The Age of the Abolitionists" and "The Age of the Harlem Renaissance," Jackson inserts "The Age of the Negro Nadir," though his dates—like Logan's—allow him to exempt Du Bois's most famous work, *The Souls of Black Folk* (1903), from this alleged cultural low.[10] Dickson D. Bruce Jr., in his *Black American Writing from the Nadir: The Evolution of a Literary Tradition, 1877–1915*, notes that "a great deal of creative work was done by black Americans" during this period,[11] but still judges it as ultimately limited.

Yet, Locke and Braithwaite's formulation of the preceding era as a time of accommodation and passivity, of false white idols and thus a literary as well as political failure, does not take into account their stake, and that of others, in casting the Harlem Renaissance as a "new" birth for black artists. Not surprisingly as well, this agenda coincided with the dominant culture's rejection of its immediate past, which it also found guilty of timidity and so-called gentility; thus white writers of the period—such as William Dean Howells and Sarah Orne Jewett—and especially women writers, were similarly discounted.[12]

Part of the success of the "Harlem Renaissance" lies in its explicit alignment with a specific cultural space.[13] Celebrating black cultural renewal in these terms helped black America envision a capital, a mecca, a ground to stand on, a dream to believe in. Ironically, though, what Harlem once stood for—community, social mobility, cultural renewal, safety—may today be read in the "reverse migrations" of African Americans to southern "chocolate cities" such as Charlotte, Atlanta, and Nashville, though Harlem, too, is poised to undergo yet another rebirth. Nevertheless, despite the continuing importance of Harlem as both symbol and reality, to let the creators of the "New Negro" movement in Harlem set the terms for retelling the history of African American cultural production, especially of the period immediately preceding it, is to fail to do justice to the work of a previous generation, and to overlook the long "foreground" that made a Harlem Renaissance thinkable at all.

Some scholars have argued for a more expansive definition of the Harlem Renaissance, citing the appearance of *Souls of Black Folk* well before the 1920s and the "trope of the New Negro"[14] at the turn of the nineteenth century. But such an interpretation splits off the Woman's Era from the post-bellum–pre-Harlem years as well as severs the ties that bound a generation together. We should not forget that many of the men and women frequently associated with the Harlem Renaissance—including Du Bois, James Weldon Johnson, and Alice Dunbar-Nelson (1875–1935)—had been born between 1862 and 1875, and often to parents who had been slaves. Much was expected of them, and they refused to set their sights low. Some, like Du Bois and James Weldon Johnson, participated in Harlem's Renaissance well into midlife, unlike their useful colleagues who fit more squarely into its confines, like Claude McKay (b. 1889), Zora Neale Hurston, Langston Hughes, and Dorothy West (b. 1907). Nevertheless, literally and figuratively, the first children born out of bondage collectively made a mark on their own time, many before they were thirty.

Du Bois is only one of many. Washington and Olivia A. Davidson (1854–1889) cofounded Tuskegee Normal School, the first school exclusively run by African Americans, in 1881; Wells-Barnett claimed international attention with her treatise *Southern Horrors: Lynch Law in All Its Phases*, in 1892. Three years later, the first national organization of black women was constituted, and in 1896, the membership elected Mary

Church Terrell (1863–1954) president of the National Association of Colored Women. Her classmate at Oberlin, Anna Julia Cooper (1858?–1964), wrote *A Voice from the South* (1892), an early African American feminist work, and became one of only a handful of women speakers at the first Pan African Conference in London in 1900. This era, too, witnessed the first organizations devoted to black history and culture. Alexander Crummell (1819–1898) established the American Negro Academy in 1897; Arthur A. Schomburg (1874–1938) and John E. Bruce (1856–1924) started the Negro Society for Historical Research in 1911; and in 1915, Carter G. Woodson (1875–1950) and colleagues founded the Association for the Study of Negro Life and History, which "for many years [sponsored] the leading black-owned press in the United States."[15] This generation of writers and leaders not only pioneered black national and international studies; they were also very much part of their own time. In moving to large, urban centers, these men and women mirrored the transformation of America from a rural to an urban and industrialized society at the turn of the twentieth century, anticipating later mass black migrations to urban, northern centers. Moreover, they were sharply attuned to developments in science and technology that were fast changing the entire planet. As Robert Hughes has written, "the speed at which culture reinvented itself through technology in the last quarter of the nineteenth century and the first decades of the twentieth century seems almost preternatural"; he notes that the camera, the car, the radio, the electric light, the moving picture, the airplane, and the principle of the rocket drive were all invented or discovered before 1900.[16] At the same time, the United States was closing its last territorial frontiers and fighting the last of its Indian battles. As America emerged as a world power, at home it faced inequities created by child labor, sweatshops, sharecropping, and the boom and bust cycles of largely unchecked corporate greed. As workers, immigrants, women, and indigenous peoples struggled for greater freedoms and opportunities, so, too, did African Americans.

While it remains difficult to decide what to call the post-bellum–pre-Harlem era, new scholarship has begun to question the frequent dismissal of this period as one of "artistic loss and setback."[17] Responsible for much renewed interest in post-bellum–pre-Harlem writers are pathbreaking scholars such as William L. Andrews, Houston Baker, Elsa Barkley Brown, Hazel V. Carby, Barbara Christian, Anne duCille, Frances Smith Foster, Henry Louis Gates Jr., Paula Giddings, Beverly Guy-Sheftall, Darlene Clark Hine, Gloria T. Hull, Nellie Y. McKay, Deborah E. McDowell, Nell Irvin

Painter, Carla L. Peterson, Marjorie Pryse, Arnold Rampersad, Hortense Spillers, Robert B. Stepto, Dorothy Sterling, Claudia Tate, Mary Helen Washington, and Richard A. Yarborough, among others. In particular, their scholarship on black women's writing has revealed that this period is called the Woman's Era for good reason. What perhaps has secured this finding, however, is not a single book by a contemporary scholar but a series of recovered primary works. The thirty-eight volumes of the Schomburg Library of Nineteenth-Century Black Women Writers, with Gates serving as general editor, reintroduced authors such as Wells-Barnett, Harper, Hopkins, and Cooper alongside lesser known poets, novelists, and memoirists such as Octavia V. Rogers Albert (1824–c. 1890), Amelia E. Johnson (1858–1922), and Olivia Ward Bush-Banks (1869–1944).

At the same time, full-length studies reassessing more generally the cultural work and major figures of this era began to appear in the 1990s. One thinks of Eric Sundquist's *To Wake the Nations: Race in the Making of American Literature* (1993); David Levering Lewis's two-volume, Pulitzer Prize–winning *W. E. B. Du Bois: Biography of a Race, 1868–1919* (1993); Kevin K. Gaines's *Uplifting the Race: Black Leadership, Politics, and Culture in the Twentieth Century* (1996); and Houston A. Baker Jr.'s *Turning South Again: Re-Thinking Modernism/Re-Reading Booker T.* (2001). And a number of other recent innovative studies—published or forthcoming—have revisited major figures and topics associated with the period. Some examples include M. Giulia Fabi, *Passing and the Rise of the African American Novel* (2001); Jacqueline Goldsby, *A Spectacular Secret: Lynching in American Life and Literature* (2005); Elizabeth McHenry, *Forgotten Readers: Recovering the Lost History of African American Literary Societies* (2002); Michele Mitchell's *Righteous Propagation: African Americans and the Politics of Racial Destiny after Reconstruction* (2004); Elizabeth-Anne Murdy, *Teach the Nation: Pedagogies of Racial Uplift in U.S. Women's Writing of the 1890s* (2002); Michele Ronnick, *Autobiography of William Sanders Scarborough: An American Journey from Slavery to Scholarship* (2004); Shawn Michelle Smith, *American Archives* (1999); Susan Harris Smith and Melanie Dawson, *The American 1890s* (2000); Karen Sotiropoulos, *Staging Race: Black Cultural Politics before the Harlem Renaissance, 1893–1915* (forthcoming); Siobhan B. Somerville, *Queering the Color Line: Race and the Invention of Homosexuality in American Culture* (2000); and Maurice O. Wallace's *Constructing the Black Masculine: Identity and Ideality in African American Men's Literature and Culture, 1775–1995* (2002).

Re-Reading Post-Bellum–Pre-Harlem African American Culture

Although African American historians have applied the term "renaissance" almost exclusively to the literary and artistic production of Harlem from the end of World War I through the Depression, periods of "intense literary and artistic production" and "intellectual awakening" are not confined, Carby asserts, "only to Harlem or to the twenties."[18] She notes that the focus on Harlem has overshadowed "earlier attempts of black intellectuals to assert their collective presence."[19]

Moreover, the idea of a "renaissance" itself suggests a particular paradigm of cultural development—a sudden and miraculous flowering, a dramatic break with the past. Although this paradigm has dominated modern critical thinking about American culture (one thinks of F. O. Matthiessen's influential *American Renaissance: Art and Expression in the Age of Emerson and Whitman* [1941] and the countless studies it has spawned),[20] it does not necessarily fit African American culture. Politics—first of fighting against slavery, then of fighting against Jim Crow and segregation, and then of fighting for civil rights and an end at last to racism—has always played a dominant role in African American cultural production. In the more than three centuries since the Declaration of Independence was signed, the struggle for Americans of African descent to gain full citizenship has been, sometimes quite literally, the same struggle, just in a new guise. The staying power of African American culture has been that it circles back to its roots to renew the fight once more.

Yet even the political struggles of the post-bellum–pre-Harlem era until quite recently did not garner the scholarly attention they deserve. At a landmark conference on lynching and racial violence in America held at Emory University in 2002, historian W. Fitzhugh Brundage pointed out that this was—incredibly—the first academic gathering ever to examine this tragic subject.[21] The new intellectual willingness to confront lynching and other forms of racial violence as a central—though hidden—aspect of American history and culture also brings the artistic and intellectual achievements of black Americans during these turbulent years into sharper focus.

Now that scholars and the general public have begun to address these horrific aspects of our past, what also comes into view is not just the massive suffering of those who were lynched as well their surviving communities—though they should never be forgotten—but also the courage, activism, creativity, and resistance of African Americans of this time. We are required to ask new questions about how to read works produced during these violent and creative decades. How did artists and thinkers intervene in the racial discourse of the era? Have the models that have dominated scholars' understandings been adequate to assess them? For example, have the binary poles of assimilation versus "authentic" black identity more often limited rather than expanded our vision? Such models presuppose that black cultural production had no influence upon white America, and also that all "white"—i.e., Anglo-European—cultural influence was inevitably negative.

Those of us who theorize African American cultural production must always remember the complex cross-pollinations of aesthetic and political endeavor that have taken place on American ground: between urban and rural black populations; between and among black and white elite, bohemian, and working classes; among art forms ranging from working-class music to high art, comic burlesque to formal poetic odes. Moreover, African American cultural development, viewed as a whole, may prove to be marked more by continuity with than by rejection of the past. We risk narrow readings when we fail to see how earlier voices and controversies have shaped later ones, and how black cultural work is the product of a long evolution that has been dynamic, fluid, polyvocal, and diverse.

Post-Bellum, Pre-Harlem presents new frameworks for investigating a maligned period's cultural work, offering original readings of artists, writers, educators, thinkers, and activists who contributed to African American culture long before Harlem was in vogue. Although in many respects they anticipated and established the groundwork for the later era, it would be wrong to evaluate them only by it. Our volume offers, then, a long overdue reexamination of a seminal period in African American as well as American culture. It also yields new insight into some of the best known figures of the time. Philip J. Kowalski reevaluates Booker T. Washington in a startling new light—in the context of the reform agenda of white, middle-class women—and Andrew J. Scheiber approaches the old conundrum of "double consciousness" formulated by W. E. B. Du Bois from a fresh angle, interpreting it as a psychic split more in need of collective than individual healing. Alice Dunbar-Nelson, discussed by three of our essayists, is here reclaimed as a major contributor to African American aesthetics in the early twentieth century. And, finally, the volume explores less familiar figures, such as pastor Emmanuel King Love, educator Lucy

Craft Laney (1854–1933), and sister poets Priscilla Jane (?–?) and Clara Ann Thompson (1869–1949).

Above all else, *Post-Bellum, Pre-Harlem* challenges facile interpretations of the role African Americans played during this complex period, reassessing a broad range of creative work and introducing new paradigms for understanding the unfolding of black art and politics in these critical decades. The contributors explore an array of forms from fine art to anti-lynching drama, from painting to ragtime and blues, and from light-hearted dialect pieces to serious fiction. Representing a variety of disciplines, they raise crucial questions relevant to ongoing discussions of race and culture in America. Throughout, major themes emerge: collaboration, activism, modernity, language, race and gender, class mobility, technology. Key figures, such as Chesnutt, Du Bois, Washington, Dunbar, Johnson, and Dunbar-Nelson, also reappear, viewed from different angles. The book progresses chronologically, revealing subtle shifts across decades in the collective strivings of black people between 1877 and 1919.

The first section, "Reimagining the Past," frames the entire volume with two wide-ranging, provocative essays. Frances Smith Foster's essay, "Creative Collaboration: As African American as Sweet Potato Pie," finds collaboration and community central to the story of how important work is produced, instead of the more familiar narratives in black history so often dominated by "Moses figures." Her collaborative model thus underscores continuity in African American thought and culture, opening the way for new interpretations. The second essay in this section, "Commemorative Ceremonies and Invented Traditions: History, Memory, and Modernity in the 'New Negro' Novel of the Nadir," by Carla L. Peterson, probes the question of why the 1890s inspired so many African American novels. Black intellectuals consciously sought to fashion a collective memory, she argues, to make sense of a past haunted by slavery as well as to grapple with the agonizing present, epitomized by the devastating Supreme Court ruling in *Plessy v. Ferguson* (1896). Her essay raises key questions about the function of history in black narrative and the way writers craft hope in a time of crisis.

The second section, "Meeting Freedom: Self-Invention, Artistic Innovation, and Race Progress (1870s–1880s)," takes up the extraordinary ways in which the first generation strove to fashion themselves in freedom, from fine artists to lady teachers, from race leaders to servants, and from bluesmen to ministers. "Landscapes of Labor: Race, Religion, and Rhode Island in the Painting of Edward Mitchell Bannister," by Gwendolyn DuBois

Shaw, divines the history of slavery and the Middle Passage in the Canadian-born artist's landscape paintings, exploring the black artist's relationship to "high" New England art and culture as well as to his own community. The next essay focuses upon women of the South, the site of barbarous racial violence during these years but also the ground of resistance and community building. In " 'Manly Husbands and Womanly Wives': The Leadership of Educator Lucy Craft Laney," Audrey Thomas McCluskey offers the pioneering educator as a blend of traditionalism and activism, shrewdly negotiating both Washington and Du Bois camps. Barbara Ryan's "Old and New Issue Servants: 'Race' Men and Women Weigh In," views Charles Waddell Chesnutt—perhaps the most influential postbellum–pre-Harlem writer—through the lens of labor history, exploring the tensions between two generations of southerners: former slaves and freeborn, wage-earning domestics. The final essay in this section also turns to the South—and the question of how black spiritual leaders constructed politicized communities and an activist press amid the era's violence and disenfranchisement. In "Savannah's *Colored Tribune,* the Reverend E. K. Love, and the Sacred Rebellion of Uplift," Barbara McCaskill evaluates how the Reverend Emmanuel K. Love's uplift publications in Georgia's black press blurred divisions between sacred and secular themes and challenged images of post-Reconstruction southern blacks as muted and passive.

"Encountering Jim Crow: African American Literature and the Mainstream (1890s)," the third section of this volume, addresses the way artists met the increasingly rigid color line. In "A Marginal Man in Black Bohemia: James Weldon Johnson in the New York Tenderloin," Robert M. Dowling argues for Manhattan's Tenderloin District as a center of black bohemia well before Harlem's role as black cultural mecca. In the second essay, "Jamming with Julius: Charles Chesnutt and the Post-Bellum–Pre-Harlem Blues," Barbara A. Baker also explores the role of music in challenging the color line, placing Chesnutt in the context of the blues, the American musical form that emerged at the turn of the twentieth century in the rural South. The final two essays of this section offer divergent readings of Paul Laurence Dunbar, though both emphasize genteel pressures upon fin-de-siècle black women's writing. Paula Bernat Bennett, in "Rewriting Dunbar: Realism, Black Women Poets, and the Genteel," rereads the trope of gentility in black women's poetry as a complex figure, as poets were torn between genteel ideals and their desire to speak the raw truth of black women's lives. However, Dunbar's fidelity to genteel aesthetics, she argues, compromised his ability to represent the harsher aspects of both pre- and post-Emancipation life. Taking a very different tack, Caroline Gebhard, in "Inventing a 'Negro Literature': Race, Dialect, and Gender in the Early Works of Paul Laurence Dunbar, James Weldon Johnson, and Alice Dunbar-Nelson," repositions these important writers as founders of an "emerging domain of 'Negro literature,'" in which questions of dialect, linguistic mastery, and gender are inevitably intertwined. Dialect, Gebhard asserts, represented a critical opportunity for the black writer; thus she reads Dunbar as artfully moving between language registers to reclaim black dialect and black themes for the black artist, yet refusing to relinquish equal claim to the language of American high culture.

The final section, "Turning the Century: New Political, Cultural, and Personal Aesthetics (1900–1917)," includes essays on the two "Moses" figures, Washington and Du Bois, who have so often defined broad—and sometimes conflicting—visions of black aspiration in this era. Yet both essays offer fresh appraisals that avoid the temptation to contrast the two simplistically. In "No Excuses for Our Dirt: Booker T. Washington and a 'New Negro' Middle Class," Philip J. Kowalski explores Washington as a conflicted political actor, who, like white, middle-class female reformers, couches a blueprint for the creation of a black middle class in a discourse of hygienic appearance and speech, even though at times he minstrelizes the very people he seeks to uplift. The essay that follows, Nikki L. Brown's "War Work, Social Work, Community Work: Alice Dunbar-Nelson, Federal War Work Agencies, and Southern African American Women," also addresses black political actors: in this case, Dunbar-Nelson, who found herself caught between multiple strata—African American and white, institutional and public, middle-class and working-class, secular and religious—in her war work with southern black women. Brown questions whether war time is truly transformative of racial practices in the United States, as has so often been contended. The third essay in this section also looks at Dunbar-Nelson. Koritha A. Mitchell, in "Antilynching Plays: Angelina Weld Grimké, Alice Dunbar-Nelson, and the Evolution of African American Drama," theorizes that black women dramatists resisted the spectacle of racial violence by focusing instead on the home as lynch victim. Their aim was to galvanize the black community to fight such violence and their achievement, the first serious black drama. Also turning to artistic production, Margaret Crumpton Winter and Rhonda Reymond's "Henry Ossawa Tanner and W. E. B. Du Bois: African American Art and 'High Culture' at the Turn into the Twentieth Century" suggests that Du

Bois's own work shows how black writers and artists could successfully operate within canonical Western art, while at the same time drawing their deepest inspiration from the wellspring of black religious tradition. This essay reveals what critics often miss: not just African American writers, but visual artists as well, meld "high" Western art themes and techniques with traditional black spiritual forms.

The concluding essay in this volume shifts the focus from historicist reframings of key figures and moments to an astute reconsideration of the rhetoric of a single work, arguably one of the most important works ever written in America, *The Souls of Black Folk*. It is fitting that Andrew J. Scheiber gestures here towards a revised analysis of the central terms of Du Bois's thought—"folk," "consciousness," and "culture"—terms that have dominated discourse about African American literature in the twentieth century. He analyzes how Du Bois positions black southern culture as the highest expression of American cultural ideals in "The Folk, the School, and the Marketplace: Locations of Culture in *The Souls of Black Folk*." He argues, however, that Du Bois goes beyond valorizing black vernacular culture: terms such as "white" and "black" serve multiple and sometimes incommensurate aspects of Du Bois's argument, whose larger purpose, Scheiber writes, is to claim continuity, rather than a disjunction, between vernacular and learned culture as a norm of psychic and social health for a multicultural society such as the United States. Thus he reads this critical text as prophetically announcing both the Harlem Renaissance and twenty-first-century concerns with the tyranny of American global capital.

Taken as a whole, *Post-Bellum, Pre-Harlem* represents a collaborative effort by a diverse group of scholars to offer new and original perspectives on the signal achievements of the black men and women of a neglected, though vitally important, period of our national past. We hope it will serve as a starting point for fresh inquiries into the meaning of the black cultural production of this era, though we are well aware that one volume must of necessity only gesture toward the directions that future scholars may take. Certain key period figures such as Wells-Barnett, Cooper, Sutton E. Griggs (1872–1933), William Sanders Scarborough (1852–1926), and many others merit more sustained attention than we can accomplish within these pages, as do other influential cultural spaces outside of Harlem, such as Washington, D.C., Chicago, and the far West. The significance of "invisible" black homosexual communities, particularly in the South, needs to be taken up as part of current discussions of the nexus of racial violence, African Americans, and the law during this period, and additional understandings of legal, educational, and religious institutions need to be articulated. In all, *Post-Bellum, Pre-Harlem* represents significant new ways of rethinking and reimagining a time when, seizing opportunities and shaping new destinies, the first generation of African Americans came of age in freedom.

NOTES

1. See Charles Waddell Chesnutt, "Post-Bellum–Pre-Harlem," in *Stories, Novels and Essays,* comp. Werner Sollors (New York: Literary Classics of the United States, 2002), 906–12.

2. Rayford W. Logan, Preface to *The Betrayal of the Negro from Rutherford B. Hayes to Woodrow Wilson,* with an introduction by Eric Foner (New York: Da Capo Press, 1997), xx.

3. Henry Louis Gates Jr. and Nellie McKay, et al., eds., *The Norton Anthology of African American Literature,* 1st ed. (New York: Norton, 1997), 464.

4. W. E. B. Du Bois, as quoted by historian Eric Foner in *Reconstruction: America's Unfinished Revolution, 1863–1877* (New York: Harper and Row, 1988), xxi.

5. Yet often overlooked is the way Logan also attends to "the roots of recovery," or the way black scholars, ministers, business leaders, journalists, and club women gradually but successfully formed a critical mass for progressive social change at the end of the era. See Logan, *Betrayal,* 314–39.

6. James Allen et al., eds., *Without Sanctuary: Lynching Photography in America* (Santa Fe, NM: Twin Palms Publishers, 2000), 13.

7. Alain Locke, *The New Negro* (1925; repr. New York: Atheneum, 1968), 8.

8. William Stanley Braithwaite, "Some Contemporary Poets of the Negro Race," in *The William Stanley Braithwaite Reader,* ed. Philip Butcher (Ann Arbor: University of Michigan Press, 1972), 52.

9. Braithwaite, "The Negro in American Literature," *Braithwaite Reader,* 78.

10. See Blyden Jackson, *A History of Afro-American Literature.* Vol. 1, *1746–1895* (Baton Rouge: Louisiana State University Press, 1989).

11. Dickson D. Bruce Jr., *Black American Writing from the Nadir: The Evolution of a Literary Tradition, 1877–1915* (Baton Rouge: Louisiana State University Press, 1989), xii.

12. For how critics generally marginalized post–Civil War women writers, see Caroline Gebhard, "The Spinster in the House of American Criticism," *Tulsa Studies in Women's Literature* 10.1 (Spring 1991): 79–91.

13. The term "Harlem Renaissance" was enshrined during the Black Studies Movement of the late 1960s and early 1970s. As Brent Hayes Edwards has noted, the term "New Negro" was claimed by those artists involved in the renaissance of

black culture in the 1920s and subsequent decades, one that arose both in America and in international sites. Our focus here is on the success of this early-twentieth-century renaissance, not when it was named. See Edwards, *The Practice of Diaspora: Literature, Translation, and the Rise of Black Internationalism* (Cambridge, MA: Harvard University Press, 2003).

14. Henry Louis Gates Jr., "The Trope of a New Negro and the Reconstruction of the Image of the Black," in "America Reconstructed: 1840–1940," special issue, *Representations* 24 (Fall 1988): 129–55.

15. See Gary Ashwill, "Woodson, Carter G.," in William L. Andrews, et al., eds., *The Oxford Companion to African American Literature* (New York: Oxford University Press, 1997), 788–89.

16. Robert Hughes, *The Shock of the New* (New York: Knopf, 1981), 15.

17. Braithwaite, "The Negro in American Literature," *Braithwaite Reader*, 69.

18. Hazel V. Carby, *Reconstructing Womanhood: The Emergence of the Afro-American Woman Novelist* (New York: Oxford University Press, 1987), 163.

19. Ibid., 163.

20. "Renaissance" is a ubiquitous concept in American literary studies; see, for example, Lawrence Buell's *Literary Transcendentalism: Style and Vision in the American Renaissance* (Ithaca, NY: Cornell University Press, 1973); Kenneth Lincoln's *Native American Renaissance* (Berkeley: University of California Press, 1983); Timothy B. Powell's *Ruthless Democracy: A Multicultural Interpretation of the American Renaissance* (Princeton, NJ: Princeton University Press, 2000); and Klaus Benesch's *Romantic Cyborgs: Authorship and Technology in the American Revolution* (Amherst: University of Massachusetts Press, 2002).

21. W. Fitzhugh Brundage, plenary address, conference on Lynching and Racial Violence in America: Histories and Legacies, Atlanta, GA, October 3–6, 2002.

Part I

Reimagining the Past

Chapter 1

Creative Collaboration
As African American as Sweet Potato Pie

Frances Smith Foster

The stories of African American collaboration—particularly the coalitions of artists and activists who worked in formal organizations and in informal communities to articulate goals and to promote progress towards racial equality, spiritual maturity, social competence, and self-esteem—are less well known in our culture than those of the rugged individualists who succeeded against the odds.[1] Particularly in narratives of African American cultural history before Emancipation, the lone fugitive, the fiery rebel, the singular sojourner, or the inspired visionary dominates our attention. Our narratives of racial progress generally feature a heroic Moses while making it seem that half of his challenge was convincing those he would rescue that if they stopped acting like crabs in a barrel, they could become a people with a purpose.

The essays of this volume counter or complement dominant narratives by emphasizing collaborative efforts of African American writers, artists, and thinkers at the turn of the twentieth century: that is, between 1880 and that era most often referred to as the "Harlem Renaissance." This essay introduces or contextualizes those discussions by describing eighteenth- and nineteenth-century creative intellectual precursors. It focuses upon a few particular examples while suggesting that they represent a tradition of collaborative creative industry that is as African American as sweet potato pie. In our communities, as in our culinary inventions, people of African descent living in the North American colonies and in the first century or so of the United States combined the materials at hand with memories in head to feed their bodies, minds, and souls. They formed families, neighborhoods, organizations, and larger, sometimes international, networks to provide for themselves the strength of numbers and the solace of like minds and similar aesthetics. Whether in creating spirituals and work songs, newspapers and novels, churches, schools, or lodges, collaboration was a necessary and nurturing part of these enterprises.

The centers of U.S. economic and artistic dominance were generally in the urban Northeast and above the Mason-Dixon line. England and its traditions, while not the sole source from which U.S. America developed its philosophical and artistic concepts, had an unusually significant impact. Thus, it makes sense to assume, as most people do, that much of African American cultural development, including its concepts of family, friendship, and fraternity, integrates Anglophone and European elements and that its spokespersons articulate their hybridity in English. Certainly the scholarship on our organizations and cooperative enterprises focuses primarily on the events and individuals in and around the bustling corridor from New England to New York and Philadelphia. However, just as the so-called Harlem Renaissance was in fact infused, influenced, and supported by writers, artists, and intellectuals from California to Oklahoma and Florida, from Jamaica and Cuba to Mexico, Senegal, France, Germany, and beyond, so, too, one very important achievement of earlier artist/activist coalitions was the diversity and pervasiveness of their influence and effect. Perhaps, therefore, the instances of collaboration among artists and intellectuals whose energies were employed in lesser discussed areas such as the pre–Civil War South and in community building among African American Muslims or Louisiana Creoles are all the more important to recall. Thus, as a way of reminding us why discussions of the achievements of African American writers, artists, and thinkers should recognize the minority as well as the majority confederations within our common heritage, this essay begins with instances of two minority communities that must not be overlooked when the achievements of African American writers, intellectuals, and artists are tallied. The second part of this essay concentrates upon organized efforts to theorize and practice progressive racial politics using combinations of education, art, and reason. Mutual aid and literary societies and the emerging African American press provide such examples.

Among the earliest African American communities were those of African Muslim slaves. From all accounts, they were a numerical minority in this country and in the local African American populations within which they resided. However, as scholars such as Sylviane A. Diouf point out, "they preserved a distinctive lifestyle built on religious cohesiveness, cultural self-confidence, and discipline," and their memoirs form "a disproportionate number" of extant African-in-America narratives.[2] Some scholars use data, such as the places in which certain texts have been found and the kinds of paper and ink with which they were produced, to hypothesize that African American Muslims, along with African Americans of other religious and cultural traditions, participated in an international network among African Americans and people of African descent in Brazil, Italy, and other parts of the world. Their work suggests collaboration and cooperation melding art and aesthetics, artifice, and activism in ways that parallel or presage certain twentieth-century Pan-African, Caribbean, and Continental integrations and interventions by Harlem Renaissance figures such as Langston Hughes, Zora Neale Hurston, Claude McKay, Marcus Garvey, Jean Toomer, and W. E. B. Du Bois. Speculations about established antebellum international and interreligious networks are intriguing and merit more concentrated research. Still, the evidence that we already have makes it clear that African American Muslims were an important part of early African American culture, and that their writers, artists, and thinkers expressed ideas and conserved traditions essential to group survival and prosperity.

Most of the extant writings from African Muslim slave communities are in Arabic.[3] Many of them can be considered as slave narratives, for they are personal accounts of lives in slavery and attempts to free themselves from bondage. However, most narratives by Muslim slaves, in emphasis and perhaps intent, are different from the more commonly discussed antebellum fugitive narratives. For example, Muslim slave narratives tend to be much briefer and to give little attention to antislavery or abolitionist rhetoric. In this, they are more similar to those by Olaudah Equiano or Venture Smith, whose memoirs tend to be more communal, more descriptive of religious, artistic, social, and familial practices and observances. Their treatments of literacy, both in their communities and in their own lives, suggest greater sophistication than that of marveling over how they learned the English alphabet or to write their names. In fact, because they are written in Arabic and they assume literacy as a given and not something snatched by stealth, such narratives imply that some intellectual traditions survived the Middle Passage and continued despite enslavement and laws designed to eradicate them. They remind us that it was not unheard of for at least some African Americans to be literate and multilingual. In narratives by African Muslim slaves, as in narratives by many other slaves who did not choose to write in the tradition of the fugitive slave narrative genre, learning to read and to write in English were less important than other endeavors, such as acquiring a greater degree of economic or physical independence or preserving metaphysical concepts and religious practices. Texts such as those written by African American Muslims may be considered early examples of African American collaboration within African America. They seem more intended to build and to preserve community, to protect themselves and others from at least some of the disintegrative aspects of U.S. American enslavement, than to argue or plead with Euro-Americans for surcease or succor.

Among the African American Muslims who wrote and provided intellectual or spiritual guidance for their communities is Umar (Omar) ibn Said. Said spent most of his life as a slave in Fayetteville, North Carolina. The legends, myths, and controversies around him, his writings, and his relationships are myriad and difficult to resolve. Some things, however, are clear. He was a leader in his community and esteemed for his intellectual acuity. A contemporary newspaper article about him deemed him "An African Scholar." Allan D. Austin writes that African Americans generally considered him "a 'pray-god to the king,' a *marabout*, or a kind of religious counselor, to non-Muslim rulers."[4] Among his fourteen extant manuscripts are excerpts from the Koran and from traditional commentaries on the Koran, lists of family members, the Lord's Prayer, and an autobiography. These topics imply concern with conservation of religious traditions, preservation of family history, and possible revisions of identity as people of African descent now living in the intersections of Christianity, Islam, and racial oppression.

Another example comes from Bilali (aka Bilali Mohamed and Ben-Ali), who lived on Sapelo Island in Georgia. An *imam* or *admaamy* of the local African Muslim community, Bilali wrote a highly unusual and controversial text generally referred to as *Ben Ali's Diary or Meditations*.[5] According to translators, a portion of the extant Bilali manuscript excerpts a tenth-century Islamic legal work that was common in the curriculum of many Muslim schools in West Africa. Excerpts of cultural history, such as this, were essential to claiming and preserving the diversity and integrity of an important aspect of African American culture. In *(Dis)Forming the American Canon*, Ronald A. T. Judy argues that Bilali's manuscript "prompts a study of the conditions of knowledge determining the field of modernity, and within that field a special order of cultural studies."[6] Judy's suggestion that Bilali's achievements in the nineteenth century can be a key influence for thinkers and scholars of the twenty-first can be applied generally to his Muslim American colleagues also.

Bilali and Umar ibn Said are but two of several early African Americans who preserved in Arabic ideals and ideas of African Americans. Their extant texts evidence a strong, if small, community of African Muslims who produced letters, autobiographies, histories, and texts that range from excerpts of the Koran and theological commentaries to strategies for political rebellion and social integrity. As Diouf summarizes, these Arabic-writing intellectuals "used their knowledge not only to remain intellectually alert but also to defend and protect themselves, to maintain their sense of self, to reach out to their brethren, to organize uprisings, and, for some, to gain their freedom."[7] In sum, they were pre-Emancipation forerunners to those in the post-bellum–pre-Harlem era and later years. Like their African American sisters and brothers of other religious persuasions, like those who wrote in English, and like those whose achievements occurred decades later, they worked to preserve cultural values and to offer alternate modes of transcendence by, for, and of people of African descent in America.

French, too, was a lingua franca for some African Americans, and the collaborative achievements of French-speaking intellectuals form part of our legacy from African American writers, artists, and thinkers before 1880. They demonstrate a way in which some people of African descent rejected external definitions that tried to conflate and to dictate the cultural ingredients they should use. Instead of following the North Star, they sometimes sought freedom by sailing to France. However, these communities did not so much deny their African ancestry as they affirmed the African American Francophonic or Creole culture they constructed. Consideration of their art and shared endeavors provides a different starting point for narratives of the development of the African American press as well as our understanding of African American literary production. For example, the life and early writings of Alice Dunbar-Nelson become more nuanced and less odd and the chronicle of the development of African American fiction changes.

To begin with the last point, if one accepts, as did the editors of the first edition of the *Norton Anthology of African American Literature* (1997), Victor Séjour's short story, "The Mulatto," as African American fiction, the earliest extant short story can be dated from 1837 rather than 1852.[8] Accepting Victor Séjour as an African American seems appropriate since he was born in New Orleans, his father was a free mulatto from Santo

Domingo, and his mother was a Louisiana native of African ancestry. Moreover, Séjour grew up within a larger African American community than many African Americans of the eighteenth-century colonies did. He was educated at Sainte-Barbe Academy, a school run by an African American writer, Michel Séligny. As a young man, Séjour went to France, where he found recognition as an artist and intellectual. In important ways, Séjour's journey parallels or prefigures those by other African Americans such as sculptor Edmonia Lewis in Italy, painter Henry Ossawa Tanner in France, violinist Portia Washington in Germany, and singer/actor Paul Robeson and writer Dorothy West in Russia.

Before leaving the United States, Victor Séjour had belonged to a dynamic literary community in New Orleans that produced in 1843 what some call the "first Negro literary magazine."[9] *The Literary Album, Journal of Young People/L'Album Littéraire, Journal des Jeunes Gens* began as a bimonthly, bilingual (French/English) compilation of "poems, editorials, sketches and short stories," but proved so popular, write Armistead S. Pride and Clint C. Wilson II, that "it soon became a semi-monthly."[10] Slaveholding New Orleans, Louisiana, was not only the birthplace of what is considered the "first" literary magazine by African Americans, but it was also home to what has been identified as "the first Black newspaper in the South," *The Union/L'Union* (1862), and in 1864, the "first Negro daily newspaper," *The New Orleans Tribune/La Tribune de la Nouvelle-Orleans.*[11] While they did not represent the majority of African Americans in the South, the French and/or multilingual newspapers and literary societies were African American intellectual collaboratives that flourished during slavery. The newspapers, magazines, and literary anthologies of Francophonic African Americans were part of a southern cultural establishment that included or led to other collectives such as *The SemiWeekly Louisianian,* edited in 1870 by P. B. S. Pinchback, and the *Southwestern Christian Advocate,* which in 1892 published Octavia Victoria Rogers Albert's serialized *The House of Bondage; or Charlotte Brooks and Other Slaves. . . .* Multilingual and other intellectual communities off, and sometimes far distant from, the Atlantic Corridor were essential to the development of the African American press. Nor were they the only such communities. Even during the period of enslavement, in southern locations that include Charleston, South Carolina, Baltimore, Maryland, Savannah, Georgia, and Natchez, Mississippi, African Americans banded together to organize schools and societies. Founders, teachers, students, and graduates of these schools were among the early editors, journalists, and publishers of

African American newspapers and periodicals. Nineteenth-century editors and publishers, writers, and readers laid the foundations upon which were built later collaboratives such as *The Colored American* (1900), *The Woman's Era* (1894), *The Crisis* (1910), *Negro World* (1918), *The Brownie's Book* (1920), and *Opportunity* (1923).

However, the best known activity among African American intellectuals and artists before the twentieth century, like that of Euro-Americans as well, occurred in and around the Atlantic Corridor from New England to Philadelphia. The data on collaborative efforts of artist/activists before the 1770s is, as of yet, still quite fragmented and inconclusive. Collaboration began, I suspect, during the Middle Passage, for it is difficult to believe that, even or especially in those most nightmarish circumstances, there were not dream weavers, griots, and storytellers who kept alive the souls within those tortured bodies. Our earliest records of African American publications include a narrative by Briton Hammon in 1760 and a poem by Jupiter Hammon in that same year, and it is probable that members of their African American communities influenced and were influenced by their thoughts. Certainly, coalitions or societies that encouraged articulate and artistic communities existed before 1760. We know, for example, that Lucy Terry Prince created the poem "Bar's Fight" about 1746. The fragment that survives is in ballad form, suggesting the work was intended as a communal offering. Historians such as Sidney Kaplan and Emma Nogrady Kaplan report that Prince and her daughter Duroxa both had reputations as poets, and her son Festus was a gifted musician.[12] In his *History of Deerfield* (1972), George Sheldon adds that the Prince household was a gathering place for African American conversation and storytelling.[13]

There is sufficient evidence from the 1770s for us to know that African Americans joined forces to articulate, to argue, and to effect social change. There were petitions such as that by "many Slaves, living in the Town of Boston, and other Towns in the Province"—sent on January 6, 1773, to Governor Hutchinson and the General Court by Peter Bestes, Sambo Freeman, Chester Joie, and Felix Holbrook "in behalf of our fellow slaves in this province and by order of their Committee"—which was published as a pamphlet in April 1773.[14] There were African American churches formed in Silver Bluff, South Carolina, that later united with congregations in Savannah, Georgia, and sent ministers to organize congregations in Jamaica and Sierra Leone.[15]

A very good example of artistic unity and collaborative support in the latter part of the eighteenth century centers around Phillis Wheatley, whose book of poetry appeared in 1773. Wheatley's circle (or circles) included Europeans, European Americans, and at least one Native American intellectual, Samson Occum; however, most relevant to this discussion is her African American collegium. Recent discoveries of letters, manuscripts, and publications by and about Wheatley suggest that Wheatley herself was at the center of an informal group who encouraged, advised, and emulated one another.[16] Such rediscoveries and reinterpretations of Wheatley's works redirect our attention from Phillis, the isolated prodigy, to Phillis, the consciously committed artist and community leader. Although casual critics generally point to Wheatley as an instinctive poet alienated from the African American community and focused more on evangelical cant than on community or intellectual matters, some evidence suggests quite the opposite. As the title of her first and only published volume of poetry declared, Wheatley wrote "On Various Subjects, Religious and Moral" (1773). Indeed, reading these poems on various subjects reveals a woman deeply concerned about issues such as art, philosophy, and political action. One need only scan the titles or read the contents of such works as "To the King's Most Excellent Majesty," "To the Right Honourable William, Earl of Dartmouth," or "To His Excellency General Washington" to realize her interest in and readiness to address major political figures of her time. "To the University of Cambridge, in New-England," "To Maecenas," "Deism," "Atheism," "Liberty and Peace," and the newly rediscovered "Ocean" illustrate her intellectual and aesthetic priorities. In fact, in "Ocean" Wheatley uses the occasion of the ship's captain casually killing an eagle who flew too close to reflect upon the meaning of seemingly random destruction of weaker humans and animals. In so doing, Wheatley reveals herself as a philosopher, and she may also be considered one of our earliest published ecological conservationists.

Phillis Wheatley's artistic/activist efforts were consciously collaborative and often racially specific.[17] For example, her poem "To S. M., a Young *African* Poet, on Seeing His Works" not only affirms her acquaintance with the works of other African American artists but also declares her idea of reciprocal inspiration and common goals. Wheatley's Boston readers would have identified "S. M." as Scipio Moorhead, another African American artist whose artistic "genius" was acknowledged by colonial New Englanders.[18] The odds are great that especially if, as many scholars believe, Scipio Moorhead drew the frontispiece portrait of Wheatley in her book, not only did Phillis the enslaved African American poet know and support

Scipio the enslaved African American painter, but she also saw their efforts as having an element of collaborative conspiracy.

In "To S. M.," the poet tells the painter that his work stimulates her imagination, that their works "conspire." She declares,

> When first thy pencil did those beauties give,
> And breathing figures learnt from thee to live,
> How did those prospects give my soul delight,
> A new creation rushing on my sight? (3–6)[19]

Later, she embraces the commonality of artistic concerns across genres by exclaiming,

> . . . may the painter's and the poet's fire,
> To aid thy pencil, and thy verse conspire! (9–10)[20]

With lines such as these, which suggest an idea of art as both aesthetic pleasure and racial affirmation, Wheatley is participating in conversations attributed to the Enlightenment in ways beyond the religious and theological. Rosemary Fithian Guruswamy's statement that "[b]ecause of the double Enlightenment appeal to . . . Christianity and . . . natural law that spoke for the essentiality of freedom, African Americans were able to participate openly in a related thread about 'black uplift,'"[21] has a particular resonance when applied to Phillis Wheatley's work.

The "essentiality of freedom" and racial relevance for this particular poem begins with its title. "S. M." is deliberately and directly identified as a "young *African* artist" (emphasis in original). This invites readers to approach this writing as being about art and especially about its function and effects for African American artists and for the tradition they are creating.

A few years after the publication of Wheatley's book, another African American writer, Jupiter Hammon, suggests that Wheatley's circle encompassed more than the African Americans of Boston, Massachusetts. Jupiter Hammon wrote from Hartford, Connecticut, to "Miss Phillis Wheatly [*sic*], Ethiopian Poetess, in Boston" on behalf of himself and "a number of his friends, who desire to join with him in their best regards to Miss Wheatly [*sic*]." In the poem entitled "An Address to Miss Phillis Wheatly, Ethiopian Poetess . . ." (1778), Hammon and friends first present a philosophical or theological premise that Wheatley is where and what she is because of God's "tender mercies." They advise this prominent African American woman that because she is a role model, she therefore has particular responsibilities to maintain her piety, both private and public: "That thou a pattern still might be, / To youth of Boston town" (21–22).[22] The word "still" acknowledges her current position as well as its vulnerability and the necessity that she protect and defend her exemplary status. "An Address to Miss Phillis Wheatly, Ethiopian Poetess . . ." is both a tribute and a testimony from one group of African Americans in one New England colony to and about their colleague in another New England colony. It suggests, at the very least, an informal concept of community and collaboration among colonial African Americans.[23]

Despite or maybe because of their slave status, Phillis Wheatley, Scipio Moorhead, Jupiter Hammon, his friends, and others understood themselves as part of a community of African American writers, artists, and thinkers who could perhaps write things right. Theirs was undoubtedly an informal or virtual mutual aid society. By the end of the eighteenth century, among freer African Americans, such communities were more formally constituted and such collaborations were more public. The work of twentieth-century archivists and academics such as Dorothy Porter and Elizabeth McHenry suggests that formalized mutual aid societies agreed with the informal evidence from our colonial artist and authors that "stimulation of reading and spreading useful knowledge" were essential to social, political, spiritual, and moral health.[24] Whether their primary or original purpose was to offer health and death insurance, support local churches, or simply provide social contact, such societies generally encouraged the creation and expression of elocution and oratory, of reading and writing, of public articulation of ideas and ideals about personal and public concerns. Like the characters who arrange the "conversaziones" depicted in late-nineteenth-century works such as Frances E. W. Harper's *Iola Leroy; or, Shadows Uplifted* (1892), these groups organized lectures and discussions and urged members to read and write, listen and critique for themselves and for others that which they read and heard. Documents such as bylaws, minutes, membership rolls, and program announcements make more visible ways in which African Americans writers, artists, and thinkers organized and collaborated not only by providing the occasions for individual members to publish their creations and argue their ideas but also by creating reading rooms, libraries, and schools. The societies did not operate in a vacuum, nor were they isolated oases existing in a desert of ignorance unaffected by and unaffecting the larger environment.

The chronology of their establishments suggests that the success of some sparked the creation of others. For example, the Reading Room Society in Philadelphia began in 1828, the Clarkston Society of New York started the next year, the Theban Literary Society of Pittsburgh was founded in 1831, and the Afric-American Female Intelligence Society of Boston dates from 1832.

Reading rooms and literary and intelligence societies developed authors and audiences whose influence extended well beyond their memberships. It was the Female and Literary Society of Philadelphia that provided many of the poems, essays, and other writings published in Garrison's *Liberator* during 1831–1832, and the Afric-American Female Intelligence Society was a site of one of Maria W. Stewart's first public lectures. In much the same way as the African American women's groups gave money and spaces for Ida B. Wells to lecture and publish her work at the end of the nineteenth century, so too did many mutual aid groups, literary societies, and other community organizations support artist/activists in the beginning of that century. They not only supported artist/activists but also created them, and they created the necessary public venues for their work. The connections among W. E. B. Du Bois, James Weldon Johnson, Alain Locke, and others underlay the founding and success of journals such as *Crisis* and *Opportunity*, whose salubrious effects upon the careers of Langston Hughes, Countee Cullen, and Nella Larsen, and the existence of what is called the Harlem Renaissance, are well documented. Nearly a century earlier, similar connections were at play. The earliest extant African American newspaper, *Freedom's Journal*, is a prime example.

Freedom's Journal, first published in New York City in 1827, began with a consortium of individuals from several states. The paper officially began after a meeting at the New York City home of Boston Crummell of several prominent African Americans, including Nathaniel Paul, an Albany, New York, abolitionist minister; A.M.E. Bishop Richard Allen of Philadelphia; John B. Russwurm, recently graduated from Bowdoin College in Maine; William Hamilton, chairman of the People of Color of New York; and the Reverend Samuel Cornish, former missionary to Maryland slaves and founding member of several abolitionist societies. About the same time, in Boston, David Walker hosted an auxiliary meeting with Thomas Paul (Nathaniel's brother), James Gould, George B. Holmes, and others. These Massachusetts leaders organized to provide financial and journalistic support for the paper. *Freedom's Journal* was, from its conception, the result of collaboration. It was intended as a national and even international forum for discussion among people of African heritage, discussion that would produce collective enlightenment and progress. Its first issue proclaimed its purpose as "the dissemination of useful knowledge among our brethren, and . . . their moral and religious improvement." Kenneth D. Nordin summarizes its basic objective as "to produce a nationally circulated newspaper which would develop a sense of fraternity, a black consciousness, as it were, among the freemen and ex-slaves living in scattered communities throughout the northern states."[25]

Like the New Negro Movement at the end of the nineteenth century, these early-nineteenth-century movers and shakers were centered in New York City and in many ways presented New York as the symbolic capital of African America. Yet they were from diverse areas, with diverse and sometimes divergent perspectives, and they intended to chronicle and to foment artistic and political change and racial self-esteem throughout the African Diaspora. Among the "authorised Agents" listed in the first edition were Ruben Ruby of Portland, Maine; George C. Willis of Providence, Rhode Island; John W. Prout of Washington, D.C.; and Theodore Wright, James Cowes, and B. F. Hughes from Princeton, New Brunswick, and Newark, New Jersey. And, as Pride and Wilson report, during the two years of its existence, the paper listed at least forty-four agents representing a dozen U.S. states and territories as well as Canada, Haiti, and England.[26]

From its inception, *Freedom's Journal* aspired to attract and affect African Americans in all the important aspects of their lives. Its motto, "Righteousness Exalteth a Nation," can be interpreted in various ways. "Righteousness" evokes "moral and religious improvement." The word "Nation" applies to the United States in which they lived and of which they demanded actions in accordance with the idealistic words of its Constitution and Declaration of Independence. "Righteousness" therefore implied that the United States should do right by itself and its citizens. But, if the opening editorial and the contents of the paper are to be taken seriously, "Nation" here also means "African America." *Freedom's Journal* was also about the building and preservation of the African American "nation." And to that end the paper promised to articulate, educate, and admonish African Americans about themselves, present, past, and future. To that end, the paper promised that "useful knowledge of every kind, and every thing that relates to Africa, shall find a ready admission in our columns."[27]

The paper was a wonderfully eclectic mix of material submitted by a large number of agents, correspondents, and contributing authors along with articles, poems, and essays reprinted from newspapers from the United States and around the world. The first issue combined "Foreign News" and "Domestic News" with a serialization of the "Memoirs of Capt. Paul Cuffee" and the "True Story" of the miraculous reunion in England of Mary Davis with her kidnapped son. *Freedom's Journal* regularly published poetry and essays by new and established writers. It sometimes mentioned significant publications such as a history of New England Indians published by "Davis Cusick, an Indian of the Tuscarora tribe" in Lewistown, New York. The paper promoted the importance of earlier African American authors such as Phillis Wheatley and George Moses Horton. Contributors from Haiti and Jamaica shared news of their communities along with reprinted items on global and economic issues such as "Chinese Fashion" and "The Egg Trade." *Freedom's Journal* noted births, deaths, and marriages, crimes and crowning achievements of African America. To stimulate intellectual interest and provide avenues for material success, the paper advertised businesses such as B. F. Hughes's School for Coloured Children of Both Sexes and Charles Mortimer's Shoe and Boot Shop. In short, *Freedom's Journal* functioned to stimulate and to nurture, to be a renaissance of and resource for cultural, historical, political, and economic identity and influence.

It is also important to recall that those who founded and represented *Freedom's Journal* not only were collaborating on this historic achievement, but they were also related to, or in relationships with, other individuals, groups, and communities that supported, influenced, and were influenced by the collective actions and attitudes that *Freedom's Journal* reflected and inflected. It worked because the founders themselves were veterans of other campaigns to create, celebrate, and cultivate African American cultural, educational, and political progress; and they would continue working with other groups in the future. Richard Allen, along with Absolom Jones and others, had founded the Free African Society in 1787 and in 1817 had incorporated what may have been the first African American publishing company, the A.M.E. Book Concern. Allen was also a poet, essayist, and autobiographer with a long history of collaboration with others on publications such as *Confessions of John Joyce* (1808) and the history of the A.M.E. Church, which appeared in the first *Discipline* (1817) of that denomination. David Walker, author of the *Appeal . . . to the Coloured Citizens of the World . . .* (1829), was also a friend and mentor to Maria W. Stewart, whose essays and lectures sought to stir men and women to higher education, greater appreciation of their African heritage

and innate abilities, and stronger public agitation for equal rights. His colleague, Thomas Paul, had officiated at Maria W. Stewart's wedding.
Thomas Paul was head of the African Church on Belnap and later
founded Abyssinian Baptist Church in New York City. He was also a mem-
ber of the Boston School Committee, husband to Catherine Paul, who
operated a private school, and father to Susan, whose *Memoir of James
Jackson* (1835) was exhibited in bookstores alongside volumes by Phillis
Wheatley and Lydia Maria Child.[28] Boston Crummell, the father of
Alexander Crummell, became the founder of the Phoenix Society of New
York in 1833. On its board of directors were *Freedom's Journal* coeditor
Samuel E. Cornish and Charles B. Ray, editor of one of *Freedom's Journal's*
successors, the *Colored American*. Charles B. Ray was father of Cordelia
Ray, whose affiliations included the *New Era,* which under the title of *New
National Era,* was edited by Frederick Douglass.

The list can go on. We would consider the work of the Annual Conventions of Free Persons of Colour and note the memberships that overlap
but also extend. We could talk about the African American antislavery and
vigilance groups that were part of the Underground Railroad. During the
Civil War and Reconstruction, an example of African American collaborative efforts is the Contraband Relief Agency, headed by Elizabeth Keckley
and strongly supported by community groups such as that from the Fifteenth Avenue Presbyterian Church. In 1881, the Bethel Literary and Historical Association was, in Jane Rhodes's words, "Washington's central
gathering place for black intellectuals and public figures," and Mary Ann
Shadd Cary, editor and founder of the *Provincial Freeman,* was one of the
"nation's distinguished African Americans [who met] to discuss the pressing issues of race and society, as well as science and letters."[29] The Bethel
Literary and Historical Association was but one of many such groups that
Daniel Payne and others had founded, and it was another direct descen-
dant of the mutual aid and literary societies that began in the eighteenth
century, perhaps even on the dreadful Middle Passage. But, hopefully, the
point has been made. Informal and formal organizations of artists, writers, and thinkers are intricately interwoven into the fabric of African
American history. Their social, religious, economic, and political organizations and associations led to institutions, such as the African American
press, which were essential to the development of African American art
and literature. These organizations were not always identical in their
scope, philosophies, or significance. Nor were the languages, rituals, and
beliefs of their members always in harmony with them or with the com-

munities they purported to impact. Cliques, class, and cultural differences were common. Criticism and controversy were never in short supply. There were also, of course, the lone individuals, the solitary thinkers and artists, the isolates and the iconoclasts whose achievements we now revere. But, and still, and nonetheless, collaboration, too, is as African American as sweet potato pie.

NOTES

1. This is not to suggest that collaborations among African Americans or the social networks and organizational activities of early African Americans have been entirely ignored. Many scholars, from Monroe Majors to Dorothy Porter, Benjamin Quarles, and James O. Horton, have discussed this topic. My point here is that despite a long history of alternative narratives, the dominant and more often cited images are of individual and singular success.

2. Sylviane A. Diouf, *Servants of Allah: African Muslims Enslaved in the Americas* (New York: New York University Press, 1998), 2.

3. Recent scholarship has provided translations. My comments are based upon the English translations.

4. Quoted in Diouf, *Servants of Allah*, 131.

5. Bilali's text defies easy translation, in part because the manuscript has deteriorated and ink seepage has rendered parts illegible, and in part because he used a mixture of what Sylviane A. Diouf states is "classical Arabic and Pulaar written with Arabic characters." In Diouf, *Servants of Allah*, 126–28.

6. See Ronald A. T. Judy, *(Dis)Forming the American Canon: African-Arabic Slave Narratives and the Vernacular* (Minneapolis: University of Minnesota Press, 1993), 24.

7. Diouf, *Servants of Allah*, 144.

8. Given the great amount of African Americana that has been destroyed, displaced, or appropriated, I am not convinced that proclaiming a text or author as "the earliest" or "the first" of anything means a great deal. However, when one tries to establish origins of or intertextuality among particular conventions and character types in African American fiction, establishing priority can be significant. For example, if one begins, as do many scholars, not with "The Mulatto" but with Frederick Douglass's "The Heroic Slave" (1853), African American fiction began with an integrated abolitionist story featuring a dark-skinned hero. Beginning with Séjour's story, published fiction started in French with a gothic revenge tale revolving around the psychological conflicts of a mulatto searching for the identity of his father.

9. Armistead S. Pride and Clint C. Wilson II, *History of the Black Press* (Washington, DC: Howard University Press, 1997), 73–75.

10. Ibid., 75.

11. Two very helpful discussions of such collaborations are Jacqueline Jones Royster, *Traces of a Stream: Literacy and Social Change among African American Women* (Pittsburgh, PA: University of Pittsburgh Press, 2000); and Janet Duitsman Cornelius, *When I Can Read My Title Clear: Literacy, Slavery, and Religion in the Antebellum South* (Columbia: University of South Carolina Press, 1991).

12. Sidney Kaplan and Emma Nogrady Kaplan, *The Black Presence in the Era of the American Revolution,* rev. ed. (Amherst: University of Massachusetts Press, 1989), 241.

13. Sheldon, *History of Deerfield* (Somersworth: New Hampshire Publishing Company in collaboration with the Pocumtuck Valley Memorial Association, Deerfield, 1972), 901.

14. Kaplan and Kaplan, *Black Presence,* 11.

15. Ibid., 91.

16. See, for example, the very excellent work of Julian D. Mason Jr., *The Poems of Phillis Wheatley: Revised and Enlarged Edition with an Additional Poem* (Chapel Hill: University of North Carolina Press, 2001); William H. Robinson, *Phillis Wheatley and Her Writings* (New York: Garland Press, 1986); and John Shields, *The Complete Poems of Phillis Wheatley* (New York: Oxford University Press, 1988).

17. For a fuller discussion of Wheatley as racial advocate and activist see Frances Smith Foster, *Written by Herself: Literary Production by African American Women, 1746–1892* (Indianapolis: Indiana University Press, 1993), 30–43.

18. See Mason, *Poems,* 104–5. According to Julian D. Mason Jr., a notation in the American Antiquarian Society's copy of Wheatley's book "identifies S. M. as 'Scipio Moorhead—Negro Servant to the Revd. Mr. Moorhead of Boston, whose Genius inclined him that way.'"

19. Mason, *Poems,* 104–5.

20. Ibid., 105.

21. Rosemary Fithian Guruswamy, "'Thou Hast the Holy Word': Jupiter Hammon's 'Regards' to Phillis Wheatley," in *Genius in Bondage: Literature of the Early Black Atlantic,* ed. Vincent Carretta and Philip Gould (Lexington: University Press of Kentucky, 2001), 191. Guruswamy offers a fascinating theory of Jupiter Hammon's work as pioneering "the discourse of 'African Americanism.'" Such a reading would offer additional support for the idea of continuities between eighteenth-century African American writers, artists, and thinkers and those of the twentieth. Like the speculations of Diouf and Judy mentioned earlier, her idea suggests great rewards to scholars who would give greater time and attention to pre-Emancipation theory and practice.

22. Henry Louis Gates Jr. and Nellie Y. McKay, eds., *The Norton Anthology of African American Literature,* 2nd ed. (New York: Norton, 2004), 165–68.

23. Other suggestions regarding Wheatley's African American sphere of influence come from her several letters to Obour Tanner in Newport, Rhode Island.

24. The quotation comes from Dorothy Porter, "The Organized Educational Activities of Negro Literary Societies, 1828–1846," *Journal of Negro Education* 5 (October 1936): 555–76. See also Elizabeth McHenry, "Forgotten Readers: African-American Literary Societies and the American Scene," in *Print Culture in a Diverse America*, ed. James P. Danky and Wayne A. Wiegand (Urbana: University of Illinois Press, 1997), 149–72.

25. Kenneth D. Nordin, "In Search of Black Unity: An Interpretation of the Content and Function of *Freedom's Journal*," *Journalism History* 4.4 (1977–1978): 123.

26. Pride and Wilson, *History*, 10, 17.

27. *Freedom's Journal* 16 (March 1827): 1.

28. Susan Paul, *Memoir of James Jackson, the Attentive and Obedient Scholar, Who Died in Boston, October 31, 1833, Aged Six Years and Eleven Months, by His Teacher, Miss Susan Paul*, ed. with an introduction by Lois Brown (1835, repr. Cambridge, MA: Harvard University Press, 2000), 1.

29. Jane Rhodes, *Mary Ann Shadd Cary: The Black Press and Protest in the Nineteenth Century* (Bloomington: Indiana University Press, 1998), 203.

Chapter 2

Commemorative Ceremonies and Invented Traditions

*History, Memory, and Modernity in the
"New Negro" Novel of the Nadir*

Carla L. Peterson

The movement of the Negro [is] more and more a mass
movement toward the larger and the more democratic
chance—. . . a deliberate flight . . . from medieval America to modern.

—Alain Locke, 1925

The American Negro must remake his past in order to
make his future. Though it is orthodox to think of
America as the one country where it is unnecessary to
have a past, what is a luxury for the nation as a whole
becomes a prime social necessity for the Negro. For him,
a group tradition must supply compensation for perse-
cution. . . . History must restore what slavery took away.
. . . So . . . we find the Negro thinking more collectively,
more retrospectively than the rest, and apt out of the
very pressure of the present to become the most enthusi-
astic antiquarian of them all.

—Arthur Schomburg, 1925

You know, never a truly indigenous novel has been written so far. Punches have been pulled to "keep things
from the white folks" or angled politically. . . . I have
decided that the time has come to write truthfully from
the inside.

—Zora Neale Hurston, 1951

The first two quotations from Alain Locke's 1925 volume, *The New Negro*, portray the African American looking to the future in anticipation of becoming modern. Schomburg's statement further emphasizes how this movement toward modernity can occur only by looking to the past in a collective retrospection designed to "supply a group tradition." And it insists that the Negro is not simply given this group tradition but must "remake" it. Lastly, in a 1951 letter Hurston suggests that it is now time for African American writers to move beyond an old, politically angled history to new representations from—and I would add—of the "inside."[1]

Post-bellum–pre-Harlem African American writers were, however, similarly preoccupied with the creation of the New Negro and similarly recognized that to achieve their goals they needed to face rather than suppress the past. In Charles Chesnutt's *House behind the Cedars* (1900), for example, John Walden proudly proclaims to his sister that "we are a new people."[2] But, even as he seeks to constitute himself as new and obliterate the old, Walden is drawn to his past by "a thousand chords of memory and affection."[3] The African American novels of this period turn to the historical past specifically to detail the ways in which slavery and its legacies have disrupted family lineages. They further suggest that such historical consciousness provides the foundation for growing consciousness of self. Hence, these texts mark—however tentatively—a probing of the "inside" from the "inside" quite new to nineteenth-century African American fiction. Yet, when historical consciousness and self-consciousness become too painful for narrators and characters alike to bear, the narratives recast secular history as sacred history. From a Christian perspective that interprets time as an everlasting present, slavery and its legacies are seen both to repeat earlier events and anticipate later ones, thus elaborating a history of providential design.[4]

Mainstream ideologies of the Gilded Age believed history to be rational and apprehensible, and articulated an optimistic vision of historical progress: humankind's destiny unfolds within a positivistic evolutionary framework of material and moral progress, embodied in the figure of the self-made man, whose values take shape within the modern bourgeois family. Yet beneath such complacent thinking lay an unease that intensified with the era's increasing social and political turmoil.[5] Modernist thought questioned traditional values of historical knowledge and rethought both historians' interpretations of history as continuous and progressive and their objective and rationalist methods of interpretation; history is envisioned neither as seamless continuity nor as progressive development. In *The Use and Abuse of History* (1874), for example, Nietzsche counseled the historian to "keep away from all constructions of the world-process, or even of the history of man." Yet he recognized that "man" cannot forget the past and believed historical consciousness to be essential to human life. According to Nietzsche, we explain the past from the point of view of our present and what is most "powerful" in it; the present redeems the past.[6] In the process, however, we create images of the past that serve our present and future; the past redeems the present. The historian becomes self-interested artist rather than disinterested scientist, and the writing of history, artistic composition.

From the vantage point of African Americans, the post-bellum–pre-Harlem era was the "nadir" of black historical experience, characterized by the emergence of increasingly virulent racist ideologies, disfranchisement, denial of public services, and white mob violence.[7] Hence, black intellectuals' response to the questioning of historical value was particularly complex and ambivalent. They too challenged dominant notions of historical continuity and evolutionary progress. In *The Souls of Black Folk* (1903), for example, W. E. B. Du Bois asserted that "so wofully unorganized is sociological knowledge that the meaning of progress, the meaning of 'swift' and 'slow' in human doing, and the limits of human perfectability, are veiled, unanswered sphinxes on the shores of science."[8] In addition, black thinkers well knew that the dominant culture had long perceived African American history to be both discontinuous in itself and disruptive of the nation's historical narrative, resulting in a consistent negative positioning of Africans and their descendants. In the 1830s, Hegel had asserted that Africans lacked awareness of an objective existence outside of themselves, and hence possessed neither culture nor history. Throughout the century, romantic racialists held black people to be incapable of progress because of an immutable nature that fixed them in childhood. At the nadir men like Frederick Hoffman located African Americans on the darker side of progress—in degeneration.

Yet, African American intellectuals also endorsed ideologies of progress, hoping that, with the advent of freedom and citizenship, they would finally be able to position themselves on the side of progress and become full participants in Western civilization; they aspired to be New Negroes. According to Henry Louis Gates Jr., the New Negro agenda was to project the image of a Public Negro Self created out of a willful act of self-negation, of a complete rupture with the past.[9] No differently from Nietzsche's "man," however, New Negroes could not forget the past. Instead, under the "pressure of the present" of post-Reconstruction policies, African Americans understood that they needed to "remake their past" and supply themselves with a group tradition through which they could confront the dilemmas of the present and successfully enter the future as modern American citizens. The thinking of Episcopalian clergyman Alexander Crummell reflects this ambivalence. In an 1885 address, Crummell counseled against an obsessive recollection of slavery that leads to "morbidity and degeneracy." Yet, at the same time he promoted imaginative remembrance of the past as "a stimulant to high endeavor."[10]

If modernist thought was marked by a questioning of historical knowledge, it was also characterized by new speculations about human self-consciousness and "psychological man." In France scientific researchers like Alfred Binet and Pierre Janet were formulating theories of the subconscious. In the United States, this interest in interior life took hold in the academic discipline of New Psychology, best represented by William James.[11] It is such self-consciousness, conjoined to historical consciousness, that Western philosophers like Hegel had denied to Africans. Along with other African American intellectuals, Du Bois, himself a former student of James, insisted on apprehending black folk from the inside in order to plumb their soul and explore their inner strivings for a life beyond their harsh material world. In the process, he came to formulate a theory of double consciousness that poignantly linked African Americans' self-consciousness to their history of oppression.[12]

The post-bellum–pre-Harlem era was indeed an age of retrospection. It gave impetus to the writing of African American history—in the works of William Wells Brown, William Still, and George Washington Williams—to the sociological studies of Du Bois, and to the beginning of serious investigation into African American folklore in the Hampton Institute's journal, *The Southern Workman*. This was also an intense period of African Americans' public commemoration—their participation in world expositions, their ongoing remembrance of historically significant events such as U.S. and West Indian Emancipation Day celebrations, as well as their innovation of ceremonies like Juneteenth. I suggest that beyond this body of scholarly research and cultural practices, the writing of historical fiction as artistic invention and imaginative remembrance constitutes an act of commemoration as well.

Far from being a literary nadir, the period 1892–1903 represents a second flourishing of the African American novel, breathing new life into a form born forty years earlier with William Wells Brown's *Clotel* (1853). This later period witnessed the publication of, among others, Frances E. W. Harper's *Iola Leroy* (1892); Charles Chesnutt's *House behind the Cedars* (1900) and *The Marrow of Tradition* (1901); Pauline Hopkins's *Contending Forces* (1901), *Hagar's Daughter* (1901–1902), *Winona* (1902), and *Of One Blood* (1902–1903). The paradox of the birth of the African American novel in the 1850s and its rebirth at the turn of the century becomes fully comprehensible in light of Mikhail Bakhtin's contention that the novel tends to make its appearance at moments of social crisis; the genre is "inseparable from social and ideological struggle, from processes of evolution and of renewal of society and the folk."[13] Of particular interest to me here is the cultural work that post-bellum–pre-Harlem novels performed for their African American readership: namely, the exploration of possibilities of "evolution and renewal of society" through a remaking of the past to recreate those group traditions obscured by the experiences of slavery.

I begin by emphasizing the fundamental similarity in the premise of the novels' plots. Such similarity invites us to consider the texts as commemorative ceremonies that embody the Nietzschean dialectic of historical forgetting and remembering, as the characters vacillate between the desire to forget the "mournful past" and the compulsion to recall it. These fictional narratives underscore the authors' desire that, following Crummell, African American readers will engage in imaginative rememberings of an unknown, suppressed, or forgotten past, no matter how painful. The novelists build upon this impulse by constructing their texts as sites of memory created, in Pierre Nora's words, at particular historical turning points when "consciousness of a break with the past is bound up with the sense that memory has been torn—but torn in such a way as to pose the problem of the embodiment of memory in certain sites where a historical continuity persists."[14]

To counter this break with the past, this tearing of memory, the novels constitute themselves as what Eric Hobsbawm has termed "invented traditions." According to Hobsbawm, social groups invent traditions at moments of crisis when rapid changes weaken social patterns that until then have been held together by old traditions. The invention of new traditions reestablishes continuities with the old, with an historic past deemed worthy of preservation; in the process, it reaffirms critical values and norms of behavior. Invented traditions are designed, then, to ensure the social cohesion of the group, the legitimation of its institutions, and the socialization of members into a particular value system. Hobsbawm refers to the invention of traditions as a response to "novel situations."[15] Yet, for African American writers not only was such invention a response to the newness of life at the nadir, but the response itself was "novel"; their novels struggle to establish continuity with a ruptured past, affirm group identity, and chart a direction for the future.

In constructing their texts as sites of memory that invent traditions, African American novelists appropriated the form of the historical romance but subverted many of its values. I rely on the term "romance" because the novelists themselves employ it; and I add the marker "historical" to situate these texts in the literary tradition inaugurated by Sir Walter Scott. The genre takes as its subject the recent history of particular societies. It perceives their members to be shaped by large historical forces and preoccupies itself with their fates. It is a form pervaded by historical consciousness, by the importance of the past to the present.[16] The plot typically pits a primitive people against a more technologically advanced one, forces of reaction against those of progress. But the African American romances I consider ask the question, Who is primitive and who is civilized? What constitutes the old, the new, the modern? In response, they present southern aristocracy as mostly a backward and reactionary people, while the North represents forces of progress and the New Negro embodies progressive potential. In some of the texts, the mulatto figures specifically as what Chesnutt boldly referred to in his journalism as "the future American." Finally, several of the romances indict the nation itself as a primitive society and suggest that modern civilization exists only on the other side of the Atlantic, in Europe or Africa.

If the endings of historical romances traditionally point to the inevitable triumph of forces of progress, even when accomplished at great cost, these African American texts question whether such forces have in fact triumphed, or ever can triumph. And if these traditional endings generally gesture toward reconciliation between the old society and the new—often in the form of marriage—the African American romances wonder whether reconciliation is at all possible. These narratives do invoke this possibility by depicting an interracial union at some point in the plot and tracing its familial consequences. Yet the conclusions are for the most part left open ended, as the novelists confess to their inability to write the future.

Family is indeed central to the traditional historical romance, as the plots often unfold by tracing the history of families over generations. The family constitutes a dynastic line that defines itself through linear succession, producing a sense of causality and genealogical destiny. The dynastic line is initiated by a founding father whose authority, derived from being first, is unquestioned. His descendants achieve identity and legitimacy through inheritance of both "blood" and property, and perpetuate lineage through proper marriage. Genealogical succession proceeds toward a determined end that validates historical progress.[17] It is primarily through this process that family members achieve historical consciousness; they think through the family to history and identity.

More complexly, in the African American romance the family functions as a site of memory, as individual family members work to remember a suppressed or forgotten past; the narrative then reconstructs this remembered history over generations.[18] It is by reenacting, or inventing, traditions that families and narrators alike strive to restore historical continuity where slavery and its legacies have caused a break with the past, a tear in individual and collective memory. The romances' premise posits a white man—a slaveholder or at least substantial man of property—as the founding father: Eugene Leroy in *Iola Leroy*, Judge Straight's unnamed friend in *The House behind the Cedars*, Samuel Merkell in *The Marrow of Tradition*, Charles Montfort in *Contending Forces*, Ellis Enson in *Hagar's Daughter*, Henry Carlingford in *Winona*, and Aubrey Livingston in *Of One Blood*. But the narratives challenge conventional values as they reconstruct the genealogical destiny not so much of the father's white descendants but of the mixed-bloods produced by the sexual union of the father and a woman whose blood is tainted by "blackness": the slave mother and daughter, Hannah and Mira, in *Of One Blood*; the freed slave women, Marie Leroy in Harper's novel, Julia Merkell in *The Marrow of Tradition*, and Hagar Enson in *Hagar's Daughter*; the free woman, Molly Walden in *The House behind the Cedars*; and Grace Montfort, the woman rumored to have black blood, in *Contending Forces*.

The romances ask whether it is possible for such mixed-blood descendants indelibly marked by slavery's violent past—Iola and Harry Leroy; Rena and John Walden; Merkell's daughter, Janet Miller; Hagar and her daughter Jewel; Winona; the Montfort children, Will and Dora Smith; and, finally, Aubrey Livingston's three children, Aubrey, Reuel Briggs, and Dianthe Lusk—to think through the family and claim a modern identity. These descendants start with different degrees of self-knowledge concerning their genealogical line, and hence adopt different subject positions. Unaware of their mother's slave past, Iola and Harry Leroy engage in unconscious passing, as does Jewel in *Hagar's Daughter* and Aubrey Livingston in *Of One Blood*. In contrast, John and Rena Walden, as well as *Of One Blood's* Reuel Briggs, are conscious passers. Will and Dora Smith openly identify as African American, as does Winona, but the history of their ancestry is shrouded in mystery. Janet Miller, finally, is also aware of her parents' identity but is ignorant of the legal status of their relationship.

The plots then seek to untangle these dynastic lines and probe the consequences. They question the legitimacy of the white founding father's authority and ask whether this authority may not be usurped by that of another founding parent, perhaps a black foremother. They emphasize the ways in which custom, force, and law are manipulated in order to disrupt the lineage of mixed-blood individuals: ties to white forebears are obscured and marriages to white men invalidated or hidden; properties of white blood and estate are disallowed, as black blood alone is deemed inheritable.[19] Finally, in positing the mixed-blood descendants as slavery's legacy to the nation—whether as sin or as salvation—the narratives wonder how these young men and women can lay claim to being modern American citizens.

African Americans were fully aware of the degree to which citizenship was based on private as well as public rights. As early as 1859, James McCune Smith had written an essay in the wake of the Dred Scott decision titled "Citizenship." In it he argued that the U.S. Constitution nowhere defined the word "citizen," obliging us to turn back to Roman law. The codes of Roman law properly spelled out both the citizen's public rights ("Jus Civitatis") and private rights ("Jus Quiritium"), which include "the right of family, of marriage, of a father, of legal property, of making a will and succeeding to an inheritance."[20] At the nadir, the creation and consolidation of stable African American families thus represented a claim to citizenship that undermined white supremacist ideology. In their fictions, then, the novelists insistently portrayed the family as foundational to the nation, and the nation itself as family.

At its most fundamental level, the African American historical romance challenged contemporary notions of degeneracy and progress. In all the texts, the white slaveholding families are characterized by lineage, succession, legacy, and inheritance. Yet several—most especially *Iola Leroy, The Marrow of Tradition,* and *Of One Blood*—emphasize the degeneration of southern aristocracy in the wake of the Civil War: men die in battle or fall prey to alcoholism; couples have difficulty procreating; heirs exhibit criminal tendencies, or are sickly and their survival doubtful. To shore up the decaying order, this class resorts to the invention of traditions under the guise of restoring the ways of the past. In *The House behind the Cedars,* for example, the white social elite to which Rena is introduced revives the medieval chivalric tournament as the sign of a South Carolinian renaissance. In *Marrow,* Major Carteret and his colleagues invent a white supremacist ideology to strengthen their class's very marrow. Both this degeneracy and its compensatory acts affirm, however, that it is whites, not blacks, who cannot function as proper citizens.

Of these romances, the earliest written, *Iola Leroy,* most radically challenges the white founding father's authority. At the outset, slaveholding and slave families alike adhere to expected social paradigms. While the former follow the laws of succession and inheritance, the latter are marked by silences and ruptures. Female slaves cannot procreate, slave mothers and fathers are separated from their children; the former slave woman, Marie Leroy, withholds her slave past from her children; after his death, Leroy's relatives ensure that they cannot inherit his estate. But the plot enacts a gradual shift in family fortunes. Even before the end of the Civil War, slave masters exhibit signs of degeneracy, and slave men become surrogate fathers to their heirs. After the Civil War it is black, not white, families that are reunited. Iola, for example, successfully reconnects "the once-severed branches of our family."[21] Reluctant to silence the secret of her slave heritage, and intuiting her white lover's apprehension that a visibly mixed-blood child might inherit his family's estate, Iola refuses to repeat her mother's mistake. She rejects the whiteness of blood and estate and reclaims her "blackness."

Blackness here signifies neither color nor blood but lived experience. As Iola's uncle Robert insists, "[W]hen a man's been colored all his life it comes a little hard for him to get white all at once."[22] The text then traces the ways in which the "white" Iola and her brother Harry become "colored." They do so first through a reinterpretation of the silences in their white familial past, and secondly through a new appreciation of the slave past—one that is "mournful" but whose "Darkness shows us worlds of light / We never saw by day."[23] Marked by darkness (as the only family member who cannot pass for white) and emblematic of slave resistance and agency, grandmother Harriet is the one who embodies this "light in darkness." By the text's conclusion, the Leroys form part of a self-contained southern community of former slaves who, through purchase, have inherited their former masters' estates. They are also reconstituted as a New Negro family in which the men are self-made entrepreneurs and professionals and the women, agents of benevolence. Although the future of African Americans within the nation is not resolved, the Leroy family remains centered around Harriet, and we sense that when she passes on, her memory will survive to provide the core values of historical remembrance, loyalty to family, and commitment to community that will guide African Americans into the modern era.

In striking contrast to *Iola Leroy,* the later romances of Pauline Hopkins and Charles Chesnutt seem more conflicted about the value of the past and eagerly anticipate the creation of "future Americans." If these texts acknowledge the ways in which African Americans have been shaped by the historical experiences of slavery and racial prejudice, several also embrace the white founding father's authority and lay claim to his inheritance as the most effective means of achieving national citizenship. Such a strategy is fully comprehensible in light of the "pressures of the present"— the *Plessy v. Ferguson* decision, Booker T. Washington's Atlanta Compromise speech, black disfranchisement, and U.S. expansionism abroad designed to subjugate peoples of color—that challenged African Americans' acquisition of full citizenship. Much as in *Iola Leroy,* in these romances New Negro modernity is based in large measure in progressive ideology, whereby the self-made male protagonists successfully enter the professions of law, education, and medicine. But, even more significantly, these texts seek to locate New Negro identity in notions of racial indifference.[24] In different ways and to differing degrees, they embrace theories of "of one blood" that either emphasize the common origins of a racially diverse family or point to the invisibility of black blood on the skin's exterior or, finally, promote Chesnutt's "future American," the product of racial mingling whose white appearance offers particular privileges: "If it is only by becoming white that colored people and their children are to enjoy the rights and dignities of citizenship, they will have every incentive to 'lighten the breed,' to use a current phrase, that they may claim the white man's privileges as soon as possible."[25]

Hopkins's *Contending Forces* exhibits a much greater ambivalence toward the past than *Iola Leroy.* Its narrative impulses are explicitly directed toward uncovering the white British origins of the African American Smith family in order to suggest the "progressive" nature of this reconstituted biracial family and its members' inheritance of white property. In the process, however, the text itself engages in acts of forgetting. As she retells her life story, Ma Smith, the repository of the family's collective memory, silences her mother's African American history. Ma Smith claims James M. Whitfield, Hopkins's own great-uncle, as her maternal grandfather. In the 1850s, Whitfield had broken with Frederick Douglass to side with emigrationists like Martin Delany, arguing that black peoples too had a "manifest destiny" and proposing the creation of a black republic in the Caribbean or Central America. By inscribing Whitfield's name within her fiction, Hopkins was perhaps seeking to revive the historical memory of this ancestor who, in striking contrast to Douglass, had died in relative obscurity. Yet, her own narrative colludes in Ma Smith's silencing of her maternal history in favor of the "romantic" story of her father's origins in the British Montfort family.

Through Ma Smith's story, Hopkins invents history: the Montforts' vast wealth is said to derive from a vibrant colonial plantation economy in Bermuda, in which the founding father, an "exporter of tobacco, sugar, coffee, onions, and other products so easily grown in that salubrious climate"[26] takes good care of his slaves. Hopkins taps here into a long-standing invented tradition that grounded Bermuda's slave system in strong affective and familial ties between master and slave. Moreover, her narrative also exaggerates the economic history of the island. Given the rockiness and aridity of its soil, Bermuda never achieved the wealth of either Jamaica or Barbados. Its colonists failed in their attempts to plant tobacco and sugar; instead, the island's economy was based on "salt, cedar, and sailors"—salt-raking in the nearby Turk's Islands, shipbuilding, and commerce.[27] After Emancipation in 1834, these industries went into decline and were replaced by low-profit agricultural endeavors. It was only the growth of the tourist industry in the 1880s that enabled Hopkins to emphasize Bermuda's "salubrious climate" and imagine vast wealth produced by a colonial plantation economy.

Nonetheless, Hopkins's fictional history of a Bermudian economy based on sugar and tobacco carries tremendous symbolic weight in *Contending Forces*. It invents both a wealthy plantocracy and a dependent servile class that generations later provide both the Smith family and their acquaintances with a legacy of conspicuous consumption (that replaces slave production). Following Fernando Ortiz's paradigm, tobacco in Hopkins's romance is wild and masculine. It is also devilish in its prominent association with two of the male characters: the North Carolinian tobacco-chewing Hank Davis, who whips Montfort's wife Grace in a symbolic rape, and the villainous John Langley, who ostentatiously smokes a cigar while betraying his race to the southern sympathizer, the Hon. Herbert Clapp. Sugar, in contrast, is feminine, civilized, indicating elite social status. It is linked to Ma Smith and Dora, whose invention of the traditions of tea parties and evening receptions around the consumption of sweets is reflective of their economic ability and status right—of their New Negro identity.[28]

At the text's conclusion, the family departs for England to reunite with British relatives and recover their Montfort inheritance. Yet this ending remains ambiguous as a foundation for New Negro modernity. Does it reaffirm the authority of the white founding father and legitimate the genealogical destiny of his mixed-blood descendants through receipt of his estate? Is such an inheritance predicated on the suppression of both a slave past as the basis of the family's wealth and an alternative black diasporic history promoted by James Whitfield? Or is it a form of reparations? Does it offer a vision of transnational identity and racial identity by emphasizing the common origin of the black and white Montforts? Or does it represent a return to origins, preparatory to a new departure that will enable the mulatto characters to recreate themselves as New Negroes in America?

Hopkins's *Hagar's Daughter* and Chesnutt's *House behind the Cedars* go further than *Contending Forces* in their initial suppression of slavery's past, given that their protagonists engage in conscious and unconscious acts of passing. Here, too, mixed-blood characters point to an already miscegenous nation forged from extralegal relationships between white men and black women. The plots then ponder the possibility of legal interracial marriage and its progenies' inheritance of the founding father's estate and privileges of whiteness. Indeed, the novels suggest that such unions might provide the basis for national reconciliation and unity.

John and Rena Walden, the protagonists of *House,* suppress their African American past and pass in order to become "new people" and create new families. To the extent that they do claim a past, it is based on invented traditions. John adopts his dead white wife's ancestors as his own, and both he and Rena participate in rituals appropriated by southern white aristocracy from European medievalism by way of Scott's historical romances. They adopt the surname Warwick, Rena is renamed after *Ivanhoe*'s heroine, Rowena, and, finally, she meets her white lover, George Tryon, at a tournament that consciously reenacts scenes from Scott's chivalric romances. In *Hagar's Daughter,* Hagar unconsciously suppresses her slave childhood and marries the white aristocratic southerner, Ellis Enson. After the uncovering of her racial identity and reconstruction of her family's slave history, Ellis abandons Hagar, but the two are reunited at the novel's end. Ostracized from polite society, they nonetheless continue to live the genteel lifestyle of southern aristocracy. Their interracial marriage is indeed novel, but it effectively erases all traces of African American-ness.

Both romances point, however, to the high cost of suppressing the past. For two of the female protagonists, the results are tragic. In *House* Rena cannot forget the memories that bind her to her familial past; her dreams of her mother, suffused with African American folkloric beliefs, lead her back home. Deserted by her white lover, she attempts to reintegrate herself into the black community, but soon dies. Unlike Rena, Hagar and Ellis's daughter Jewel of *Hagar's Daughter* cannot accept the fact of her "black" blood; and unlike Harper's Iola and Harry Leroy, she is unable to appreciate the value of slavery's "mournful past" and of being "colored." Thus, when her white lover discovers her racial identity and rejects her, she is unable to withstand the shock.

Despite the characters' belief in their capacity to know blood, both narratives suggest a threatening racial indeterminacy. As Judge Straight points out in *House*, much of this indeterminacy stems from the southern states' differing definitions of whiteness and blackness. Interestingly enough, it also resides in the murkiness of several of the white characters' parentage. George Tryon comes from the borderless region between North and South Carolina, and his father remains unnamed. In *Hagar's Daughter*, Elise Bradford, the lover of Ellis's brother, St. Clair, is raised by an aunt in the border state of Kentucky; it is she who confesses that "black blood is everywhere—in society and out."[29] Both Chesnutt and Hopkins make use of such racial indeterminacy to hold out the possibility that mixed-blood descendants can in fact inherit white property. After the revelation of his racial identity, John Walden disappears anonymously into white society, and readers may assume that his mixed-blood son will inherit his white mother's estate. Hagar and Ellis Enson become parents to St. Clair and Elise's son, who is now heir to their estate. In both situations, however, the conditions of inheritance are qualified: "blackness" is either not confirmed or remains hidden.

In contrast to these two narratives, in *Winona* it is the white father's lineage that has been suppressed and that the plot uncovers. This romance would seem at last to offer its readers a vision of racial reconciliation

based on an openly interracial marriage and inheritance of white property: it concludes with Winona's marriage to a British gentleman and, as
with the Smiths in *Contending Forces,* the reinstatement into her British
father's family, and inheritance of his fortune. In the process, however,
Winona must not only reject her mother's "primitive" African American
heritage but also sever ties with barbaric America and relocate to civilized
England.

In the last novel published during his lifetime, *The Marrow of Tradition,*
Chesnutt acknowledged the arbitrary and irreducible power of white
supremacy, and rejected the fantasy of passing and interracial marriage.
Marrow constitutes a call for all those who, through a common history,
identify as African American to bond in community. Its characters
embrace their families' slave past and accept the differing legacies
bequeathed them. The laborer, Josh Green, keeps alive the memory of his
father's murder at the hands of a white supremacist and his mother's subsequent insanity. Dr. Miller uses the money inherited from his hard-working father to become a doctor and build a hospital for the black
community; he becomes a New Negro. In contrast, it is the white characters who suppress events from the past, most notably Samuel Merkell's
legal marriage to Julia Brown (and thus his daughter Janet's right to a portion of his estate).

Marrow pointedly associates interracial unions with a primitive past
rather than a modern present. Throughout the text, Janet craves familial
recognition from her white half-sister, Olivia. Given the many references
to the sisters' exact resemblance, the narrative repeatedly gestures toward
ideas of racial indifference. But the race riot that occurs midway through
the text clarifies for characters and readers alike just "how inseparably the
present is woven with the past."[30] At the end, the secrecy surrounding
Janet's parents' marriage, and the conspiracy of the town's white supremacist leaders, are fully exposed. In the very last pages, Janet rejects the privileges of "whiteness" offered by her sister's recognition not only of their
kinship but more importantly of her legitimacy and right to their father's
estate. Here, neither intermarriage nor inheritance is sufficient to overcome slavery's dark legacy.

For the protagonists of these romances, the burden of the past is slavery
and its legacies. I suggest that such historical consciousness leads at critical
moments in the narratives to a movement toward interiority, a marker of
modernity as important as the acquisition of history, citizenship, and
material wealth. The result is a tentative exploration of African American

self-consciousness that later flourishes in such texts as Johnson's *Autobiography of an Ex-Colored Man* (1912) but that Hurston claimed in 1951 had still not received full representation. One manifestation of this turning inward is double consciousness, a concept that Du Bois adapted from William James's notion of the multiple consciousnesses of split personalities. Among its many meanings is the

> sense of always looking at one's self through the eyes of others, of measuring one's soul by the tape of a world that looks on in amused contempt and pity. One ever feels his twoness,—an American, a Negro; two souls, two thoughts, two unreconciled strivings; two warring ideals in one . . . body.[31]

Double consciousness manifests itself most particularly in Chesnutt's characters who face a pressing racial dilemma. It is most obvious in the mixed-blood characters, like Rena, who engage in passing. Once she agrees to her brother's scheme, Rena experiences double consciousness. Embraced by the white aristocratic society around her, but worried about the morality of such deceit and fearful of discovery, Rena tries "to place herself, in this passing upon her own claims to consideration, in the hostile attitude of society toward her hidden disability." After her secret is discovered and she returns home to engage in the uplift of the former slaves in her community, Rena is still plagued by a double consciousness born of her double past—her African American childhood and (brief) white womanhood: "Doubly equipped, she was able to view them at once with the mental eye of an outsider and the sympathy of a sister."[32]

Significantly, several of Chesnutt's white characters also suffer from double consciousness as racial crises force them to question their easy acceptance of white supremacist ideology and slave law. With the knowledge of Rena's impending death, George Tryon is obliged to look at himself from the outside. He recognizes that his life has been ruled by external custom rather than inner moral standards, encouraging him to be "dazzled by his own superiority."[33] In *Marrow*, Olivia's wrongful act of burning her father's papers forces her to question her own moral standing and consider slavery from the point of view of the disinherited as "a great crime against humanity." Similarly, at the narrative's end her husband is able to place himself in Dr. Miller's position and understand the latter's refusal of aid: "For a moment the veil of race prejudice was rent in twain, and he saw things as they were. . . . In Dr. Miller's place, he would have done the same."[34]

The African American historical romances of the nadir ultimately acknowledge that the process of creating New Negro individuals and families out of slavery's legacy had reached an impasse. In fact, fissures and fault lines are manifest within the texts. Many of them are inhabited by solitary Old Negro figures, who either do not belong to the newly constituted New Negro household or whose relationship to it is marginal. Unlike *Iola Leroy*'s Harriet, they lurk at the periphery, but cannot entirely be discarded. Positioned against the New Negro protagonists, these Old Negroes—former slaves or Africans still strongly attached to the continent —appear backward and primitive, characterized by dialect speech, superstitious beliefs, and visionary religious practices. Whether portrayed in positive or negative terms, they complicate the stock figure of the "darky" who pervaded white plantation fiction; most to the point, all of them speak important racial truths.

Chesnutt's characterization of such Old Negro figures is infused with an ambivalence that acknowledges African Americans' present position "on the borderline between two irreconcilable states of life."[35] In *House*, the self-acceptance of Rena's faithful friend Frank is contrasted to her mother's inability to abandon outdated distinctions of color, caste, and class. In *Marrow*, Aunt Jane and her son Jerry are portrayed as self-hating Old Negroes who derive their identity from their status as former slaves and current servants to the Carteret family. Jerry applies bleaching substances to his skin in hope of becoming white, while Jane subsumes her identity to that of the Carterets, holding the family's collective memories, preserving their health, and finally giving her life for them. Jerry, however, is shown fully to understand white privilege, while Mammy Jane's conjure practices challenge the supremacy of white modern science.

Much less ambivalently, Hopkins's romances invoke an ancestral black mother, a figure of wisdom and prophecy, who embodies the collective memory of African American as well as African history; she foreshadows the novelist's direct evocation of Africa in *Of One Blood*. In *Contending Forces*, Sappho's aunt, Madam Frances, is said "to be skilled in the occult arts which were once the glory of the freshly imported African."[36] In *Winona*, Aunt Vinnie appears at the end of the narrative to prophesize the end of slavery: "Dis is de year of Jubilee, / Send dem angels down. / De Lord has come to set us free, / O, send dem angels down."[37] These peripheral black mother figures turn back to the text's center to question the authority of the white founding father. Their intrusion problematizes notions of historical continuity and progress, challenging the values traditionally attached to the Old and the New.

Ultimately, the romances conclude that neither new interracial marriages nor Old Negro figures are possible pathways to citizenship in modern America. As a consequence, in yet another narrative fracturing, these fictions seek to reconsider the basis of citizenship by charting a movement from secular to sacred history, by working against chronological order to transcend historical time. Following emerging modernist ideology, the novelists turn to concepts of mythic time—what Nietzsche called the "superhistorical"—whereby human experience is viewed *sub specie aeternitatis* rather than *sub specie saeculi.* For Nietzsche, the "superhistorical" consists of the power to turn "the eyes from the process of sheer becoming to that which gives existence an eternal and stable character—to art and religion."[38] Gillman has cogently argued that in the writings of Hopkins and Du Bois this transcendence of historical time is grounded in "occult history."[39] Yet the romances of the nadir are equally embedded in the Judeo-Christian ethos that structured the belief systems of nineteenth-century African Americans. The result is a syncretic vision that combines African diasporic mysticism and biblical traditions in order to supply a group tradition.

From this perspective, collective memory is transmitted not only through family but through religious history as well. Individuals remember through commemorative religious practices—the enactment of ritual, the reciting of scripture, the singing of hymns. Additionally, the narratives suggest typological readings that work toward the collapse of chronological time. The plots are recapitulative: current events are prefigured in the biblical past and reenacted in the present. But they are also adumbrative since events are seen as yet to come. Time is an everlasting present, the Old is identical to the New, and history holds out the promise of redemption.[40] Such fictional mythmaking thus remakes African American history from the point of view of biblical history. It invites readers to consider how they might work to achieve the "already known" of the African American future.

In many of the romances, this movement to sacred Judaeo-Christian time is only tentatively explored. In *Iola Leroy,* the emergent black leaders envision the solution to post-bellum–pre-Harlem problems in terms of a national imitation of Christ; Lucille Delany speaks for all when she asserts that "my life is . . . part of a divine plan."[41] *Marrow* proposes—with mixed results—that the novel's characters must abide by two biblical injunctions of humility: the first, voiced by Dr. Miller, is that "the meek shall inherit the earth"; and the second, proclaimed in the narrator's post-riot warning, is that " 'vengeance is mine' saith the Lord, and it had not been left to Him."[42]

To a much greater extent than Harper's and Chesnutt's works, Hopkins's romances are typological narratives that rewrite the Bible. Hopkins begins from a Christian perspective in *Contending Forces* by reimagining the Christ story. In several iterations, Will Smith's fiancee, Sappho, the emblem of black America, repeats the Easter story of suffering for the sins of others, spiritual death, and rebirth. *Hagar's Daughter* and *Winona* return to Christianity's origins by reenacting different episodes from the Old Testament's history of Canaan. The first text rewrites the familial history of Israel's founding father such that Abraham and Hagar give birth to a daughter rather than a son. Egypt's curse on Israel is the curse of those mixed-blood women whose presence so troubles the house of the white founding father. Yet the novel's ending holds out hope for reconciliation between the two nations. In *Winona,* the war between abolitionist and proslavery forces in Kansas explicitly reenacts the holy war between Israelites and Philistines in Canaan. John Brown, Parson Steward, and Ebenezer Maybee are all prophet figures derived from 1 Samuel, and Winona's step-brother Judah is the very embodiment of the kingdom established by David. Repeating the victory of the Israelites, they predict the eventual triumph of the antislavery movement.

Hopkins's last romance, *Of One Blood,* neatly recapitulates the themes analyzed above and, like *Marrow,* expresses disillusionment in the fantasy of passing and interracial marriage. The text invokes, only to reject, the conciliatory possibility of the future American, that racially mixed figure empowered "to claim the white man's privileges." It emphasizes instead the racial nightmare of the genealogical destiny of slave descendants as two brothers, Reuel Briggs and Aubrey Livingston, end up marrying their sister, Dianthe Lusk. Passing for white in Boston's medical community but disillusioned with his prospects for the future, Reuel Briggs travels to the Old Continent, Africa. At this point, the ideology of the future American gives way to the invented tradition of Ethiopianism, providing Reuel with an Old World history. Reuel affirms his common heritage with Africa, which, despite its supposed obscure present, is revealed to have had a brilliant past and, under his leadership, will rise again. Incorporating historical accounts from William Wells Brown's *The Rising Son; or, The*

Antecedents and Advancement of the Colored Race (1874) and George Washington Williams's *History of the Negro Race in America from 1619 to 1880* (1883) in her fictional narrative, Hopkins leads Reuel to the discovery of the ancient Ethiopian civilizations of Meroe and Telessar. Here the Old is equated neither with the past nor with the primitive, as these civilizations are represented as present and proto-modern.

Hopkins also elucidates the ways in which self-consciousness is linked to historical consciousness. In so doing, she acknowledged a direct debt to William James's essay "The Hidden Self" (1890); it provides the subtitle to the romance, and in the opening chapter Reuel is found reading the essay (although the narrator refers to it as "The Unclassified Residuum" by Alfred Binet). As critics have noted, Hopkins racializes James's notion of a hidden self. Dianthe Lusk closely approximates James's case studies of individuals who, when mesmerized or induced into trances, manifest different selves. She is revived by Reuel's scientific skill but loses all memory of the past and hence unwittingly passes for white. It is only through the involuntary singing of spirituals that her hidden African American self reemerges. For the conscious passer Reuel, it is his trip to Africa that reveals to him the secrets of both African history and his inner self, symbolized by the hidden city of Telessar.[43] Through this exploration of interiority, Reuel overcomes the double consciousness suffered while passing in the United States.

It would seem that in this return to Africa, Reuel turns from embracing whiteness to embracing blackness. Yet Hopkins's romance does not promote essentialist notions of race. Instead, it validates concepts of "of one blood" by asserting Ethiopians as humankind's source. Whites have simply evolved away from humanity's original color, and Ethiopians themselves range in skin color from "creamy tint to purest ebony," and in hair texture from "soft waving curls to the crispness of the most pronounced African type." The text's protagonists are indeed all mulattos, but its racial theory works to undermine the significance of visible racial signs. In Africa, Reuel discovers that the leopard can indeed change its spots: "The moon played on the spots of its body. The dark spots became silvered, and relapsed into darkness."[44] The narrative concentrates instead on cultural formation as the measure of progress. It envisions the creation of a syncretic culture that offers readers a mythic version of modernity, what Paul Gilroy has called a "counterculture of modernity."[45]

Gillman has argued that this counterculture results from Hopkins's fashioning of an occult history that combines the invented traditions of

Egyptology and Ethiopianism, placing the former at the service of the latter.[46] What needs to be emphasized, however, is that Hopkins deliberately situates this occult history within the framework of Judeo-Christianity. "But the Biblical tradition is paramount to all," maintains the archeologist Professor Stone. Stone here explicitly displaces more recent historiographical traditions, which credit the world's "advancement to the Romans, Greeks, Hebrews, Germans, and Anglo-Saxons," to return to a biblical genealogical tradition that privileges Ethiopianism. Noah begets several sons among whom is the Ethiopian Ham. Ham in turn begets "Cush and Mizraim and Phut and Canaan," who constitute the originators of "the four races—Egyptians, Ethiopians, Libyans and Canaanites," from whom all modern peoples descend.[47] Moreover, in coming to Telessar Reuel brings with him elements of Christian and American culture that merge with its ancient civilization. To the dismembered and resurrected Egyptian god Osiris, Reuel adds the figure of Jesus. To Ai, the embodiment of Ethiopian collective memory, he adds his grandmother, Aunt Hannah, the emblem of American slavery and its legacies. Both biblical figure and sphinx, Hannah is the prophet who alone can unravel the Livingston family's tangled skein of genealogy.

This syncretic "counterculture" that fuses Egyptian, Ethiopian, and Christian elements promises that Africa shall rise again. Thus, Reuel's recovery of self and of the historical past takes place in Africa within the framework of mythic Judeo-Christian time. Through his name, Reuel evokes Moses's surrogate father; through his actions, he suggests a reincarnation of Philip the Evangelist who, according to Acts 8, was the first to send Christianity to Ethiopia's Queen Candace. Consequently, Hopkins's biblical representation of Reuel is both recapitulative and proleptic, as elucidated by the lines engraved on Telessar's sphinx but drawn from Ecclesiastes 3:15: "That which hath been, is now; and that which is to be, hath already been; and God requireth that which is past."[48]

Yet a tension persists in *Of One Blood* between mythic and chronological time—a tension that coalesces around Hopkins's inability ultimately to transcend notions of patrilineal genealogical succession. Patrilineal inheritance accounts for Cush's foundation of Ethiopia, and it regulates dynastic succession, as Reuel is inserted back into a royal lineage that originated with king Ergamenes, continued through his grandmother Hannah and his mother Mira, and is restored through his marriage to Queen Candace.[49] Yet, under the aegis of Ethiopianism a racially mixed founding father now replaces the white. Hopkins's last romance, then, embodies the very tension between progressivist and modernist tendencies that characterized New Negro thinking at the nadir.

In 1987 Toni Morrison wrote a brief essay, "The Site of Memory," in which she outlined the genesis of *Beloved* (1988). She recalled her frustration when reading antebellum slave narratives in which the ex-slaves repeatedly "pull[ed] the narrative up short" to "'drop a veil over these proceedings too terrible to relate.'" As she saw it, her task became that of ripping aside this veil in order to expose, explore, and narrate what slave narrators had hidden from their white audiences: the monstrosity of the slave system and the interior lives of those it held captive. To do so, Morrison asserted, required "certain things. First of all, I must trust my own recollections. I must also depend on the recollections of others. Thus memory weighs heavily in what I write. . . . But memories and recollections won't give me total access. . . . Only the act of imagination can help me."[50] Morrison failed, however, to recognize that this was precisely the task that post-bellum–pre-Harlem novelists had set for themselves nearly one hundred years earlier: to record the experience of slavery and the inner life of the enslaved by means of memory and imagination. In so doing, she engaged in her own act of forgetting, reminding us that our literary history is indeed a story to be remembered and passed on.

NOTES

1. The sources of the three epigraphs are Alain Locke, *The New Negro* (New York: Charles Boni, 1925; New York: Atheneum, 1986), 6; Arthur Schomburg, "The Negro Digs Up His Past," in Locke, *The New Negro,* 231; and *Zora Neale Hurston: A Life in Letters,* ed. Carla Kaplan (New York: Doubleday, 2002), 655–56.

2. Charles Waddell Chesnutt, *The House behind the Cedars* (1901; repr. Athens: University of Georgia Press, 1970), 83.

3. Ibid., 12.

4. A different version of this essay, "Modernity and Historical Consciousness in the 'New Negro' Novel at the Nadir (1892–1903)," appeared in *African Diasporas in the New and Old Worlds,* ed. Geneviève Fabre and Karl Benesch (Amsterdam: Rodopi, 2004), 161–80. The essay adds to earlier scholarship on the nadir. See Claudia Tate, *Domestic Allegories of Political Desire: The Black Heroine's Text at the Turn of the Century* (New York: Oxford University Press, 1992); Kevin K. Gaines, *Uplifting the Race: Black Leadership, Politics, and Culture in the Twentieth Century* (Chapel Hill: University of North Carolina Press, 1996); Shawn Michelle Smith,

American Archives: Gender, Race, and Class in Visual Culture (Princeton, NJ: Princeton University Press, 1999); and, most especially, Susan Gillman, *Blood Talk: American Race Melodrama and the Culture of the Occult* (Chicago: University of Chicago Press, 2003), whose concerns are similar to mine.

5. T. J. Jackson Lear, *No Place of Grace: Antimodernism and the Transformation of American Culture, 1880–1920* (Chicago: University of Chicago Press, 1994), 7–26.

6. Friedrich Nietzsche, *The Use and Abuse of History,* trans. Adrian Collins (1873; repr. Indianapolis: Bobbs-Merrill, 1957), 59, 40.

7. See Rayford W. Logan, *The Negro in American Life and Thought: The Nadir, 1877–1901* (New York: Dial Press, 1954).

8. W. E. B. Du Bois, *The Souls of Black Folk,* ed. Henry Louis Gates Jr. and Terri Hume (1903; repr. New York: Norton, 1999), 162.

9. Henry Louis Gates Jr., "The Trope of a New Negro and the Reconstruction of the Image of the Black," *Representations* 24 (Fall 1988): 132.

10. Alexander Crummell, "The Need of New Ideas and New Aims for a New Era," in *Civilization and Progress: Selected Writings of Alexander Crummell on the South,* ed. J. R. Oldfield (Charlottesville: University of Virginia Press, 1995), 121–23.

11. See Cynthia Schrager, "Pauline Hopkins and William James: The New Psychology and the Politics of Race," in *The Unruly Voice: Rediscovering Pauline Elizabeth Hopkins,* ed. John Gruesser (Urbana: Illinois University Press, 1996), 189–209.

12. Du Bois, *Souls,* chapter 1.

13. Mikhail Bakhtin, *The Dialogic Imagination,* ed. Michael Holquist (Austin: University of Texas Press, 1981), 269.

14. Pierre Nora, "Between Memory and History: Les Lieux de Memoire," in *History and Memory in African-American Culture,* ed. Geneviève Fabre and Robert O'Meally (New York: Oxford University Press, 1994), 284.

15. Eric Hobsbawm and Terence Ranger, eds., *The Invention of Tradition* (Cambridge: Cambridge University Press, 1983), 2.

16. George Dekker, *The American Historical Romance* (Cambridge: Cambridge University Press, 1987), 38–46. See Gillman, *Blood Talk,* 58–59, for her use of the term "race melodrama" to describe many of these novels.

17. Patricia Drechsel Tobin, *Time and the Novel: The Genealogical Imperative* (Princeton, NJ: Princeton University Press, 1978), 3–16.

18. Gillman's *Blood Talk* also underscores the importance of family structures in the "race melodramas" of this period.

19. For a fuller development of these points, see Eva Saks's essay "Representing Miscegenation Law," *Raritan* 8 (Fall 1988): 39–69.

20. James McCune Smith, "Citizenship," *The Anglo-African Magazine* 1.5 (May 1859): 143–50.

21. Frances E. W. Harper, *Iola Leroy; or, Shadows Uplifted* (1872; repr. Boston: Beacon Press, 1987), 215.

22. Ibid., 43.

23. Ibid., 273.

24. Walter Benn Michaels, *Our America: Nativism, Modernism, and Pluralism* (Durham, NC: Duke University Press, 1995), 53–60.

25. Charles Waddell Chesnutt, "The Future American: A Stream of Dark Blood in the Veins of Southern Whites," in *Charles W. Chesnutt: Essays and Speeches,* ed. Joseph R. McElrath Jr., Robert C. Leitz III, and Jesse S. Crisler (1900; repr. Stanford, CA: Stanford University Press, 1999), 134.

26. Pauline E. Hopkins, *Contending Forces: A Romance Illustrative of Negro Life North and South* (1901; repr. New York: Oxford University Press, 1988), 22.

27. Frank E. Manning, *Black Clubs in Bermuda: Ethnography of a Play World* (Ithaca, NY: Cornell University Press, 1973), 9–10.

28. Fernando Ortiz, *Cuban Counterpoint, Tobacco and Sugar,* trans. Harriet de Onís (New York: Knopf, 1947), 75, 3–46; and Sidney Mintz, *Sweetness and Power* (New York: Viking Press, 1985), 173.

29. Pauline E. Hopkins, *The Magazine Novels of Pauline Hopkins* (New York: Oxford University Press, 1988), 160.

30. Charles Waddell Chesnutt, *The Marrow of Tradition,* ed. Robert M. Farnsworth (1900; repr. Ann Arbor: University of Michigan Press, 1969), 112.

31. Du Bois, *Souls,* 11.

32. Chesnutt, *House,* 76, 194.

33. Ibid., 292.

34. Chesnutt, *Marrow,* 266, 321.

35. Ibid., 42.

36. Hopkins, *Contending Forces,* 200.

37. Hopkins, *Magazine Novels,* 437.

38. Nietzsche, *Use and Abuse,* 69.

39. Gillman, *Blood Talk,* 26.

40. Sacvan Bercovitch, *The American Jeremiad* (Madison: University of Wisconsin Press, 1978), 40–44, 75–80.

41. Harper, *Iola Leroy,* 255.

42. Chesnutt, *Marrow,* 62, 309.

43. Gillman, *Blood Talk,* 61; and Schrager, "Hopkins and James," 188–200.

44. Hopkins, *Magazine Novels,* 521, 545, 571.

45. See Paul Gilroy, *The Black Atlantic: Modernity and Double Consciousness* (Cambridge, MA: Harvard University Press, 1993).

46. Gillman, *Blood Talk,* 36.

47. Hopkins, *Magazine Novels,* 531, 533.

48. Ibid., 552.

49. Ibid., 547.

50. Toni Morrison, "The Site of Memory," in *Inventing the Truth: The Art and Craft of Memoir,* ed. William Zinsser (Boston: Houghton Mifflin, 1987), 109–10.

Part II

Meeting Freedom
*Self-Invention, Artistic Innovation, and Race Progress
(1870s–1880s)*

Chapter 3

Landscapes of Labor
Race, Religion, and Rhode Island in the Painting of Edward Mitchell Bannister

Gwendolyn DuBois Shaw

From his arrival in Providence, Rhode Island, in 1869, until his death there in 1901, Edward Mitchell Bannister (1828–1901) painted the landscape of southern New England in a style that has often been described as derivative of the Barbizon school. However, unlike the Barbizon painters, who sought to create pastoral scenes of idyllic peasant life in the French countryside, Bannister frequently depicted farms and other rural locations that evoke the history of Rhode Island chattel slavery. He first emigrated from New Brunswick, Canada, to Boston, Massachusetts, in 1850, and his life exemplifies many of the challenges and achievements that creative African Americans faced and attained during the second half of the nineteenth century. Similar to the paintings of Henry Ossawa Tanner, or the neoclassical sculpture of Edmonia Lewis, Bannister's compositions provide a window on the intellectual and creative terrain that socially concerned artists of the period confronted. In a short catalog entry on the undated painting *The Haygatherers* (c. 1893), art historian Corrine Jennings suggests that "the presence of Black figures, relatively uncommon in Bannister's work, has raised speculation that the painting stands as an oblique reference to the plantation system of Rhode Island's past and to its role in the slave trade."[1] Indeed, paintings such as *The Haygatherers* and *Workers in the Fields* (c. 1890) reveal a space in which the artist could explore a legacy of racial oppression within a contemporary international artistic language of landscape and noble peasantry. In this way Bannister was able both to commemorate the rapidly disappearing evidence of Rhode Island's plantation history and to elevate the labor of its still disempowered black folk.

Bannister accomplished this radical move in two ways: first, by referencing the African American religious tradition; and second, by subverting the visual vernacular of French landscape painting and its then current vogue for semirealism and the rural picturesque. His status as a privileged artist allowed him to negotiate these issues of class and race. In his work he identifies with the social issues facing former slaves while simultaneously escaping them via his own freeborn status and through the patronage of both the black and the white bourgeoisie.

We witness this paradox in the rectangular canvas of *Haygatherers,* within whose borders a large, green-and-brown hay field set beneath a low-lying horizon opens before the spectator. The field is framed from below by a bit of wild grass that sprouts wildflowers and dandelion puffs, and on the left by a group of three trees that anchors the composition by extending all the way to the top margin of the painting. The third tree, at the far left of the canvas, is only partially visible, giving the effect of the continuation of the imaginary space beyond the picture frame. In the middle ground and to the right, within the yellow-brown of the hay field, two dark-skinned women labor at what appears to be the work of gathering hay to place atop the large hay wain at the back of the composition. Their presence in the middle ground rhymes nicely with the two trees at left, and is further emphasized by the placement of two smaller trees directly above and behind them in the far distance. With this twinning, the two women make up the lower corner of a pyramidal arrangement that finds its apex in a third group of treetops that rises behind the hay wain and its minute attendants.

The women are lost in the space of the hay field, which swirls about their knees, truncating them and blocking their forward progress. There is no visible path behind them to indicate the direction from which they have come, nor is there any sign that they have cleared the crop and are now gleaning the remains. As their right arms reach forward in tandem, toward the pastoral field of wildflowers and the stand of trees that borders the two spaces, they appear to be swimming across a great sea of grass, the trampled blades that surround them arching like waves. This swimming motion moves them apart from the other figures, as though they have strayed from the distant harbor of the hay wain and the life of labor that it represents, and are now approaching the pastoral promise that rises in the foreground.

In *Haygatherers,* Bannister creates for the spectator a world in which the drudgery of daily life and the curse of humble birth can be challenged,

Edward Mitchell Bannister. *The Haygatherers*, c. 1893. Oil on canvas. 17 1/8 x 23 1/8 inches. Private collection.

if not overcome or transcended. He renders a world in which crossing over, the action of moving from one reality to another, from labor to leisure, can be achieved by fording a river of grass as though it were the River Jordan. He shows these black bodies as analogous to the Israelites, who wandered in the wilderness for forty years waiting for the ultimate reward of the Promised Land, yet still within the control of the plantation system that had enslaved their ancestors, still within Pharaoh's reach. This ability to depict an unpopular reality in a popular mode makes Bannister's work in general, and *Haygatherers* in particular, some of the most dynamic landscape painting of the late nineteenth century.

The post-bellum–pre-Harlem period when Bannister completed his mature work brought great changes to the American art world. This important half-century saw the exponential expansion of national interests, as the barely reunited country promoted industrialization at home and new-found imperialist opportunities abroad. It also witnessed the size of the artisan class retract as the professional and working classes grew.

Just as those who practiced crafts felt the increasing competition of the mechanized workplace, so did critical changes occur in the demographics of those who were able to produce so-called fine art. With the rise of photography, they no longer needed painted portraits to decorate their homes; they now longed for intimate landscapes and tasteful objects to grace their parlors.

These economic and social changes came in the aftermath of significant antebellum agitation by the abolitionists and women's rights adherents who, prior to the war, had taken great interest in the creative potential of African Americans. This focus, which centered on artistic achievement as a way to emphasize the humanity of black slaves and their free counterparts and their worthiness to participate in the American democracy, laid a foundation for notable, but extremely limited, African American artistic success in abolitionist enclaves centered in Boston, Philadelphia, and Cincinnati.

Bannister was among several African American artists who received their initial support from individual abolitionists and from antislavery societies, and then went on to garner prizes and acclaim from the mainstream art world following the Civil War. The landscape painter Robert Scott Duncanson (1821–1872)[2] and the sculptor Lewis[3] are two other prominent artists to emerge from these environments. Bannister was freeborn and had a mixed racial heritage. His father may have been from Barbados; however, there is compelling evidence that his family immigrated to New Brunswick, fleeing the newly established United States as Loyalists following Britain's defeat in the Revolutionary War.[4] Once they were settled in Canada, his grandfather may have worked as a "servant" for the prominent Hatch family. Following the death of his parents, a youthful Bannister worked on the estate belonging to Harris Hatch before serving as a sailor on one of the many ships that plied the northeastern seaboard between Nova Scotia and New York.[5] This experience on a plantation in eastern Canada must have impacted his thinking about the racial politics of field labor when he approached it as artistic subject matter much later in his life. This is perhaps why he is so sympathetic to the plight of the figures that swim across the river of grass in *Haygatherers*: in many ways they repeat his experience of leaving a life of field labor for one of self-determination.

The foundational support that Bannister received through abolitionist patronage, while he struggled for artistic recognition and creative acceptance from the dominant culture, cannot be understated. Yet support from his immediate community during the mid-nineteenth century was also crucial. By the late 1840s Bannister had settled in Boston with his brothers and had begun working as a hairdresser while painting on the side. As his skills developed, he began to pick up work painting portraits of the local white abolitionists and the growing numbers of black bourgeoisie in the area.

One of Bannister's earliest known portraits, *Dr. John Van Surley DeGrasse* (c. 1848), is of a noted black physician and antislavery activist who subsequently served as the first black surgeon in the Civil War.[6] The image presents the doctor as a well dressed, middle-class professional. Bannister's painting joined others in the DeGrasse family collection, including one of Isaiah DeGrasse, the doctor's father, by the African American painter and print maker Patrick Reason. Several years later, Bannister also completed a pastel portrait of Cordelia Howard, the future Mrs. DeGrasse, which joined a painting by the European American William Matthew Prior of Cordelia's mother, Margaret Gardner.[7] That the DeGrasse and Howard families were able to afford multiple painted portraits of family members, and that these works remained in the family through the late twentieth century, speaks to the solidity and dynamism of the African American social system that had developed in Boston during the nineteenth century. The portrait of Dr. DeGrasse is a visual testament to Bannister's involvement in the abolitionist work in Boston and to his status as a midlevel, but well established, artist.

Like many other freeborn African Americans before him, Bannister used his talent to support the cause of abolition numerous times during the 1850s, and just a year into the Civil War he made a full-length, posthumous portrait of Colonel Robert Gould Shaw (location unknown) that was sold at a charity auction. His portrait of the white leader of the Massachusetts Fifty-fourth, the first black regiment commissioned in the Union Army, joined a number of other commemorations of the fallen hero, including a bust by Lewis.[8] Comparable to Cincinnati's abolitionists, who applauded and supported the career of the African American painter Duncanson, the Boston antislavery community was vigorous in its promotion and utilization of free black creativity to propagandize for the cause.[9]

This involvement in Boston art and politics enabled Bannister to make inroads into the mainstream art establishment during the late antebellum period and the Civil War. It helped him to grow and develop despite the hostile racial environment of the United States during this era. In addi-

Edward Mitchell Bannister. *Dr. John V. DeGrasse,* c.
1848. Oil on canvas. 23 inches. Kenkeleba House, Inc.

tion, his wife Christiana Carteaux, whom he met in the 1850s, was unques-
tionably his greatest patron and supporter. Carteaux, who had roots in the
Native American communities around Providence, was a fellow hairdresser who owned her own salon. She was also active in the antislavery
movement (during the war she served in the Colored Women's Auxiliary),
and when they married in 1858, her financial acumen enabled Bannister to
devote nearly all his time to his art. During this period he received some
formal art training at Boston's Lowell Institute under the painter William
Rimmer and began to expand his repertoire from portraits to religious
subjects, genre, still life, and later, landscape painting.

Unfortunately, much of the social progress that Bannister made in the
1860s was challenged during the post-bellum–pre-Harlem decades as the
dominant culture of the United States became increasingly hostile to black
creativity. This negative attitude retarded the spread of African American
artistic culture during the Gilded Age. Following the Civil War the climate

for African Americans living in Boston had changed dramatically. Many displaced former slaves had begun making their way north in search of work and opportunity. Within a few years the community of free black professionals to which the Bannisters belonged, many of whom had been in the area long before the war, began to see their social status slip. They were no longer readily identifiable within an increasingly large black population, and they faced racist slights on the streets and elsewhere in the public sphere. As freedmen skilled primarily in farm work flooded the increasingly industrialized labor markets of northern cities, working-class whites (who were themselves mostly immigrants from Ireland and other impoverished European countries) adopted racist attitudes about the right to work. Further, the white community that had supported the abolitionist cause was now far less interested in the current situation for African Americans, having been more enamored by the idea of freedom than by the reality of the free blacks who now filled their city.[10] This tense climate led in some cases to race riots and generally made the environment of the city unbearable for many middle-class black families, who increasingly found that their presumption of social privilege was not a protection against racially motivated violence.

In 1869 Bannister and Carteaux, possibly threatened by the continued erosion of race relations and their own social status, removed themselves to the significantly smaller city of Providence. At the time, the city was home to a small community of artists, and its environs were characterized by the remnants of what had once been a large system of plantations and shipping businesses linked to the slave trade. Some members of Rhode Island's African American population, exemplified by Carteaux's own family, had mixed with Native Americans from the area, creating a dynamic ethnic community. It was during this period, in this fresh location, that Bannister's style fully matured. His landscapes began to show the influence of the Barbizon school, the anticlassical style of painting that began in the French countryside with the work of Théodore Rousseau, which focused on the spiritual and emotional properties of landscape. These serene spaces featured peasants who seemed to coexist peacefully with the beasts of the field; they were explorations of humanity's harmonious interaction with God's creation. In opposition to the studio-produced epic oil paintings, the "Great Pictures" of the Hudson River school style that artists like Duncanson had painted at the height of his career in the 1860s, Barbizon-influenced landscapes were generally done outdoors and were intimate in scale. That American art critics and consumers shifted their taste in landscape painting from epic to contemplative in the 1870s is evident not only in the rapid decline of Duncanson's reputation following his death in 1872 but also in the survival of Bannister's career, which embraced the new style.

Following his relocation to Rhode Island, Bannister developed his method of painting through first-hand study of the regional landscape around Providence. Here he found a welcoming arts community and in 1873, with his colleagues George Whitaker and Charles Stetson, he helped to found the Providence Art Club. Still in existence today, the club proved to be an influential organization. Its proximity to Newport and the well-heeled summer populations that the region attracted enabled members to exhibit and sell their work to an influential bourgeoisie and upper-class clientele. Testifying to his involvement in its foundation, a silhouette of Bannister's profile is visible behind the front door of the clubhouse.

Through his affiliation with the Providence Art Club, and his work in founding the Rhode Island School of Design in 1878, Bannister saw many of his works move into private collections. Eventually, he was able to devote all his time to painting, traveling up and down the New England coastline, exploring the many islands in Narragansett Bay in his small yacht. In this way he became familiar with the various locations that had factored heavily in the Rhode Island slave trade, its many ports where Africans had been put ashore. If in *Haygatherers* Bannister had raised the legacy of slavery and the presence of black folk in the landscape to a biblical level, then the paintings that he made of these historically loaded sites did something just as powerful, if more covert. In these compositions he records the industrial revolution altering the pastoral world and, as Corrine Jennings has rightly argued, "his use of rivers and the sea reflects a lost ancestral heritage and the longing for freedom, and his ships have been identified as signifying freedom."[11]

This belief in the power of landscape to retain history, empowering the terrain to stand as witness to the past, is evident in the seascape *Fort Dumpling, Jamestown, Rhode Island* (c. 1890). *Fort Dumpling* is a rectangular composition divided by diagonal lines and pyramidal forms. In this scene of leisure, four figural groups, made up of light-skinned men, women, and children, relax along the seashore. Three children in yellow straw hats hunch within the shadow of the cliff at the lower right of the composition, as though examining a newfound treasure. Close by them, at the center of the space, is a group of three adult figures, a man and two women. One woman stands with her back to the spectator, facing the sea and holding a red parasol, while another sits at her feet. The man faces them both.

Together, the three adults, with their triangular arrangement and the arresting red of the parasol, draw the spectator's gaze up and into the dark block that is Fort Dumpling. The fort, whose upper form line is clearly visible against the white clouds of the sky, rises like a forbidding piece of the living rock on which it is perched. As a military installation on Narragansett Bay, it references both the forceful conquest of Coanicut Island from the Wampanoag and Naragansett peoples, Christiana Carteaux's ancestors, and Rhode Island's establishment as a slaveholding state and a leader in the triangular, transatlantic slave trade. During the period between 1709 and 1807 nearly one thousand slaving voyages were made to Africa by vessels registered in the Naragansett Bay region.[12] The nearby town of Warwick, for example, was named for the second Earl of Warwick, who established Providence Plantation and had the dubious distinction of bringing the first black slaves to the British colonies in 1619. In the colonial era that followed, the area surrounding Narragansett Bay had the largest population of slaves in New England. They could be found working in South County plantations or as servants in merchant households. When read through the lens of history, the ship in the water to the fort's left ambivalently references both the horror of the Middle Passage and Bannister's own love of sailing.

Bannister's landscapes of the 1890s, such as *Fort Dumpling,* which features the maritime legacy of slavery in seemingly idyllic surroundings, or *Haygatherers,* in which black bodies attempt to ford a river of endless labor, may be read as subtle visual metaphors of the Middle Passage, attempts to pass over racial barriers as well as into the heavenly reward. In this way a river painted by Bannister can be read both as surrogate for the journey that slaves made as they fled from slavery to freedom in the northern states and as an allusion to the biblical River Jordan that the Israelites crossed to the Promised Land after having wandered in the wilderness for forty years following their flight from Egypt.[13] Fort Dumpling itself stands as though it were the Sphinx, a witness to the passage of many stolen and enslaved black bodies before its cliff side.

The identification of the plight of African Americans with biblical figures—even after the end of slavery—that we see in *Haygatherers* is also present in the work of Lewis and Tanner. In 1869 Lewis created a marble sculpture of Hagar, the Egyptian handmaiden of the barren Sarah who is forced to lie with her mistress's husband Abraham and is then cast into the desert once she conceives her master's heir. As a woman abused by and separated from patriarchy, the subject of Hagar constituted a fitting way for Lewis to comment on the social disadvantages faced by black women in the United States both under and after slavery.[14]

In contrast to the water imagery of Bannister, or the metaphorical transposition of Lewis, Tanner approached biblical subject matter and its relationship to African American religious culture in his paintings by using the people of North Africa, whom he came to know through his travels in the region, as his models. Having expatriated to France in the 1890s, Tanner made numerous paintings of biblical scenes using Moroccans and other North Africans as models, and depicting their living cities as though they were ancient scenery.

Art historian Adrienne Childs has argued that Tanner's use of African models for biblical characters seems to have been a solution that he reached to deal with the vexing criticism that was heaped upon him when he stopped painting African American characters following *The Banjo Lesson* (1893) and *The Thankful Poor* (1893–1894).[15] Tanner was never forgiven by some critics for having abandoned the sympathetic treatment of African Americans found in these two images of black men passing on their cultural capital, in the form of music lessons and piety, to young boys. In fact, it is for these works that he is most often remembered, even though they are not representative of his mature style or of the biblical subject matter to which he was most frequently drawn. Rather, *The Banjo Lesson* and *The Thankful Poor* were explorations of ways to render the popular motif of the folk in American terms. Tanner sought to represent African Americans as an authentic folk, the rustic peasants that peopled so many French paintings of the 1880s and 1890s. In fact, during the period between 1893 and 1895 in which he painted these authentic black folk, he also executed *The Bagpipe Lesson* (1894) and *The Young Sabot Maker* (1895), two images of Brittany peasants teaching their offspring the joys of music and the skill of shoemaking.[16]

Just as his younger colleague Tanner was searching for a compelling way to paint African Americans, so too was Bannister investigating modes for depicting black bodies as the folk inhabitants of the countryside. And in the same vein as Tanner, he chose to render them as though they were not only the French peasants Barbizon painters had so adored but also biblical heroes. And yet, despite the emphasis on the contemplative and transcendent power of landscape that we find in Bannister's work, *Fort Dumpling* and *Haygatherers* must become more than idyllic retreats for the spectator, for they speak to the struggle with racial representation that the artist grappled with throughout his career. After having begun his artistic practice painting many black Bostonians—a body of work that included commissioned portraits such as those for the DeGrasse-Howard family as well as a personal portrait of his wife that is now at the Newport Museum—in his landscapes he rarely included any African American characters. This absence of black bodies in his images may be read as a survival mode by which he submerged his blackness beneath a generic landscape aesthetic that called for a benign white presence in the composition, an assumed white producer of the object, and an ideal white spectator standing before it.

This sublimation into whiteness that we see in much of Bannister's painting, with obvious notable exceptions, was also apparent in the covert manner he submitted his work to exhibitions, often keeping his racial identity a secret. For example, in 1876 he entered an already much lauded work, *Under the Oaks* (location unknown), in the competition at the Philadelphia Centennial Exposition. There it won first prize for painting and gave rise to one of the most frequently recounted stories of nineteenth-century African American art history, one that reflects the racism and difficulties with which post-bellum–pre-Harlem black artists contended:

> I learned from the newspapers that "54" had received a first prize medal, so I hurried to the Committee Rooms to make sure the report was true. There was a great crowd there ahead of me. As I jostled among them many resented my presence, some actually commenting within my hearing in a most petulant manner what is that colored person in here for? Finally when I succeeded in reaching the desk where inquiries were made, I endeavored to gain the attention of the official in charge. He was very insolent. Without raising his eyes, he demanded in the most exasperating tone of voice, "Well what do you want here any way? Speak lively." "I want to enquire [*sic*] concerning 54. Is it a prize winner?" "What's that to you," said he? In an instant my blood was up: the looks that passed between him and others in the room were unmistakable. I was not an artist to them, simply an inquisitive colored man; controlling myself, I said deliberately, "I am interested in the report that *Under the Oaks* has received a prize; I painted the picture." An explosion could not have made a more marked impression. Without hesitation he apologized, and soon everyone in the room was bowing and scraping to me.[17]

This type of national success must have been bittersweet for Bannister because, while it garnered him recognition from black and white communities outside New England, it also exposed him to the tide of racism that had continued to rise in the United States. And it was just this type of reception that probably caused him to shy away from black characters and from overtly racialized subject matter. To the white officials and attendees of the Philadelphia Centennial Exposition, like the Bostonians he had left behind, he would never be distinguishable from the blacks that labored in the hay fields he painted. Nevertheless, he continued to exhibit nationally, in 1879 at the National Academy of Design, and in 1880 at the New Orleans Cotton Centennial Exposition.

The artistic production of Bannister, and that of his colleagues Duncanson, Lewis, and Tanner, speaks to the changing modes of visualizing the global African experience that occurred in the second half of the nineteenth century, and it retells the obstacles they encountered due to their socially proscribed identities as they negotiated spaces of race and representation. Because of the reactionary historical oppression of black creativity, today we are familiar with the work and careers of only a handful of the African American artists who were active between 1865 and 1920. This is due in part to the limited critical reception they received during their lifetimes, and also to the institutional racism that kept their work out of most museum collections until the late twentieth century. Further, after finding the dominant art world at best unresponsive and, more typically, openly hostile to their efforts, many of these artists, with the exception of Duncanson, who died in 1872, chose alternate avenues for their careers. Bannister, of course, left Boston for the relative isolation of Providence, where he was able to develop a strong reputation amidst a growing colony of regionally motivated landscape artists. Lewis expatriated permanently to Rome after the mid-1870s, where she entered a community of American sculptors, many of them women. And Tanner sought the unique status and relative racial freedom of France, where he lived permanently from 1895 until his death in 1923.

Following their deaths at the turn of the century, the reputations of both Lewis and Bannister suffered a rapid descent into obscurity, as the styles in which they had painted and sculpted fell rapidly out of fashion. Their work, and that of Tanner as well, was further marginalized by critics during the subsequent "Harlem Renaissance," who found it derivative and imitative of white aesthetics rather than authentically African American.[18] Up until the last decades of the twentieth century there was little appreciation for Bannister's landscapes; his paintings were largely unknown to historians of American art and virtually unseen outside of Rhode Island collections. There were few eyes to look into the sea of grass and out across the bay waters to search for the struggle of racial representation that Bannister engaged in his landscapes of Rhode Island's plantation past.

NOTES

1. *Edward M. Bannister: A Centennial Retrospective* (New York: Kenkeleba House, 2001), an exhibition catalog, 22.

2. The best source of biographical information on Duncanson is Joseph D. Ketner's *Emergence of the African American Artist* (Columbia: University of Missouri Press, 1993). Ketner's exhaustive research established an extensive biographical history for Duncanson, as well as reproducing a large number of the artist's paintings for the first time.

3. For recent work on Lewis, see Kirstin Buick, "The Ideal Works of Edmonia Lewis: Invoking and Inverting Autobiography," in *Reading American Art,* ed. Marianne Doezema and Elizabeth Milroy (New Haven, CT: Yale University Press, 1998), 190–207; and Marilyn Richardson, "Edmonia Lewis's *The Death of Cleopatra*: Myth and Identity," *International Review of African American Art* 12.2 (1995): 36–52.

4. According to the website of the Nova Scotia Museum, the Bannister surname appears in the *Book of Negroes,* which lists "Black passengers leaving New York on British ships in 1783." Only three copies of this handwritten book survive that give "a name, age, physical description, and status (slave or free) for each passenger, and often an owner's name and place of residence." This list is the starting point for research about black Loyalists. See Nova Scotia Museum, "Remembering Black Loyalists: Black Communities in Nova Scotia," Nova Scotia Museum, http://museum.gov.ns.ca/blackloyalists/index.htm.

5. Corrine Jennings, interview with author, January 26, 2002. Significant work on Bannister has been done by, and under the auspices of, collector and independent art historian Corrine Jennings. Through Jennings's New York City gallery, Kenkeleba House, two retrospectives of Bannister's work—at the Whitney Museum of American Art at Champion and the Roger King Gallery in Newport, Rhode Island—have been mounted in the last decade. The catalogs for these two shows, *Edward Mitchell Bannister, 1828–1901* (New York: Kenkeleba House, 1992; Stamford, CT: Whitney Museum of American Art at Champion; New York: distributed by Harry N. Abrams, 1992) and *Edward M. Bannister: A Centennial Retrospective* (New York: Kenkeleba House, 2001) are the primary sources for information on the artist.

6. Dr. DeGrasse gave Bannister his first nonportrait commission in 1854 for

The Ship Outward Bound (Edward M. Bannister, 5). More information on the DeGrasse Family and their role in African American life in nineteenth-century Boston can be found in the DeGrasse-Howard papers at the Massachusetts Historical Society.

7. Reason, who was probably based in Philadelphia, is better known for his print "Am I Not a Man and a Brother?"—after the late eighteenth-century Josiah Wedgewood plaque that first showed a shackled and kneeling slave pleading for freedom—than for his paintings. Almost as little is known about the life of Prior, who is often called a "plain painter" or a "limner," terms that refer to the flat linearity of his images. Many of the extant portraits he did are of black sitters, including one of the abolitionist and Underground Railroad conductor William Whipper (1848), which would seem to indicate his own antislavery sentiments quite clearly.

8. Art historian Katie Mullis Kresser has written a very interesting unpublished paper on the *Shaw Memorial* that argues in part that the white Brahmin community of Boston sought to wrest the memory of Shaw's sacrifice from what they deemed to be the inappropriate hands of black artists like Bannister and Lewis by systematically marginalizing and discounting black participation in various memorial efforts. She states that Shaw, as a favorite scion of Boston's prosperous Brahmin community, was greatly mourned when he fell at Fort Wagner in the campaign to take Charleston, South Carolina, in 1863. Over the next fifty years his memory would be increasingly revered in art work until his martyrdom reached a Christlike level in the *Shaw Memorial* (1893) on Boston Common, by the white sculptor Augustus Saint-Gaudens, which shows him on horseback as though he were entering Jerusalem. Katie Mullis Kresser, "A Special Precinct: The Shaw Memorial and Brahmin Self-Definition in Late Nineteenth-Century Boston" (unpublished paper, 2003).

9. Up until the Civil War, Duncanson found patronage from abolitionists for his artistic career. But this generous, politically motivated support came with certain thematic strings attached. At least once, as evidenced by his 1853 painting of *Uncle Tom and Little Eva* (Detroit Institute of Arts), Duncanson uncharacteristically opted to render popular subject matter from Harriet Beecher Stowe's *Uncle Tom's Cabin* (1852). It is likely that the painting was commissioned, since nothing else like it appears in Duncanson's oeuvre.

10. Holland, "Reaching behind the Veil," in *Edward Mitchell Bannister, 1828–1901*, 27.

11. Ibid., 4.

12. According to Jay Coughtry's book *The Notorious Triangle: Rhode Island and the African Slave Trade, 1700–1807* (Philadelphia: Temple University Press, 1981), the slave ships would travel first to the Gold Coast, where they would collect kidnapped Africans in exchange for rum and brandy. Then they would proceed south to the West Indies, where they would offload the majority of the slaves and take on

a cargo of molasses before returning home to Rhode Island, where the remaining Africans would be sold as slaves and the molasses made into rum. Through this type of triangular trade over one hundred thousand Africans, nearly one-fifth of the total number of slaves imported to North America during the period, found themselves on vessels owned by Rhode Islanders.

13. This idea of a racialized landscape, in which African American religious culture can be read into the natural surroundings, is one first put forth by art historian David Lubin in his fine essay on Duncanson. See Lubin's *Picturing a Nation: Art and Social Change in Nineteenth-Century America* (New Haven, CT: Yale University Press, 1994), 107–57.

14. Kirstin Buick's essay "The Ideal Works of Edmonia Lewis: Invoking and Inverting Autobiography," in *Reading American Art,* ed. Doezema and Milroy, 190–207, argues that the artist used both white racial features and biblical subject matter to approach difficult racial topics and to push for the inclusion of black females into the cultural space of womanhood.

15. Art historian Adrienne Childs proposes that Tanner was the first black American professional artist to go to Africa. She investigates the significance of his depiction of black figures in his biblical and orientalist genre scenes in "Tanner, Orientalism, and the Development of African American Art" (paper presented at the "Laying Claim" conference, Colgate University, October 25–27, 2001).

16. Judith Wilson presents a strong case for Tanner's desire to make black folk into ideal American peasants. See her "Lifting the 'Veil': Henry O. Tanner's *The Banjo Lesson* and *The Thankful Poor,*" in *Critical Issues in American Art,* ed. Mary Ann Calo (Boulder, CO: Westview Press, 1998), 199–219.

17. As recorded in George Whitaker, "Edward Mitchell Bannister," undated typescript, 4–5, Edward Mitchell Bannister Papers, Archives of American Art, Smithsonian Institution, Washington, DC.

18. See Alain Locke, *The Negro in Art: A Pictorial Record of the Negro Artist and of the Negro Theme in Art* (Washington, DC: Associates in Negro Folk Education, 1940).

Chapter 4

"Manly Husbands and Womanly Wives"
The Leadership of Educator Lucy Craft Laney

Audrey Thomas McCluskey

The few extant photographs of Haines Normal and Industrial Institute founder and educational activist Lucy Craft Laney (1854–1933) span several decades and show a young, middle-aged, then elderly woman with an increasingly serious mien, close-cropped natural hair, dark brown skin, and gentle eyes. She looks into the camera with a trace of a smile—composed and self-contained. The portraits—head shots of Laney in plain, long-sleeved dress—do not conform to the formal style preferred by many of her contemporaries among the first generation of college-educated black women. Educators and women's club leaders such as Anna Julia Cooper (1858?–1964), Mary Church Terrell (1863–1954), and Janie Porter Barrett (1865–1948) were often photographed in parlor settings, exuding style and status in a manner purposely oppositional to perceptions of black women in society at large. As Kathryn A. Canas argues, such accoutrements as parasols, floor-length dresses, gowns, capes, and wraps were part of the "rhetorical paradox" of these women as they entered the public sphere for the first time.[1]

In the early 1900s such images conveyed a middle-class respectability that mirrored these women's white counterparts in dress and mannerisms. As captured by the Atlanta-based African American photographer William T. Askew, these images meant to "answer the slander" against blacks and to create "a new black visual aesthetic" for public consumption.[2] Although Laney was known as one who "had but a few dresses, and hopelessly out of style hats,"[3] her disregard for fashion reflected her no-nonsense style of teaching and leadership,[4] not a different opinion about race uplift. Her

Lucy Craft Laney. Moor-
land Spingarn Research
Center. Howard University.

Mary Church Terrell.
Moorland Spingarn
Research Center. Howard
University.

willingness to buck fashion trends set her apart, but her nimble navigation between the views of the two towering male figures of the post-bellum–pre-Harlem era—Booker T. Washington and W. E. B. Du Bois—distinguished her as an educational visionary.

As the acknowledged spokesmen of black America, Washington and Du Bois took contrasting positions on racial advancement—including whether to emphasize industrial or classical/academic education—that framed the discourse among African American intellectuals. A parallel female-centered discourse defined their contemporary Laney's work. Her broad agenda for race uplift relied upon education and distinct gender roles within the family that incorporated both viewpoints. This essay traces her development as an educational activist in the context of the people, events, and social currents that influenced and engaged her during this transitional era.

Laney's personal qualities and leadership were widely noted by associates, although she did not view herself as a leader or seek the spotlight. Her Atlanta University (AU) classmate, Richard R. Wright Sr., then a high school principal in Augusta, Georgia, recalled that Laney, besides being "the loveliest, most energetic and attractive brown skin girl he had ever met," intrigued him by "her unwillingness to give up." She spurned his romantic advances and challenged him in class when she thought he was erring.[5] Du Bois called her "the vestal virgin who kept the fires of Negro education fiercely flaming."[6] Laney visited Tuskegee to attend workshops and was a friend of Washington's third wife, Margaret Murray Washington. Washington and Laney's interactions are not documented, but he did praise her for "interesting and important work" at Haines. By astutely placing "industrial" in the school's name, she appeared to ally herself with Washington, while defusing hostilities of white southerners who feared that blacks would be educated out of their "natural station."[7]

In addition to attracting white support, "industrial" connoted a resourcefulness and personal responsibility that reflected Laney's Victorian mores. She chartered Haines in 1886, only five years after Washington founded Tuskegee Institute with the help of his first wife, Olivia Davidson Washington. That Laney succeeded in offering a curriculum with some industrial courses, but weighted toward academic studies, at a time when Washington's brand of industrialism and political accommodation was sweeping the South was not surprising. Mary McLeod Bethune, who apprenticed with Laney in 1896 before opening her own school in Daytona in 1904, attributed Laney's success to "her fearlessness, her amazing touch

Mary McLeod Bethune. Moorland Spingarn
Research Center. Howard University.

in every respect, an energy that seemed inexhaustible, and her mighty
power to command respect and admiration from her students and all who
knew her. She handled her domain with the art of a master."[8]

Laney embraced the notion of a divided sphere that focused on
women's "natural" and "innate" abilities as nurturers of children. Such
thinking showed the impact of the "cult of true womanhood," a mid-nine-
teenth-century ideal of female purity, piety, submissiveness, and domesticity, designed for the "protection" of middle- and upper-class white women
within the home.[9] While Laney reified marriage in her public speeches,
she spurned it for herself and directed her energies toward her work.
Hazel V. Carby, among others, notes that African American women elites
used the concept of true womanhood as a restorative for black women's
virtue, which had been damaged in the enslaved, sexually exploited
group.[10] Laney's appropriation of some of its elements infused gender into
the male discourse of race uplift in the post-bellum–pre-Harlem era.

To women uplifters, removing the taint of immorality would come through "purifying" home life, which they saw as a prerequisite to social acceptance. This compelled them to downplay their sexuality and adopt what Darlene Clark Hine calls a "culture of dissemblance" about their private lives.[11] Laney's reference in her speeches to "self-sacrificing" and her frequent mention of "purity" and "cleanliness" are compatible with the usages of other race leaders like Du Bois and Washington, who stressed the value of hygiene and comportment.[12] Du Bois's description of her as a "vestal virgin" underscores the era's link between female sexual purity and fitness to teach. Organizations like the American Missionary Association (AMA), and many public school systems, required that women teachers remain single.[13]

Despite her unmarried status, her advocacy of home life bestowed a halo of spiritual motherhood upon Laney.[14] Her focus on domestic roles sought to elevate black women, who were denied political expression by the Fifteenth Amendment, which extended suffrage only to black men. She believed that it was largely the job of black mothers to eliminate the class-based gap between the educated and the masses.

Laney's trajectory as an independent-minded educational leader can be attributed to her unique childhood in Macon, Georgia, and her educational influences. Her parents, and the family life they created, were her domestic model. David Laney, her father, bought his freedom and moved from South Carolina to Macon, where he became a master carpenter, lay minister, and one of three black men ordained in the Presbyterian Church. He married the slave Louisa and bought her freedom. The seventh of ten children of that union, Lucy viewed her mother and father's relationship as ideal. She described it as a caring one in which her father "would never let my mother do heavy work."[15] It was a relationship of mutual nurturance and care, in which gender roles were distinct, but equal. Both her mother and father provided income for the family. She said of her father, "He didn't forget my mother in anything. I never heard him say a harsh word to her . . . when she was determined to have her way—he would say, so tenderly, 'Now, Louisa, be careful.' And usually she listened." Recalling her childhood, and how she learned to read along with her mother, Laney said, "[W]e were always comfortable, had books to read and such fun we children had."[16] By age twelve she was reading and translating Latin, igniting a lifelong love for the subject.[17]

Laney's social and intellectual development was further enhanced by the post-bellum–pre-Harlem era's enthusiasm for building black schools and promoting political empowerment.[18] In Macon, five AMA schools opened, including the John R. Lewis High School that Laney attended. African Americans of Macon responded to the general white hostility toward black education and fickle funding by taxing themselves to support their own schools.[19] Blacks in Macon also helped to elect African Methodist Episcopal Bishop Henry McNeal Turner (1834–1915) to the state legislature in 1868. He was then expelled by white legislators, but eventually reseated. In a speech before the legislature on September 3, 1868, Turner defiantly stated, "I hold that I am a member of this body . . . I shall neither fawn nor cringe before any party, nor stoop to beg them for my rights. I am here to hurl thunderbolts at the men who would dare cross the threshold of my manhood."[20] His expulsion marked the rise of reactionary Democrats and racist assaults in the state. Laney's proclamations against racial prejudice in her speeches were not as strident as Turner's, and focused more on women and families. But her instinct to preserve black control of schools, rather than trust their fate to public funding by white-elected bodies, may have been the lesson of such events in her home state.[21]

East of Augusta, the newly established Atlanta University was another pivotal part of her intellectual and social development. Chartered by the AMA in 1867, AU presented the most visible example of faith in the educability of blacks. Its curriculum emphasized the classics, reflecting founding president Edmund Asa Ware's views. The Yale-educated Ware recruited like-minded northern teachers through the Freedman's Bureau and developed a curriculum that "followed closely the best New England colleges." He established an academically rigorous environment, despite hostility from members of Atlanta's white community, who considered the school a threat to the racial status quo.[22] Later, AU's academic reputation helped to recruit young professor Du Bois to the faculty.[23] Just as Hampton Institute's founder Samuel Armstrong molded Washington to the doctrine of industrial education for blacks, Ware's orientation inspired Laney's love of the classics and an academic education.

When she graduated with honors in 1873, Laney was a budding intellectual, dedicated to teaching the "whole person" and spreading the gospel of service to the race.[24] She and her three other women classmates were among the increasing numbers of service-minded women entering the "helping professions" of teaching and nursing, virtually the only ones open to southern black women.[25] This trend was aided by the popular belief that women were endowed with a gift for nurturing and care giving.[26]

Laney began teaching with stints in Macon and Augusta. Before founding Haines, she also taught in the public schools of Milledgeville and
Savannah. She counted upon the assistance of Augusta's receptive black
community, who had welcomed church-sponsored educational initiatives,
including those of the AMA and the Baptist Home Mission Society. The
city was the home of the African American activist ministers and educators Charles Walker, who founded Paine College, and William J. White,
who founded the Augusta Baptist Institute, which later became Morehouse College.[27]

Du Bois admired Laney as a teacher, but more for her principled,
uncompromising advocacy on behalf of black people. He visited Haines in
1917 to lecture on the difference between industrial education and his own
views on preparing the "talented tenth" for race leadership.[28] Afterwards
he wrote,

> There is fighting in Augusta, a Little Battle in the Dark; a lone, little black
> woman waging war, not only against entrenched prejudice (the kind that
> keeps thousands of colored school children out of school), but also with
> traitors and hypocrites in her own race; men who know how to work with
> tourists for tidy sums by cringing and kowtowing. Yet, Lucy Laney triumphs
> even when her school is poor and half equipped.[29]

Although Washington had died two years earlier, Du Bois's praise of Laney
can be read as a salvo against servile racial behavior and the accommodationist politics associated with Washington. Nevertheless, in the same editorial, he stated that although there is "no pretense of a school, with
dishwashing substituted for English, . . . it is a home and center of learning."[30] Demonstrating either a lapse or a misreading of the evidence, his
assessment was at odds with the school's academic subjects and the
accomplishments of its students.

John Hope, who became the first black president of AU in 1929, was
taught by Laney in Augusta. Again illustrating Laney's ability to navigate
the ideological divide in black education, his biographer notes that she
brought a "vast practicality" to the field of education.[31] While intellectually compatible with Du Bois, Laney valued the focus in industrial education on thrift and personal rectitude. Her greatest difference with
Washington was that she viewed an industrial curriculum as the beginning of an education, not the final goal. The program at Haines was thus

comprehensive rather than narrowly defined. It showed the influence of Laney's own broad learning[32] and pragmatism.

Haines's core curriculum included college preparatory courses such as English, classical and romance languages (Greek, Latin, and French), history (including African American history) and geography, science (biology and physics), music, and religious education.[33] But the school's rapid growth was enabled by its offering of utilitarian classes such as sewing, and its "Christian" rather than industrial orientation. Laney depoliticized the curriculum by integrating the "kingdom of knowledge" with the kingdom of God and sidestepping the fractious politics of the industrial/academic schism. She became known as "not only an institution builder, but a character builder."[34]

When Du Bois invited her to the Amenia Conference in 1916, an interracial conclave of leaders assembled to discuss the future of the race, Laney was already a national figure. She had been a regular participant in Du Bois's Atlanta University Conferences, and was also among the black educators who attended the Farmers' Conferences first organized in 1890 at Tuskegee, thus making valuable contributions at both poles of black educational thought.[35] In addition, Laney became active in the new National Association of Colored Women organized in 1896, which represented black women's emerging activism.

The Farmers' Conferences became the Hampton-Tuskegee Negro Conferences, but continued to concentrate on blacks in rural communities, with little attention to demographic shifts created by the throngs migrating to the cities.[36] In contrast, the Atlanta Conference highlighted urban African Americans and addressed issues affecting them, such as mortality, poverty, wages, and labor.[37] Under Du Bois's leadership, it reached its pinnacle when it generated the first social science studies on city-dwelling blacks. Its publications established a benchmark for such scholarship, earning accolades and international recognition for Du Bois and AU. With his goal of using social science to argue for enlightened public policy toward African Americans, he included prominent alumni such as Laney among his core investigators. Her report to the First Atlanta Conference in 1896 was on the "Causes of Excessive Mortality: Poverty."[38] It was an unadorned description of the conditions under which different "classes" of blacks live in city "settlements." "The rank and file of the race [keep] . . . most ignorant," she noted, going on to decry conditions in black homes, where, she reported, mothers were required to work twelve hours a day, with no time for guiding their children, and fathers labored all day for seventy-five cents to one dollar and twenty-five cents, which left families little option but to huddle in unhygienic one-room houses. For the "class" who had overcome ignorance and learned to live clean and industrious lives, societal conditions denied them opportunities to own businesses or to find decent employment. Laney hoped that the conference would produce a plan for bringing relief to these sufferers of neglect and racism.[39]

At the second Atlanta Conference, Laney established the tone for the Women's Meeting, a cluster of presentations that included speeches on topics such as "Friendly Visiting," "Mothers' Meetings," "Need of Day Nurseries," and "Need of Kindergartens." Each speaker proposed some special way in which African American women could or should be more useful to their communities. Dubbed the "mothers' meetings," these became the media for bringing effective instruction and practical strategies to the masses in matters religious and moral. For example, they endorsed day nurseries where children would receive the highest level of instruction and attention while their mothers worked.[40]

The gender segregation at the conference suited Laney's female-directed message to women. She extolled motherhood as "the greatest joy, a crown more costly than pearls of royalty." For her, gender roles were very important. The race needs "manly, God-fearing husbands" and "womanly, God-fearing wives," she declared. The mother is the "chief joy" in the home and has the "privilege and authority, God-given," to develop young lives. Recalling her parents' relationship, she did not consider special rights and privileges for mothers as acceptance of inequality or a subordinate status. Yet, in the same speech, she warned against establishing a "double standard" for boys and girls in the home. If one exists in her home or community, the intelligent mother must "tear it down," she said.[41]

Some felt hostile toward Washington and the Hampton-Tuskegee model, but not Laney. She delivered her 1899 "Burden of the Educated Colored Woman" speech at the Hampton Negro Conference, a stronghold of Washington's followers. Women have a "burden," she expounded, because of their special endowment for improving society that begins with their "maternal instinct" for teaching young children. She exalted black women who had been uplifted by education to assist others in overcoming five different types of injustice that slavery had produced: poor education, negative home life, racial prejudice, and "ignorance and immorality." The cure she prescribed—"clean homes, pure homes, better schools, more culture, more thrift and work in large doses"—illustrated her woman-centered ethos grounded in domestic values.[42] Laney also condemned the unjust prison sentencing of black men, a fight for social justice she continued all her life.

On the topic of the "moral regeneration of black women," Laney agreed with Cooper, who was one of the several African American delegates to address the World Congress of Representative Women at Chicago's 1893 Columbian Exposition. Cooper also promoted a rigorous, classically based curriculum, although her M Street School in Washington, D.C., also offered industrial education. A staunch defender of higher education for women, she refused to be pigeonholed. In an article in *The Southern Workman*, a Hampton Institute journal supporting industrial education, she celebrated the virtues of family and pronounced marriage "sacred," but also defined it as a contractual relationship in which the domestic partner —the wife—"earns a definite part of [the husband's] wage" because of her duties at home.[43] Similarly, Laney's prescriptions for family life intended to uplift the race by adhering to conventional, but expanded, gender roles.

Laney's championing of black control of education must be viewed in the context of the political geography of her state. During the post-bellum–pre-Harlem decades, Georgia ranked among the most racist of the southern states: that slaves' descendents comprised nearly half of the population made whites jittery and inclined to contain, rather than educate, them. Du Bois dubbed the state not only the geographical center of black America but also the epicenter of African American problems.[44] Whether the issue was the convict lease system, disenfranchisement, lynching, or hostility to education, Georgia's white citizenry usually adopted an antiblack stance.

From the years 1882 through 1923 Georgia led the nation in lynchings, with 505 on record. While this form of violence declined in other states between 1900 and 1920, the number of African Americans lynched in Georgia actually outpaced the record of the previous twenty years. A single event that illustrates this hostile racial climate happened in Atlanta in 1906. Five days of frenzied "Negrophobia" engulfed the city, leaving ten blacks killed and scores wounded.[45] Draconian laws were enacted to deny African Americans their political rights and human dignity. In Macon, black women were arrested and fined under an ordinance that mandated them to find employment, regardless of their economic situations.[46] This racist and misogynistic tactic meant to force them into domestic service. A similar mindset led the attempt to undermine black public education, which in some counties meant hiring the least qualified teachers for black schools, and paying them poorly. These conditions made Laney a long-time skeptic of public education and reluctant to concede education for blacks to state control.

Compared to the climate in Macon and other Georgia cities, Augusta fostered a more hospitable environment for blacks. In the 1880s it boasted two African American newspapers, a Masonic lodge, and Paine College.[47] Between 1900 and 1921 only two lynchings are listed for the county. By no means a racial oasis, Augusta also was the site of a grand jury hearing that questioned the value of spending any public money on educating black Americans, based on the supposition that "it spoils good farm hands."[48] This was part of a general belief that blacks needed only rudimentary education: their ownership of property and accumulation of wealth did not prevent demeaning treatment.[49]

An event that defined Augusta's worsening racial climate was the closing of Ware, the only public high school for blacks in the city.[50] The Supreme Court decision in *Cumming et al. v. The Board of Education of Richmond County* had ruled that such closures did not violate the Fourteenth Amendment. This ruling devastated the mainly mulatto "aristocracy of color" in Augusta, and it hastened their retreat from racial politics.[51] Race leaders such as Laney, however, who preferred black control of their own private schools to the capricious supervision of their children's education by whites, may have even welcomed Ware's closing. Nevertheless, the issue remained a sensitive one, and Laney herself kept reticent on the topic.[52]

In the midst of such deteriorating racial relations, Laney assumed more political and social involvements in Augusta. She joined or spearheaded antilynching campaigns, voter registration drives, and community improvement projects. She presided over the Georgia Federation of Colored Women's Clubs, and in 1919 was a founder of the Augusta chapter of the NAACP (National Association for the Advancement of Colored People). Aside from her dedication to Haines, her most sustained uplift work was with the vanguard of black club women mentioned earlier, who believed that they, not the titular patriarchs of the race, held the keys to social progress.

The belief that women could best leverage race advancement coexisted with the view that women's clubs would exert a "civilizing" influence. Sometimes this emphasis could mean stamping out practices associated with folk culture. For Laney, it included condemning "Egypt-walking," a celebratory event among blacks in Augusta that she thought merely rein-forced negative stereotypes.[53] Her stature in the community allowed such interventions, while her Haines Institute contradicted perceptions of blacks as uneducable.

Decades earlier, as a teacher and principal at the prestigious Institute for Colored Youth in Philadelphia, Fannie Jackson Coppin (1837–1913) demonstrated similar goals. She had showed that black students could master the most demanding classical curriculum, and that she herself pos-sessed the ability, character, intelligence, and vision to lead such an institu-tion.[54] Like Coppin's Institute for Colored Youth, Laney's Haines Institute symbolized the possibilities inherent in a female-centered uplifting mis-sion. Both institutions became centers of academic excellence that quietly integrated academic and industrial courses.

By aligning a traditional view of women's roles with an oppositional intent, Laney confirmed the scholar Carol Allen's view that post-bellum–pre-Harlem black women intellectuals "returned to traditions [in order to] modify them."[55] Her very strong advocacy of women as the levers of civilization and uplift proved empowering for many African American educators. Women school founders who acknowledged her mentorship include Mary McLeod Bethune of the Daytona Normal and Industrial School, Charlotte Hawkins Brown of the Palmer Memorial Institute, and Nannie Helen Burroughs of the National Training School for Women and Girls. Like their mentor Laney, they saw no contradiction in instituting a curriculum comprised of both industrial and academic courses, or prag-matism and idealism. With hindsight, the implications of such black women's collective acceptance of the "burden" for racial salvation seem problematic. But under troubling circumstances—racial repression and discord, insecure black male suffrage, the warring ideals of divisive black male leadership—Laney erected, through Haines and her extensive race work, both an edifice and a legacy of educational achievement that ren-dered simplistic dichotomies of racial advancement moot.

NOTES

1. Canas defines the "rhetorical paradox" as the tension created among edu-cated African American women by whites' negative assumptions about black cul-ture, and their use of a white standard to resist and refute such stereotypes.

Kathryn A. Canas, "Managing the Rhetorical Paradox of Black Womanhood: Mary Church Terrell and the Problem of Identity Formation" (master's thesis, Indiana University, 1993).

2. The Library of Congress, *A Small Nation of People: W. E. B. Du Bois and African American Portraits of Progress* (New York: HarperCollins, 2003), 29, 55.

3. Anne W. Kendall, "Lucy Craft Laney: The Mother of the Children of the People" (Atlanta University Archives, 1978), 12.

4. Mary White Ovington, *Portraits in Color* (New York: Viking, 1927), 54.

5. Elizabeth Ross Haynes, *The Black Boy of Atlanta* (Boston: House of Edinboro Publishers, 1952), 37.

6. Edward T. James, ed., *Notable American Women* (Cambridge, MA: Harvard University Press, 1971), 351.

7. Audrey Thomas McCluskey, "We Specialize in the Wholly Impossible: Black Women School Founders and Their Mission," *Signs: Journal of Women and Culture in Society* 22.2 (1977): 407.

8. Audrey Thomas McCluskey, "Mary McLeod Bethune and the Education of Black Girls" (Ph.D. diss., Indiana University, 1991), 135.

9. Linda M. Perkins, "The Impact of the 'Cult of True Womanhood' in the Education of Black Women," *Journal of Social Science Issues* 39.3 (1983): 18.

10. Hazel V. Carby, *Reconstructing Womanhood: The Emergence of the Afro-American Woman Novelist* (New York: Oxford University Press, 1987), 32.

11. Darlene Clark Hine, "Rape and the Inner Lives of Black Women in the Middle West: Preliminary Thoughts on a Culture of Dissemblance," *Signs: Journal of Women in Society* 14.4 (Summer 1989): 912–20.

12. See, for example, Anson Phelps Stokes, *Tuskegee Institute: The First Fifty Years* (Tuskegee, AL: Tuskegee Institute Press, 1931); and Philip J. Kowalski's essay in this volume.

13. Perkins, "Impact of the 'Cult,'" 17–33.

14. The author and Haines graduate Frank Yerby wrote a poetic eulogy about Laney that included the following lines: "You have been called the mother of a race, / But you are more than leader; more than friend; / You were a flame, a torch, an era's end, / A new days' dawn, a lamp before our face." *Golden Jubilee Program,* Haines Institute, n.d.

15. *Haines Journal,* Laney Vertical File, Moorland-Spingarn Research Center, Howard University.

16. Lucy Notestein, "Nobody Knows the Trouble I See," National Missions of Presbyterian Church, William E. Harmon Collection, Library of Congress, Manuscript Division, n.d., 3–4.

17. Mary Jackson McCrorey, "Lucy Laney," *The Crisis* (June 1934): 161.

18. Paul Michael Johnson, "The Negro in Macon, Georgia" (master's thesis, University of Chicago, 1968), 19–31.

19. James D. Anderson, *The Education of Blacks in the South, 1865–1935* (Chapel Hill: University of North Carolina Press, 1988), 156.

20. Johnson, "Negro in Macon," 93.

21. Reportedly, Laney gave a deposition in the important case of *Cumming et al. v. The Board of Education of Richmond County,* which reached the Supreme Court in 1899. Siding with the white school board, the Court effectively ended high school education for African Americans until 1937. See J. Morgan Kousser, "Separate but Not Equal: The Supreme Court's First Decision on Discrimination in Schools," Social Science Working Paper No. 204, California Institute of Technology, 1978.

22. Clarence Bacote, *The Story of Atlanta University: A Century of Service, 1865–1965* (Princeton, NJ: Princeton University Press, 1969), 69, 37, 109.

23. David Levering Lewis, *W. E. B. Du Bois: Biography of a Race, 1868–1919* (New York: Henry Holt, 1993), 198.

24. A. C. Griggs, "Lucy Craft Laney," *Journal of Negro History* 19.1 (1934): 97–102.

25. Darlene Clark Hine and Kathleen Thompson, *A Shining Thread of Hope: The History of Black Women in America* (New York: Broadway Books, 1998), 221–22.

26. Perkins, "Impact of the 'Cult,'" 18.

27. See Henry Allen Bullock, *A History of Negro Education in the South from 1619 to the Present* (New York: Praeger Publishers, 1970), 175; and Gloria T. Williams-Way, "Lucy Craft Laney: Mother of the Children of the People" (Ph.D. diss., Georgia State University, 1998), 378.

28. Lewis, *W. E. B. Du Bois,* 527; and Mary Magdalene Marshall, "Tell Them We're Rising: Black Intellectuals and Lucy Craft Laney in Post–Civil War Augusta, Georgia" (Ph.D. diss., Drew University, 1998), 122.

29. W. E. B. Du Bois, Editorial, *The Crisis* 13.6 (1917): 269.

30. Ibid., 169.

31. Ridgely Torrence, *The Story of John Hope* (New York: Arno Press, 1969), 47.

32. Mrs. Lucille Laney Ellis Floyd, aged eighty-nine, a Laney namesake who attended Haines, recalled how the educator would sometimes substitute teach on any subject, including Greek, Latin, or mathematics. She would ask the class what they were studying, then proceed to teach without a textbook. Lucille Laney Ellis Floyd, interview by Audrey Thomas McCluskey, 25 April 2003.

33. Marshall, "Tell Them We're Rising," 111.

34. Britt Edward Cottingham, "The Burden of the Educated Colored Woman: Lucy Laney and Haines Institute, 1886–1933" (master's thesis, Georgia State University, 1995), 2.

35. Audrey Thomas McCluskey and Elaine M. Smith, *Mary McLeod Bethune: Building a Better World* (Bloomington: Indiana University Press, 1999), 5.

36. Stokes, *Tuskegee Institute*, 23.

37. Lewis, *W. E. B. Du Bois*, 217.

38. Published as Lucy Craft Laney, "General Mortality among Negroes," in the *Atlanta University Publications*, ed. W. E. B. Du Bois (1903; repr. New York: Arno Press, 1968), 18–20.

39. Laney, "Mortality."

40. Lucy Craft Laney, "Address Before the Women's Meeting," Atlanta University Conference, Atlanta, GA, 1898.

41. Ibid.

42. Lucy Craft Laney, "The Burden of the Educated Negro Woman," Proceedings of the Hampton Negro Conference, *Southern Workman and Hampton School Record* (September 1899): 343.

43. Anna Julia Cooper, "Colored Women as Wage-Earners," *Southern Workman and Hampton School Record* (August 1899): 296.

44. John Dittmer, *Black Georgia in the Progressive Era, 1900–1920* (Chicago: University of Illinois Press, 1977), 5.

45. Mark Bauerlein, *Negrophobia: A Race Riot in Atlanta, 1906* (San Francisco: Encounter Books, 2001), 218.

46. Dittmer, *Black Georgia*, 146.

47. Lloyd P. Terrell and Marguerite S. Terrell, *Blacks in Augusta: A Chronology* (Savannah: Georgia Historical Society, 1977), 10.

48. Edward J. Cashin, "Paternalism in Augusta: The Impact of the Plantation Ethic upon an Urban Society," in *Paternalism in a Southern City*, ed. Edward J. Cashin and Glenn T. Eskew (Athens: University of Georgia Press, 2000), 36.

49. Kent Anderson Leslie, "No Middle Ground: Elite African-Americans in Augusta and the Coming of Jim Crow," in Cashin and Eskew, eds., *Paternalism in a Southern City*, 111.

50. June Patton, "The Black Community of Augusta and the Struggle for Ware High School, 1880–1899," in *New Perspectives on Black Education*, ed. James D. Anderson and V. P. Franklin (Boston: G. K. Hall, 1978), 54.

51. Kousser, "Separate but Not Equal," 45–46.

52. Ibid., 24.

53. McCluskey, "Mary McLeod Bethune," 216–27; and Audrey Thomas McCluskey, "The Educational Leadership of Lucy Craft Laney and Mary McLeod Bethune," in *Women of the American South: A Multicultural Reader*, ed. Christie Ann Farnham (New York: New York University Press, 1997), 200.

54. Linda M. Perkins, "'Heed Life's Demands': The Educational Philosophy of Fanny Jackson Coppin," *Journal of Negro Education* 51.3 (1983): 190.

55. Carol Allen, *Black Women Intellectuals: Strategies of Nation, Family, and Neighborhoods in the Works of Pauline Hopkins, Jessie Fauset, and Marita Bonner* (New York: Garland Press, 1998), 4.

Chapter 5

Old and New Issue Servants
"Race" Men and Women Weigh In

Barbara Ryan

In 1899, W. E. B. Du Bois confronted complaints about "new issue" servi-tude in a sociological study called *The Philadelphia Negro*. "New issue" cooks and maids were a vexing social ill for those Americans whose comfort and leisure were supplied by "negros who have grown up in freedom, utterly untrained as cooks, housemaids, or nurses," and thus, for one aggrieved commentator, "ignorant of all that goes to make a desirable servant or household help."[1] Unfair, riposted Du Bois, in his counterargument based on the research-ratified finding that "new issue" attendants were "principally young people who were using domestic service as a stepping-stone to something else; who worked as servants simply because they could get nothing else to do; [and] who had received no training in service because they never expected to make it their life-calling." Emphasizing harsh and indefensible limits on African American employment, to heighten the political implications of his one-city study, this rising "race" man attested that

> to-day the ranks of Negro servants, and that means largely the ranks of domestic service in general in Philadelphia, have received all those whom the harsh competition of a great city has pushed down, all whom a relentless color proscription has turned back from other chosen vocations; half-trained teachers and poorly equipped students who have not succeeded; carpenters and masons who may not work at their trades; girls with common school training, eager for the hard work but respectable standing of shop girls and factory hands, and proscribed by their color. . . .[2]

This was a brilliant dissection of the effect that racist prejudice had on African Americans' ability to advance. Yet it was gapped, insofar as Du Bois downplayed the fact that service could be a relatively good job when employers paid wages fairly and on time. He also sidelined the status that domestic staff could enjoy in the African American community, while bracketing servingwomen's vulnerability to sexual harassment. Earlier commentators had been more confrontational about the latter, and not only during slavery days. "The opinion that a private house is a safer retreat for a good girl than a store or factory is often proved untenable," Mrs. N. F. Mossell asserted in 1886, "as very many, in fact quite a large percentage of recruits to the ranks of the disreputable testify they were first led astray by their employers."[3]

Though this was a grave concern for Americans of restricted job options, so was employability. "Your people all trained you to do service work," an ex-servant named Bernice Reeder recalled of this period. "It was what they all knew you had to learn—period."[4] Recognizing as much, Tuskegee Institute required female students to take courses in domestic science. The official line was that this prepared them to be better wives and mothers. Yet Tuskegee's head, Booker T. Washington, spoke glowingly of black attendance to white audiences. Thus, in the "Atlanta Exposition Address" (1895), Washington drew evocative word pictures of African Americans who had fully "proved our loyalty to you in the past, in nursing your children, watching by the sick-bed of your mothers and fathers, and often following them with tear-dimmed eyes to their graves."[5] This was one part purposeful stroking to two parts pragmatism, since Washington realized how many black Americans would spend part or all of their working lives in white people's homes.

Sutton E. Griggs advanced a similar but updated position in his novel, *The Hindered Hand* (1905), in a speech that denounces whites' attempt to enlist African Americans in societal overthrow. Despite turmoil, his minister-character avows, and flagrant injustice,

> "Negro servants continue to abide in white families, with no thought of leaving or of being dismissed. Negro men sit in carriages by the side of the fairest daughters of the Southland and take them in safety from place to place. The Negroes do the cooking for the whites, nurse their babies, and our mothers hover about the bedside of their dying. This they do while their hearts are yearning for a better day for themselves and their kind."[6]

This was no roseate vision, since Griggs acknowledged the threat of sexual victimization when black women accepted service posts. Instead, it was an attempt to show that all "new issue" attendants did not simmer with rage or act as what the Bible calls "eye-servants"—faithful only when under surveillance. The snag was, of course, how little Griggs's minister addressed Du Bois's painstaking research and stirring moral claims.

Du Bois was a radical, since most nineteenth-century activists praised black servants for their fidelity, efficiency, and willingness: see, in this context, not only *Uncle Tom's Cabin* (1852) but also Frank J. Webb's *Garies and Their Friends* (1857), Hannah Crafts's *Bondwoman's Narrative* (c. 1859), and Harriet Wilson's *Our Nig* (1859). None of these antebellum texts or writers discussed attendance in Du Bois's terms. Instead, each stressed the complex nature of the mistress-servant relationship, while yearning for the kind of home and family (or, at least, social) life that was difficult for workers kept at constant beck and call. Decades later, Alice Childress and Idella Parker would join the list of writers who, having served in non-kin homes, had much to say about how attendance looked and felt to those who shouldered the drudgery. Neither would revive the opinions of Washington and Griggs.

In the post-bellum–pre-Harlem era, emotionalism about the so-called servant problem reached an all-time high. A special brand of mean-spiritedness was reserved for attacks on freedpersons who tried to take charge of their working lives. Ex-slaves "are very troublesome servants to keep," sighed the *Atlantic Monthly* of 1877, "so that they rarely remain anchored long in any one vicinage."[7] A leading bone of contention was black cooks' and maids' refusal to "live in," as this was a step toward regulating their working days. "They seem to think," a southern mistress sniped in 1883, "that it is something against their freedom if they sleep where they are employed."[8] Laced through this and similar comments were comparisons between servants raised to live as slaves and those brought up as free. Exaggerating the difference between these groups, Marion Harland, the single most successful purveyor of post-bellum–pre-Harlem advice literature, disparaged "the dusky-cheeked Victoria-Columbia-Celeste of the present generation," the better to extol the attendance of African American women trained before the Civil War. "Let it be noted," she announced in 1889, "that the middle-aged mother or aunt of the smart colored damsel furnishes us with the best 'help' to be had in this, or any other country."[9] Lucy M. Salmon, author of the first academic book about U.S. service, agreed, warning homemakers in 1897 against employing the sort a male contemporary labeled the "shiftless sister in black."[10]

Not long afterward, Fannie Barrier Williams urged younger African Americans to take pride in service work. A "black clubwoman" who had experienced racism but also seen her husband favored by the Tuskegee Machine, Williams was right to say that domestic service "is the one field in which colored women meet with almost no opposition."[11] Her sense that service was a job deemed "ours almost by birthright" was not news in 1903. Yet that was precisely the problem, Du Bois charged in *The Philadelphia Negro*, adding that African Americans who resigned themselves to service "are often discontented and bitter, easily offended and without interest in their work."[12]

Into this debate stepped two gifted black belletrists, Charles W. Chesnutt and Pauline Elizabeth Hopkins. Both esteemed Washington's work at Tuskegee, but were attracted to Du Bois's more assertive politics; just as salient, both believed that creative expression should strive to change hearts and minds. Aiming for a decent, though not necessarily wealthy, audience, both kept quiet about certain issues; most noticeably, to contemporary readers, neither confronted the topic of sexual predation. From the safety of hindsight, we can criticize this omission as quietist. Yet by muting problems no literary author could solve, Chesnutt and Hopkins could broach others, while discrediting tributes to those African American attendants who had expected to live and die as property.

Chesnutt's tales of a freed coachman focus on the ex-slave's new role of waged servant. In his "conjure" stories emerging in the late 1880s, his character Julius McAdoo is pleasant, respectful, and willing to work. The tales he tells are not neutral: each reveals that slaves had never been contented or completely powerless. Chesnutt delves even further in his "Mars Jeems's Nightmare" (1898). It is not incidental that Julius "recalls" this story directly after his white employer fires Tom, his grandson. Tom's dismissal is understandable, since he is not very handy and displays no appetite for labor. But it catalyzes his grandfather Julius's discussion of a severe master who has a change of heart. "'Dis yer tale goes ter show,'" Julius explains,

> "dat w'ite folks w'at is so ha'd en stric', en doan make no 'lowance fer po' ign'ant niggers w'at ain' had no chanst ter l'arn, is li'ble ter hab bad dreams, ter say de leas', en dem w'at is kin' en good ter po' people is sho' ter prosper en git 'long in de worl'."[13]

By taking service work outside the home, some African American women gained the sort of authority memorialized by this comic song. Sheet music cover. "Now I Wants Ma Pay." New York and Chicago: F. A. Mills, 1899. Rare Book, Manuscript, and Special Collections. Perkins Library, Duke University.

This axiom marks a sharp departure from the ambiguity of an earlier Chesnutt story about a freedservant and her ne'er-do-well progeny. In "Aunt Mimy's Son," written in the mid-1890s, the lad in question—also named Tom-refuses to spend his life in service, only to die a broken man who may be a fugitive from the law. William L. Andrews has suggested that this sorry end was supposed to demonstrate the error into which young African Americans may fall if they fail to develop virtues such as thrift, patience, and pride in a job well done.[14] This interpretation makes sense, if we think of Chesnutt as a Washingtonian didact. If, however, we distinguish between the voice of a fictive narrator and a writer's personal opinions, it is surely germane that Chesnutt went on probing the question of "new issue" service in "Mars Jeems's Nightmare" and *The Marrow of Tradition* (1901). Evidence to support the contention of continued probing includes his use of servant pairings that put "old issue" paragons in a new light. This recurring motif suggests that a committed "race" man worried a freighted topic by crafting versions of it diversified by doubles, foils, and gender shifts.

If so, his efforts culminated in a novel that ironizes the death of a devoted freedservant. Space does not permit me to review the plot of *Marrow*. Yet few will have forgotten the passage in which "Mammy Jane" Letlow dies at the hands of a mob. Beaten, shot, or trampled in a race riot (the specifics of her death are not made clear), the ex-slave uttered last words hinting that she has confused a privileged white woman with the heavenly host. "Comin', missis, comin'!" are her final words. "Mammy Jane had gone," the omniscient narrator rasps,

> to join the old mistress upon whose memory her heart was fixed; and yet not all her reverence for her old mistress, nor all her deference to the whites, nor all their friendship for her, had been able to save her from this raging devil of race hatred which momentarily possessed the town.[15]

This authorial interpolation recalls another, early in *Marrow,* an *en passant* reference to a young nursemaid who

> had neither the picturesqueness of the slave, nor the unconscious dignity of those of whom freedom has been the immemorial birthright; she was in what might be called the chip-on-the-shoulder stage, through which races as well as individuals must pass in climbing the ladder of life,—not an

interesting, at least not an agreeable stage, but an inevitable one, and for that reason entitled to a paragraph in a story of Southern life. . . .[16]

A minor character, and unnamed, this servant character is unattractive. Yet she is Jane's obvious foil insofar as she is not shown to die painfully due to whites' resentment of fellow citizens of African descent. Nor is there anything covert about these tactics, once Chesnutt depicts the ex-slave woman drawing the contrast with disdain. "None er dese yer young folks ain' got de trainin' my old mist'ess give me," Jane harrumphs grouchily. "Dese yer newangle' schools don' l'arn 'em nothin' ter compare wid it."[17] Quieter but even more illuminating is the finding that, taken together, "Aunt Mimy's Son," "Mars Jeems's Nightmare" and *Marrow* yield four freedservants and four "new issue" attendants as if, again, generational difference fretted Chesnutt as he wondered what sort of African American attendance to promote or decry.

Kinship binds six of these characters into pairings—Mimy and Tom, Julius and Tom, and Jane and Jerry—that foreground generational change. All of the "old issue" servants are able workers, getting on in years, yet much appreciated by whites. Inasmuch, however, as two are female and one is male, it is intriguing that all three of the "new issue" servant characters are young men (two being sons and the third a grandson) of distinct temperament: one refuses to serve, one serves unwillingly, and one—Mammy Jane's son—is a scrounging lickspittle for whom Chesnutt shows scant sympathy. While Chesnutt displays concern about service and African American masculinity, he also scrutinizes the effect that older freedwomen's devotion to whites has had on their time and energy for, as much as interest in, parenting. Thus, just as Mammy Jane's devotion to a white mistress may have left her boy to grow up alone, Mimy could be judged guilty of the same dereliction of motherhood. In contrast, by confronting the employer they share, Julius of the "conjure" stories finds his grandson Tom a job and helps him keep it.

The three most explicit pairings emphasize kinship ties. Yet another pair may be the most important, since it contrasts a fully characterized freedserving-man to an unnamed nursemaid. The freedserving-man, Sandy Campbell, is prominent in *Marrow*. His most powerful appearance culminates in a moving speech that leaves readers pondering what selfless service might mean to the attendant. His speech reveals the traps of selflessness for those whose hearts are kind and sentiments true. Though a freedman like Julius, Sandy is no trickster or storyteller; on the contrary, he is made a trick-ee by the caddish nephew of his ex-master and present employer, the frail but honorable Colonel Delamere. Trying to prevent his old owner from figuring out what he has already realized—that the crime for which he is imprisoned, for which a mob waits in readiness to lynch him, was committed by Delamere's own nephew—Sandy reckons a debt of gratitude. "I'll die knowin' dat I've done my duty ter dem dat hi'ed me, an' trusted me, an' had claims on me," he explains. "Fer I wuz raise' by a Delamere, suh, an' all de ole Delameres wuz gent'emen, an' deir principles spread ter de niggers 'round 'em, suh; an' ef I has ter die fer somethin' I did n' do,—I kin die, suh, like a gent'eman!"[18] The multiple ironies of this passage include the facts that the source of Sandy's troubles is a not-so-old Delamere who is morally bankrupt; that Sandy shows more concern for the Delameres' family pride than the young "gentleman"; and that Sandy's protection of his aging master recalls the notion that the best servants are "part of the family." Just as telling is that the character who comes closest to living like the Colonel's villainous nephew (i.e., trading on a forebear's good fame and cadging where he can) is "Mammy Jane's" loutish mixed-race son.

Sandy's speech illuminates why an intelligent person might refuse to display the self-abjection that some employers prized. In two versions of a comic story, the second appearing in his last published novel, Chesnutt conveys a similar sense of irony. Though not one of his finest efforts, "The Dumb Witness" will interest all who recognize the acerbity with which it exposes the fallacy that steadfast attendance, from a person free to go, always bespeaks loyalty.

In both of its incarnations, "The Dumb Witness" recounts the decline of a white family when the documents recording a valuable legacy are lost. By the time the action begins, their ruin is nearly complete. The badly gone-to-seed master clings to hopes that the freedwoman Viney, who knows where the papers are hidden, will reveal their location. She cannot speak, however, her voice robbed during slavery days as punishment for "tattling" on her former master's misdeeds. Despite this cruelty, Viney (once, Chesnutt hints, a favored concubine) did not leave the estate after Emancipation. "There was some gruesome attraction in the scene of her sufferings," the white northern narrator surmises, in the first version of the tale, "or perhaps it was the home instinct."[19] What actually transpires, though, at the story's conclusion, is the attraction of the torturer for her victim. As it turns out, Viney has actually retained her voice over the last four decades, and she could have led her former owner to the papers at any time. The story takes an even more lurid turn when reused in *The Colonel's Dream* (1905), Chesnutt's last novel to go to press, for, in this version, the silent freedwoman knows all along that there is no fortune to recover. Here is a darkly humorous subversion of the tributes to former chattel who "stayed on and on," coupled perhaps with an indictment of whites who expected African Americans to make them rich, effortlessly.

Better crafted than *The Colonel's Dream,* and more buoyantly humorous, are the servant characters Pauline Hopkins introduced in her serialized novels for the *Colored American Magazine.* Contrasting freedservants and "new issue" staff, as Chesnutt had previously, her *Of One Blood* (1903) introduces the character Jim as "a Negro of the old regime who felt that the Anglo-Saxon was appointed by God to rule over the African."[20] This is no throw-away line, since he is both venal and weak. More developed, however, are Hopkins's servant characters in *Hagar's Daughter* (1901–1902). Those introduced at the beginning of the novel are slaves: the rascally Isaac, upstanding Henny, and her daughter Marthy. Later, when the plot has moved forward into the 1880s, we meet two servant characters who were born "free": John from New England, and Venus, the daughter of Marthy and Isaac. Due to her courage, love of kin, and extraordinary derring-do, Venus stars on this list, even though a "new issue" servant.

Taking these characters in order, Isaac is a bad lot. Even his owner is suspect, since the white man is a cheat: Henny underscores this when she addresses Isaac as "you lim' ob de debbil," adding that if his master plans to do a good turn, then "de debbil turn' sain."[21] Henny is a faithful servant: diligent, warm-hearted, efficient. But she is not powerful in her master's household, for she is unable to forestall the tragedy she foresees. Nor can she prevent her daughter's attraction to Isaac. Employed as a "free" servant, decades later, Venus does find a better man. However, since her new lover, New England John, is rather dull, it is uncertain at the novel's end that Venus will marry him, or anyone at all.

African Americans do better, Hopkins shows, during post-bellum–pre-Harlem years, since Marthy works from home as a laundress while Henny finds steady employment as a janitor; in addition, Henny's grandson is sufficiently freed of money-earning responsibilities to devote himself to his education. Venus's employment with benevolent whites is additionally helpful, because of the income she earns and her employer's patronage of her grandson. They are supportive too once Henny is kidnapped and the intrepid Venus sets out to find her.

There is more to *Hagar's Daughter* than servant characters' exploits. While no shame is imputed to Henny's janitorial work or Venus's non-kin attendance, it is patent by the novel's close that, if society were fair, the younger woman could do more with her abilities. This point is not explicit; nor does *Hagar's Daughter* encourage African Americans in or out of service posts. Instead, echoing servant-writers like Harriet Jacobs and Idella Parker, Hopkins shows that Henny's affection for those she serves comports with self-respect. At the same time, *Hagar's Daughter* emphasizes that attendants possess lives apart from their labor in other people's homes. This authorial decision may not sound bold, yet it enacted unembarrassed defense of the perquisites hard won by freedpersons, who sought ways to realize what liberty entailed.

Though overlooked by Du Bois and finessed by Washington, coresidence was of vital interest to white mistresses. "When you said you wanted to work days, you left there," a retired maid named Dorothea Lewis recalled. "She told you, you'd not be able to come back."[22] In so hostile an environment, Hopkins's affirmation of incremental gain is both meaningful and brave. Chesnutt's stories may be found wittier or more polished. But Hopkins's vision of a serving girl who can turn detective on her own say-so must have thrilled and inspired, and leaves this reader, at least, wishing that Venus had enjoyed the longevity of Nancy Drew. More centrally, that Hopkins wrote so positively about a "new issue" servant makes *Hagar's Daughter* forward-looking. Some may take issue with my sense that Chesnutt was hard on freed African American servingwomen, where Hopkins seems unimpressed with black male attendants. But there should be consensus that, where his ironies were directed at whites, her innovative characterizations targeted African Americans likely to have servants among their friends, neighbors, worship communities, and kin. Neither Chesnutt nor Hopkins was satisfied with what supposed experts—black or white—were saying about African American attendance. Just one small segment in a long, rich, and complex history, concern about "new issue" service challenged "race" men and women to reshape attitudes, practices, and literature.

NOTES

1. Mrs. Orra Langhorne, "Domestic Service in the South," *Journal of Social Science* 39 (1901): 171.

2. W. E. B. Du Bois, *The Philadelphia Negro* (Philadelphia: Published for the University of Pennsylvania, 1899), 137–38.

3. Mrs. N. F. [Gertrude] Mossell, "Servant Girl Question," in "Our Woman's Department," *The New York Freeman* 2.7 (2 January 1886): 1.

4. Elizabeth Clark-Lewis, *Living In, Living Out: African American Domestics in Washington, D.C., 1910–1940* (Washington, DC: Smithsonian Institution Press, 1994), 43.

5. Booker T. Washington, *Up from Slavery: An Autobiography,* ed. William L. Andrews (1901; repr. New York: Norton, 1996), 100.

6. Sutton E. Griggs, *The Hindered Hand; or, The Reign of the Repressionist* (Nashville: Published by the author, 1905), 217.

7. "South Carolina Society," *The Atlantic Monthly* 3 (1877): 675.

8. Quoted in Tera W. Hunter, *To 'Joy My Freedom: Southern Black Women's Lives and Labors after the Civil War* (Cambridge, MA: Harvard University Press, 1997), 59.

9. Marion Harland, *House and Home: A Complete Housewife's Guide* (Philadelphia: Clawson Brothers, 1889), 93.

10. See Lucy Maynard Salmon, *Domestic Service* (New York: Macmillan, 1897), 123; and Walter Fleming, "The Servant Problem in a Black Belt Village," *Sewanee Review* 13 (1905): 11.

11. Fannie Barrier Williams, "The Problem of Employment for Negro Women," *Southern Workman* 32.4 (1903): 437.

12. Du Bois, *Philadelphia Negro,* 138. I must acknowledge Isabel Eaton's contributions to this tome. Yet I wonder how useful Du Bois found his white research assistant's work since, if he had been wholly satisfied with her "Special Report on Negro Domestic Service in the Seventh Ward, Philadelphia," it is hard to see why he would have written as much, and as forcefully, as he did about domestic service in the body of *The Philadelphia Negro*. It is also known that he did most of the interviewing with the servants on whom she reported. For another point of view, see Mary Joe Deegan, "W. E. B. Du Bois and the Women of Hull House," *American Sociologist* 19.4 (Winter 1988): 304–6.

13. Charles Waddell Chesnutt, *The Conjure Woman and Other Conjure Tales,* ed. Robert M. Farnsworth (1899; repr. Ann Arbor: University of Michigan Press, 1969), 100.

14. William L. Andrews, *The Literary Career of Charles W. Chesnutt* (Baton Rouge: Louisiana State University Press), 32.

15. Charles Waddell Chesnutt, *The Marrow of Tradition,* ed. Robert M. Farnsworth (1901; repr. Ann Arbor: University of Michigan Press, 1969), 296–97.

16. Ibid., 42.

17. Ibid., 41.

18. Ibid., 208.

19. Charles Waddell Chesnutt, *The Short Fiction of Charles W. Chesnutt,* ed. Sylvia Lyons Render (Washington, DC: Howard University Press, 1974), 161–62.

20. Pauline E. Hopkins, *The Magazine Novels of Pauline Hopkins* (New York: Oxford University Press, 1988), 511.

21. Ibid., 42.

22. Elizabeth Clark-Lewis, *Living In,* 158.

Chapter 6

Savannah's *Colored Tribune,* the Reverend E. K. Love, and the Sacred Rebellion of Uplift

Barbara McCaskill

African Americans living in the post-bellum–pre-Harlem South ventured their most important ideas concerning politics, economics, and education in the pages of their periodical press. More than twelve hundred newspapers were born between 1866 and 1905, over 70 percent in the South.[1] It would seem that for every masthead sporting conventional titles such as "Journal," "Herald," and "Times," there was an African American paper with a moniker evoking militant and patently martial themes: in Georgia, the Athens *Blade* (edited by William A. Pledger) and the Augusta *Weekly Sentinel* (edited by Silas X. Floyd), for example. It was as if a post-Emancipation cultural practice, when many former slaves, asserting their freedom and autonomy, changed the spelling of their surnames to distinguish black family members from the white ones,[2] had followed African American editors and writers to the printing press. Yet more was at work here.

The newly freed slaves greeted the tenuous peace by foregoing the violent revenge many whites had predicted to take up a politics of reconciliation between the races and educational and economic advancement within their own. They launched a war of ideas that attacked the disenfranchisement and sexual and racial violence that troubled African American communities. *The Colored Tribune* newspaper and the minister-journalist Emmanuel King (E. K.) Love, voices of Savannah's African American community in the 1860s, 1870s, and 1880s, stand as representative examples of how the black church occupied the center of an effort to circulate news and opinion that commingled the rhetoric of reconciliation with direct, intrepid challenges to an increasingly oppressive status quo. The new insights about southern black writers and readers before the end of the Reconstruction that these newspapers bring expose information that we did not know about the breadth and dimensions of the nineteenth-century African American periodical press. And they are exemplary of the way the nonsacred papers substantiate what we do know: that, since slavery days, black Christianity, which "separated the message of Christian love from people who had no love for them,"[3] has been intertwined with the secular world of political reform and community building.

It is a widely held yet apocryphal notion that southern African American journalists muted calls for reform when the grip of Jim Crow tightened during post-bellum–pre-Harlem years. As with Rayford W. Logan's infamous "Nadir" discussion, we can reliably trace this misunderstanding to its source, in this case what is still one of the definitive resources for nineteenth-century African American journalism history, Penelope L. Bullock's *Afro-American Periodical Press, 1838–1909*. Before the digital revolution, which has made it relatively affordable, fast, and easy to preserve and provide access to early black American periodicals on visually arresting and researcher-friendly online databases, Bullock's 1981 book, which succeeded I[rvine]. Garland Penn's older *Afro-American Press and Its Editors* (1891), was an essential introduction to the history of early black newspapers. It still provides valuable, hard-to-find criticism and biographies concerning the scope and intentions of these periodicals and the lives of the men and women who published them. Yet, Bullock's assessment is misleading when she begins her chapter on the post-Reconstruction press:

> None of the periodicals initiated before 1865 were still in existence when the Civil War ended, and the publishing of black periodicals did not begin again until the decade of the 1880s. This hiatus can be attributed largely to the optimism that pervaded the black population. Negroes anticipated that legal measures taken by the federal government would guarantee first-class citizenship and place them in the mainstream of American life. Thus, the periodical, as an agent for the vindication of equal rights, was no longer needed.[4]

"The sole periodical of the Reconstruction era [*The Freedman's Torchlight*]," Bullock notes, "was published in Brooklyn in 1866."[5] Galvanized by efforts such as Georgia's Historic Newspaper Project, scholars have recovered publications such as *The Colored Tribune* that disprove Bullock's statements. Not only were a few black periodicals produced before the 1880s—many, like *The Colored Tribune,* appearing before Reconstruction was dismantled in 1877—but also their attitude about the permanence of the Reconstruction's gains was hopeful yet guarded. They vigilantly recorded and mobilized resistance to efforts to roll back the clock, and when the retrograde motion started, their outcries grew louder and more strident.

Like numerous newspapers extant from the deep South during this era, the weekly *Colored Tribune* (1875–1876), edited by John H. Deveaux (1848–1909), who hailed from one of the mulatto families of Savannah's "colored aristocracy," comes down to us as tattered issues with missing pages and incomplete runs.[6] It would seem logical to conclude that post-bellum–pre-Harlem periodicals published by southern blacks faced diminished prospects of survival, perhaps because of difficulties obtaining substantial numbers of regular subscribers, as well as agents to find and collect from them, or the dangers of undercapitalizing in a business that necessitated a reliable printing press and steady streams of ink and paper. Even publications composed before the Civil War by and for free black Americans up North—such as New York City's *Freedom's Journal* (1838), the nation's first African American newspaper, or Frederick Douglass's Rochester-based *North Star* (1847–1851?)—indicate that the odds were greater for floundering and folding during an initial two- to three-year period than for prospering. Similarly, the *Cherokee Phoenix* (1828–1834), a Native American newspaper founded in rural New Echota, Georgia—the first by a Native community in the United States—had a very brief lifespan compared to the runs of large city weeklies.[7] However, urban, abolitionist newspapers such as the *Liberator* (1831–1865) and *National Anti-Slavery Standard* (1840–1870), which also circulated among nonwhites as well as white audiences, boasted long, influential runs. The sustainability of a post-bellum–pre-Harlem newspaper such as *The Colored Tribune* thus seems less contingent upon the ethnicity or race of its readers, and more connected to a mixture of timing, location among an urban or rural constituency, literacy rates, and intersection with and patronage from a specific religious or educational institution or reform or political cause.

As the historian Robert E. Perdue informs us, "At first the *Tribune* included sermons on the front page of the paper."[8] Bringing forward into freedom the faith, forgiveness, and optimism that had sustained them during enslavement, *The Colored Tribune*'s black readers saw mirrored back to them literal reflections of their religious values and concerns: letters to the editor supporting prayer in schools; directories of Sunday School and worship services at A.M.E., Episcopal, Baptist, and Congregational churches in Savannah; and announcements of debates, spelling bees, and other educational and cultural activities in these houses of worship.

The well-known local A.M.E. minister and politician, Bishop Henry McNeal Turner, who won a seat in the state legislature as black representative for Bibb County in 1868, exerted his influence, even though *The Colored Tribune's* editor Deveaux "disagreed with Turner's colonization schemes."[9] Examples of Turner's reach within *The Colored Tribune* include a sermon from a service at his St. James Tabernacle on the folly of defying God, and his recommendation of a school for young women of the race.[10] Turner shared with many post-bellum–pre-Harlem ministers a journalistic disposition: he "founded and edited several journals [including the monthly *Voice of Missions*] and wrote a history of the A.M.E. church."[11] "[I]n a period when almost 45% of the black population was illiterate," African American preachers were typically not college trained but nonetheless were very likely to possess some degree of literacy; they were almost uniformly men who "[by] the turn of the century fell in between the categories of illiterate country preachers and the still fairly small group of college-educated and seminary-trained clerics."[12]

To regulate their slaves' interpretations of the Bible, and to reduce the prospects of their "property" running away or raising an insurrection, slaveholders had prohibited literacy, and learning to read even the Good Book became a punishable offense and an act of insubordination for unmanumitted black men and women.[13] Juan Williams and Quinton Dixie write that one step blacks took to respond to these restrictions was to create schools within the relative privacy of their churches.[14] To use the pen and written word as well as the pulpit and sermon for the benefit of their congregations must thus have carried the weight of both an ancestral command and a humanitarian mission to minister-journalists like Turner. Edward L. Wheeler positions them as the avatars of what he dubs "a theology of uplift," which combined traditional and mainstream beliefs about sin, salvation, heaven, and hell with commitment to the social reforms needed to admit black Americans specifically into the national community.[15]

Where the scholarship on the post-bellum–pre-Harlem era has fallen short is in its examination of the ostensibly secular African American press, such as the Republican-driven *Tribune,* as an effective, necessary, and logical current for cohering otherworldly concepts and social transformation. In his discussion of nineteenth-century southern black churches and nationalism, for example, William E. Montgomery unfurls a long history of religious newspapers and magazines produced by and for black communities, beginning with the influential A.M.E. *Christian Recorder* (1847–1960) and continuing through the 1890s with primarily Baptist and Methodist periodicals. I support his conclusion that, by informing about secular issues and regulating social aspirations, the Reconstruction-era sacred press continued and even amplified slavery's legacy of a black religion that was "not merely an otherworldly . . . institution . . . [but] very much a part of this world."[16] However, I am venturing further to propose that the record of post-bellum–pre-Harlem publications down South is incomplete unless we recognize that this combination of "otherworldly" and worldly strains was not confined to religious periodicals, but encompassed a broader spectrum of African American productions that includes the secular and sectarian *Colored Tribune*.

As was customary for English-language newspapers, *The Colored Tribune* reprinted liberally from other publications. Columns entitled "Learn a Trade" and "Paddle Your Own Canoe" anticipated themes of initiative, hard work, self-help, reciprocity between the races, and economic advancement that Booker T. Washington, Lucy Craft Laney, W. E. B. Du Bois, and other black leaders would codify into the uplift movement. Heedful of the time-worn adage that nothing is new under the sun, *The Colored Tribune* included lessons for its post-bellum–pre-Harlem readers that inscribed a genealogy of all-American values and traits derived from sources such as Benjamin Franklin's *Poor Richard's Almanack* (1733), Ralph Waldo Emerson's *Self-Reliance* (1841), and Lincoln's Gettysburg Address (1863).[17]

Indeed, the paper's masthead-"WITH MALICE TOWARD NONE; WITH CHARITY FOR ALL"—quotes from Lincoln's second inaugural address (March 4, 1865)[18] to announce the paper's affiliation with those whom this president's Emancipation Proclamation had liberated from slavery, and with the republican principles that, in liberating the slaves, Lincoln and the Union had affirmed. Shelly Fisher Fishkin and Carla L. Peterson identify this language as "the rhetoric of John Locke and the Founding Fathers, which invokes the inalienable rights of man; appeals to the natural principles of liberty, equality and justice; and inveighs against all forms of tyranny and oppression."[19] I would argue that *The Colored Tribune* also links itself here to a tradition of early black American writers and speakers from David Walker to Phillis Wheatley,[20] who invoke sentiments from Enlightenment-inspired texts, such as the Constitution and Declaration of Independence, in order to shame Americans into extending the protections to every human being that they reserved exclusively for elite white males.

However, to embrace such revolutionary discourse, as *The Colored Tribune* did, was more than a tactic for demanding equality and civil rights enjoyed by white folk and raising optimism and self-regard among black folk. By featuring among its religious fare this and similar rhetoric in discussions of secular topics such as suffrage, public education, and lynching, *The Colored Tribune* voiced the particular aspirations of African Americans living in the deep South who saw Christian visions of community harmony as intertwined with the occasionally down-and-dirty politics of racial elevation and national reunion.

An example of this marriage of sacred and secular is the April 8, 1876, weekly issue. The "Church Directory," announcing sabbath schools, evening Bible study classes, and prayer meetings, occupies its accustomed layout position in the first column of the third page. Where readers would anticipate more church-related news, or features on charity benefits, cultural and musical groups, and fraternal and benevolent societies, in the next column, the editor Deveaux instead inserts an article on the fifteen-year-old Emma Rhodes, who "under threats of whipping and hanging" (accompanied, probably, by the actual application of beatings and physical abuse) had been jailed by a mob and pressured to accuse her uncle of the murder of a "Mrs. Cochran" and her daughter. In the violent act of imprisoning Emma and torturing her body looms the fracture and dismemberment of black Georgia's body politic. Deveaux makes this danger lucid to his readers by opining within his report, as was customary in his day, on the legal and civil ramifications of Emma's abduction. "No man's life is safe," he writes, "when such desperate measures are resorted to obtain witnesses."[21] In the April 22, 1876, issue, again creating a collage of religious and secular matter on the same page, he declaims that Emma calls to mind "the recent slaughter of three colored men without any proof whatever that they had been guilty of any crime. . . . [Ferret] out and punish crime no matter by whom committed, white and black alike."[22]

The framing technique that Deveaux uses, literally surrounding the bulletins on Emma Rhodes with the matter-of-fact and even perfunctory "Church Directory" and "Briefs" on religious activities and individuals, accompanied by the occasional obituary, conveys multiple levels of meaning. For example, his reduction of the teen's name to "Emma" is absent a respectful honorific such as "Mrs." or "Miss" that codes of racial deference would automatically confer to a white woman. On the other hand, its familiarity may be a deliberate strategy to suggest Emma's affinity with Savannah's black community as one whose civil rights go unprotected and unsecured.

Where readers find patterns of naming opposed to those of southern whites are the "Church Directory" and "Briefs." Here Deveaux parades the surnames of prominent black Savannahians, prefaced by religious titles such as Reverend or Bishop, and concluding with academic titles that vivify what Deveaux calls the "couple of scores of B.D.'s, B.A.'s, A.M.'s, D.D.'s, and L.L.D.'s in [the A.M.E. Church's] ministerial ranks."[23] It would not go unnoticed by the *Tribune's* black readers that this "host . . . of Reverends and Professors" who "at this enlightened period [should] be the creators of thought, and a sentiment two [*sic*] valuable to be lost,"[24] are the moral and philosophical equivalent of the very same "good citizens"[25] that Deveaux has mobilized with his partisan political discourse on due process for Rhodes.

This overlapping of the sublime and the everyday is further reinforced by Deveaux's inclusion of tax notices for black men and women who are property owners, and his admonishments to black men under sixty years of age to pay their poll taxes and thus become eligible to register to vote. In the context of religious matter that derides soporific church attendance and that promotes active, involved stewardship—uplifting, "enlighten"ing, and educating one's lessers—as a spiritual obligation, Deveaux's material advice on the same pages about southern black people asserting their rights as citizens and testing the promises of the Reconstruction blurs the differences between both discursive streams: a Christian vision of community means extending the full rights of citizenship to black Americans.

For additional evidence of this conjoining of religious and secular purposes in *The Colored Tribune,* one need look no further than to its founders, all members of the city's black elite, who, as well as the college-educated Deveaux, included Louis B. Toomer, a postal worker and banker, and another university-trained civil servant, Louis M. Pleasant. While their *Colored Tribune* made utterances of the soul and spirit as prominent as the local news, and vice-versa, all three were active standard bearers of the Republican Party platform in Savannah's black community. Throughout the late 1860s and 1870s they organized campaigns of African American candidates for local and state political offices, and they retained black

Americans' loyalty to the party of Lincoln with speeches and attendance at state conventions.[26]

This interconnectedness of politics and religion was a continuity from slavery days, when surreptitious worship services in remote fields or praise houses and "religious meetings in the quarters, groves, and 'hush harbors'" also became sites of resistance, offering opportunities for revolutionaries, including Virginia's Nat Turner, inspired by scripture and divine revelation, to preach the gospel of collective revolt.[27] Or such sacred spaces welcomed fugitives such as Harriet Tubman to convert slave worshippers to the idea of rebelling by escaping for freedom. As the scholar Albert J. Raboteau writes, "To describe slave religion as merely otherworldly is inaccurate. . . . [S]lave religion had a this-worldly impact."[28] We know from the narratives of former slaves such as Douglass and Harriet Jacobs that Protestant ministers who supported abolition found phrases in the Holy Bible to connect the divine commandments of Providence to the worldly comings and goings of lawyers and politicians who lobbied to free the captives. It was therefore not incidental that "churches were early and dependable supporters"[29] of *The Colored Tribune.* In post-bellum–pre-Harlem papers such as Savannah's pioneering *Colored Tribune,* hidden in plain view is that sacred notions of individual perfectibility and the moralizing influence of families and communities, and secular aspirations for the race's advancement in business, education, and politics are inseparable.

While less remembered and less well known than Turner, the marvelously named E[mmanuel]. K[ing]. Love (1858–1900) left no less a legacy. Andrew Billingsley concludes that "during the crisis of emancipation and Reconstruction, no voice had been more eloquent, persistent, or effective in social reform than . . . pastor . . . Love."[30] Born a slave and ordained as a Baptist preacher in 1875, he pastored many churches, including Savannah's influential First African Baptist, where the nation's oldest and largest black congregation prayed. He followed the example of papers like the *Tribune* by using the southern black press, as well as other formats such as pamphlets, conference proceedings, and published sermons, to disseminate his ideas and opinions on a spectrum of subjects from temperance and marriage to lynching and the vote. Like his fellow African American ministers in the post-bellum–pre-Harlem South, Love divined that much was both expected and required of him, and he rose to meet these expectations and requirements with unflagging energy and a staggering, prolific written output. He cofounded, wrote for, and/or edited numerous publications, including the denominational *Baptist Truth, Georgia Sentinel,* and *Centennial Record,* as well as the secular *Augusta Weekly Sentinel* and *Albany Watchman.* To redress the dearth of black voices in the Baptists' official journals, and the racial slights and slurs of the white-controlled, segregationist American Baptist Publication Society, he united with other African American pastors to propose the creation of a separate black Baptist publication group.[31] The bibliographer Daniel A. P. Murray, commissioned by Du Bois to compile a list of black-authored books and pamphlets for the 1900 Paris Exposition, included Love's *History of the First African Baptist Church* (1888) in his catalog.[32]

After the Civil War, the Atlanta-Augusta-Savannah corridor, where Love and other black preachers ministered to thriving congregations, emerged as an epicenter for progressive normal and industrial schools dedicated to the instruction of Georgia's black men and women. The innovators of these institutions included Laney and Richard R. Wright of Augusta and the "Georgia fugitives" William and Ellen Craft, who returned to Georgia, where they once had been enslaved, from their Hammersmith, London, home to build educational farms for freedmen and freedwomen, including their Woodville School outside of Savannah.[33] The valedictorian of his class, Love earned a B.A. at Augusta Institute, which would later move to Atlanta and become Morehouse College, and enthusiastically joined this institution building. He lobbied in the legislature to fund the state's first black college, Savannah State, and then he successfully endorsed his colleague Wright for appointment as its first president.[34]

In pamphlets of his sermons reprinted by the Georgia Baptist Printing Company, Love intensifies the sacred-secular combination apparent in papers like *The Colored Tribune.* With its call to "our lovely Southland" that "[s]ensible Negroes and conservative whites should unite," his November 5, 1893, "Sermon on Lynch Law and Raping" proposes a "kind-hearted" appeal "to white people as our friends" in conciliatory and deferential tones reminiscent of Deveaux's commentary: "I am uncompromisingly opposed to race intermingling on any terms, legal or otherwise." In this, one of his most memorable sermons, he describes rapists as members of "a vile class" who are justifiably accused of their crimes as "blood-thirsty, savage" "brutes . . . not worthy to live among good people," and he reminds his readers that "even in Africa" such a crime is considered heinous enough to warrant execution.[35]

Yet, in step with the international crusades against lynching lead by Du Bois, Ida Wells-Barnett, Anna Julia Cooper, and others, Love risks his own safety (there were whites observed in the crowd of over fifteen hundred who came to hear him preach this message) to confront the racism that underlies the current mob-led hysteria based on assumptions that a rapist is a black man and his victim, a white woman. Arguing that "crimes are laid at our door even if the accusers are mistaken," he invokes the law to sort out fact from fiction. While he does not exonerate all southern blacks of wrongdoing, he maintains that "my race especially" knows "that our only hope and safety lie in the strictest obedience to the law and our unqualified support of the officers of the law." This is not mere self-congratulation, but also a not-so-subtle dig at white southerners who flout the courts and commit "foul play" by handing down biased, extralegal judgments against black innocents—a flagrant violation, Love points out, of the Constitution's guarantee of due process. "The ravishers can be punished far more effectually by law," he says, "and be killed just as dead by an officer of the law as by 500 masked outlaws."[36] Love seals his assertion that "[a]s horrible as raping is, lynching is infinitely worse." It is worse, Love argues, because it goes against a model of Christian community governed by rule of law. He evokes a discourse of church as well as state to contend that model Christians make model citizens.[37] Therefore, it is the "[c]ivilized Christian manhood" of upstanding black and white citizens, he concludes, that will change hearts through the press and the pulpits and thus protect the younger generations from the immoral and corrupting effects of racial violence.[38]

Such discursive strategies of Love and those who wrote in the pages of *The Colored Tribune* would not fade as the post-bellum—pre-Harlem decades segued into the twentieth century. Martin Luther King Jr., Andrew Young, Ella Baker, and the numerous unsung "foot-soldier[s] for equal justice"[39] in Georgia would respond to violence and oppression with double-edged appeals to the political and the material. The "sacred rebellion" that unfolded in the journals and pamphlets of race uplift thus gained a second life in the national debates about race and rights that swirled during the 1950s, 1960s, and 1970s. As we turn into another century, as we face another set of pressing issues that threaten to divide the globe—AIDS and HIV, global warming, terrorism, genocide—we may find our way to similar words in order to save ourselves.

NOTES

1. Henry George La Brie III, "A Profile of the Black Newspaper: Old Guard Black Journalists Reflect on the Past, Present, and Future" (Ph.D. diss., University of Iowa, 1973), 30.

2. See Herbert G. Gutman, *The Black Family in Slavery and Freedom, 1750–1925* (New York: Vintage, 1977), 230–56; and Lucille Clifton, *Good Woman: Poems and a Memoir, 1969–1980* (Rochester, NY: BOA Editions, 1987).

3. Juan Williams and Quinton Dixie, *This Far by Faith: Stories from the African American Religious Experience* (New York: HarperCollins, 2003), 7.

4. Penelope L. Bullock, *The Afro-American Periodical Press, 1838–1909* (Baton Rouge: Louisiana State University Press, 1981), 64.

5. Bullock, *Afro-American Periodical Press,* 2, 152. See also Patricia A. Young, "Roads to Travel: A Historical Look at *The Freedman's Torchlight*—An African American Contribution to Nineteenth-Century Instructional Technologies," *Journal of Black Studies* 31.5 (2001): 671–98.

6. For biographical information on Deveaux, see Robert E. Perdue, *The Negro in Savannah, 1865–1900* (New York: Exposition Press, 1973), 91, 93. *The Colored Tribune* (Savannah, GA) 1, nos. 9–34 (Dec. 4, 1875–July 22, 1876). I have digitized and encoded *The Colored Tribune* 1, nos. 17–21 (March 25, April 8, and April 22, 1876) for access and searchability online in the Georgia Historic Newspapers databases of the Digital Library of Georgia. My discussion derives from these issues. Access *The Colored Tribune* online at http://neptune3.galib.uga.edu/ssp/cgi-bin/tei-news-idx.pl.

7. One of the best sources for discussions of the *Phoenix* and its first editor, Elias Boudinot, who was inducted in the Georgia Writers Hall of Fame in Spring 2005, is the online *New Georgia Encyclopedia (NGE).* See the *NGE* reference articles entitled "Cherokee Phoenix" and "Elias Boudinot (1804–1838)" by Angela F. Pulley. http://www.georgiaencyclopedia.org.

8. Perdue, *Negro in Savannah,* 93.

9. See, for example, H[enry]. M[cNeal]. Turner, "Short Sketch of a Sermon Preached in the Tabernacle, Sunday April 18th, 1876," *The Colored Tribune* 1.21 (April 22, 1876): 1; and H[enry]. M[cNeal]. Turner, "Scotia Seminary," *The Colored Tribune* 1.17 (March 25, 1876): 2. For information about Turner's political activities, see Andrew Billingsley, *Mighty Like a River: The Black Church and Social Reform* (New York: Oxford University Press, 1999), 48, 51, 211; Edward L. Wheeler, *Uplifting the Race: The Black Minister in the New South, 1865–1902* (Lanham, MD: University Press of America, 1986), 61–65; Williams and Dixie, *This Far by Faith,* 115–18; and the chapter "Black Minister in Politics" in Stephen Ward Angell, *Bishop Henry McNeal Turner and African-American Religion in the South* (Knoxville: University of Tennessee Press), 81–107.

10. H[enry]. M[cNeal]. Turner, "Short Sketch of a Sermon Preached in the

Tabernacle, Sunday April 18th, 1876," *The Colored Tribune,* 1.21 (April 22, 1876): 1; and H[enry]. M[cNeal]. Turner, "Scotia Seminary," letter to the editor, *The Colored Tribune* 1.17 (March 25, 1876): 2.

11. Billingsley, *Mighty Like a River,* 52; and William E. Montgomery, *Under Their Own Vine and Fig Tree: The African-American Church in the South, 1865–1900* (Baton Rouge: Louisiana State University Press, 1993), 236.

12. Wheeler, *Uplifting the Race,* 49; and, Montgomery, *Under Their Own,* 319.

13. Albert J. Raboteau, *Slave Religion: The "Invisible Institution" in the Antebellum South* (1978; repr. New York: Oxford University Press, 2004), 239–43; Montgomery, *Under Their Own,* 142–45.

14. Williams and Dixie, *This Far by Faith,* 3.

15. Wheeler, *Uplifting the Race,* 37–59.

16. Montgomery, *Under Their Own,* 238.

17. Benjamin Franklin, *Poor Richard's Almanack* (Waterloo, IA: U.S.C. Publishing Company, 1914); Ralph Waldo Emerson, *Essays: First Series* (Boston: J. Munroe, 1841); Abraham Lincoln, *The Gettysburg Speech and Other Papers by Abraham Lincoln, and an Essay on Lincoln by James Russell Lowell; with Introductions and Notes* (Boston: Houghton Mifflin, 1888).

18. The second-term president ended his brief speech by expressing a wish for peace and comfort:

> With malice toward none, with charity for all, with firmness in the right as God gives us to see the right, let us strive on to finish the work we are in, to bind up the nation's wounds, to care for him who shall have borne the battle and for his widow and his orphan, to do all which may achieve and cherish a just and lasting peace among ourselves and with all nations.

By appropriating Lincoln's words, *The Colored Tribune* announced an interest in reaching out to local white Georgians, who might view free black Savannahians as suspicious and threatening, with assurances that they simply intended to cultivate harmonious relations and to go quietly about their own business. See the "Second Inaugural Address of Abraham Lincoln," The Avalon Project at Yale Law School, http://www.yale.edu/lawweb/avalon/presiden/inaug/lincoln2.htm. Accessed March 28, 2005.

19. Shelly Fisher Fishkin and Carla L. Peterson, " 'We Hold These Truths to Be Self-Evident': The Rhetoric of Frederick Douglass's Journalism," in *The Black Press: New Literary and Historical Essays,* ed. Todd Vogel (New Brunswick, NJ: Rutgers University Press, 2001), 72. This is a slightly different version of an essay originally appearing in *Frederick Douglass: New Literary and Historical Essays,* ed. Eric J. Sundquist (Cambridge: Cambridge University Press, 1990).

20. See David Walker, *Walker's Appeal, in Four Articles, Together with a Preamble to the Colored Citizens of the World, but in Particular, and Very Expressly to Those of the United States of America,* ed. Sean Wilenz (New York: Hill and Wang, 1995); and Phillis Wheatley, *Complete Writings,* ed. Vincent Carretta (New York:

Penguin, 2001). Stephanie L. Gordon invites us to expand this tradition by including the self-inventive, best-selling autobiographies of two post-bellum–pre-Harlem black cowboys. See her unpublished essay, "Self-Made Ex-Slaves: Bass Reeves, Nat Love, and the Cultures of the American Frontier."

21. "Emma Rhodes to Make a False Statement," *The Colored Tribune* 1.19 (April 8, 1876): 3.

22. "The Grand Jury of Effingham," *The Colored Tribune* 1.21 (April 22, 1876): 3.

23. "Proposed Establishment of a Quarterly Review," *The Colored Tribune,* 1.19 (April 8, 1876): 3.

24. Ibid., 3.

25. "The Grand Jury of Effingham," *The Colored Tribune,* 3.

26. Perdue, *Negro in Savannah,* 56–68, 131.

27. Raboteau, *Slave Religion,* 318; and Williams and Dixie, "God Has a Hand in It," in *This Far by Faith,* 11–41.

28. Raboteau, *Slave Religion,* 318.

29. Billingsley, *Mighty Like a River,* 45.

30. Billingsley, *Mighty Like a River,* 53.

31. For information about Love's antidiscrimation activism, writings, and advocacy of African American education and a black Baptist press, see the following: Sandy Dwayne Martin, "E. K. Love (1850–1900)," in *The New Georgia Encyclopedia,* http://www.georgiaencylopedia.org/nge; Sandy D[wayne]. Martin, *Black Baptists and African Missions: The Origins of a Movement, 1880–1915* (Macon, GA: Mercer University Press, 1989); Billingsley, *Mighty Like a River,* 41; Montgomery, *Under Their Own,* 242–43, 246–48; and James Melvin Washington, *Frustrated Fellowship: The Black Quest for Social Power* (Macon, GA: Mercer University Press, 2004), 147–50, 159–70, 183. See Giulia Fabi's unpublished essay entitled "White Lies: Amelia E. Johnson's Sunday School Fiction and the Politics of Racelessness" for an examination of the works of Johnson, the first black writer whose novels were published by the American Baptist Publication Society, which Love and his minister colleagues separated from to strike out on their own.

32. Daniel A[lexander]. P[ayne]. Murray, *Preliminary List of Books and Pamphlets by Negro Authors: For Paris Exposition and Library of Congress* (Washington, DC: U.S. Commission to the Paris Exposition, 1900). From The Exhibit of American Negroes: Daniel Murray's Bibliography, http://www.fofweb.com/Onfiles/Afhc/afparis1900/exhibit_lit_booklist.htm. Accessed January 5, 2005.

33. For information on the Crafts' efforts to educate the freedmen, see Richard J. M. Blackett, *Beating against the Barriers: Biographical Essays in Nineteenth-Century Afro-American History* (Baton Rouge: Louisiana State University Press, 1986); and Dorothy Sterling, *Black Foremothers: Three Lives,* 2nd ed. (New York: Feminist Press, 1988). For an example of how their story was used to teach the former slaves literacy, see William and Ellen Craft, *Running One Thousand Miles for Freedom* (Athens: University of Georgia Press, 1999), 101–5.

34. Billingsley, *Mighty Like a River*, 41.

35. Ibid., 41–45; and Martin, "E. K. Love (1850–1900)."

36. E. K. Love, *A Sermon on Lynch Law and Raping* (Augusta, GA: Georgia Baptist Print., 1894), preface (unnumbered), 8, 12. From the Library of Congress American Memory site, Pamphlets from the Daniel A. P. Murray Pamphlet Collection, 1818–1907, http://memory.loc.gov./ammem/aap/aaphome.html. Accessed March 12, 2005.

37. Ibid., 5, 6.

38. Ibid., 12.

39. See Maurice C. Daniels, *Horace T. Ward: Desegregation of the University of Georgia, Civil Rights Advocacy, and Jurisprudence* (Atlanta, GA: Clark Atlanta University Press, 2001), as well as his documentary films including *Foot Soldier for Equal Justice: Horace T. Ward and the Desegregation of the University of Georgia, Parts I and II* (2000, 2001).

Part III

Encountering Jim Crow
African American Literature and the Mainstream
(1890s)

Chapter 7

A Marginal Man in Black Bohemia
James Weldon Johnson in the New York Tenderloin

Robert M. Dowling

In the post-bellum–pre-Harlem period, the bulk of New York City's African American population shifted from Greenwich Village (around Bleecker and Mercer) to the notorious Tenderloin district (from Fifth Avenue across to Seventh and from Forty-second Street down to Twenty-fourth). Within the greater Tenderloin—legendary for its proliferation of dance halls, brothels, cabarets, and gambling clubs—a dynamic "black Bohemia" materialized that would later serve as a model for the celebrated New Negro Renaissance of the 1920s. Southern black migrants congregated there, and unavoidable feelings of homesickness and disorientation were accompanied by radical, and often disastrous, moral and psychological changes. New York at the century's turn was already a vital testing ground for disenfranchised southern black families and vagabonds alike; and these migrants sought not only to escape the racial injustices of the post-Reconstruction South but also to take advantage of the opportunities available in the country's greatest, most modern metropolis.

Once the center of white middle-class respectability, by the late 1870s the Tenderloin proper was a major theater district, and the subsequent army of pleasure seekers chased its "respectable" residents uptown. Tenderloin landlords then faced a difficult choice: either turn the brownstones into multiple-family tenements for the crush of immigrant arrivals from Southern and Eastern Europe, or lease them to gambling proprietors and brothel owners who could afford significantly higher rents.[1] They chose the second option, and seemingly overnight the Tenderloin became the most infamous center of vice in New York history.

The Tenderloin's black section was located along Sixth Avenue in what is now Chelsea. Anticipating Harlem life in the 1920s, this region catered to African American musicians, stage performers, and athletes, along with gamblers, prostitutes, white "slummers," and frequenters of the "black and tans" (racially integrated bars that often provided interracial assignations and drew considerable public scorn). Many blacks moved to the Tenderloin for its racial tolerance and professional opportunities. The Great Migration of African Americans escaping the horrors of Jim Crow and lynching was just beginning, but it accelerated when New York's center of black life moved from the Tenderloin to Harlem. Regardless, the midtown Tenderloin district offered black Manhattan a bohemian locale that shared many traits with the future "Renaissance," including artistic innovation, theatrical energy, moral experimentation, interracial contact, and professionalism.

In 1901, James Weldon Johnson, the African American educator, lawyer, diplomat, writer, and civil rights activist, migrated from Jacksonville, Florida, to the Marshall Hotel on West Fifty-third Street in New York City. There he collaborated with his brother, J. Rosamond Johnson, and Bob Cole, and the trio composed over two hundred popular songs, librettos, and light operas, including the hits "Nobody's Lookin' but de Owl and de Moon" (1901) and "Under the Bamboo Tree" (1902). The Marshall was an off-shoot of what Johnson referred to as the "flourishing black Bohemia" that emerged in the Tenderloin during the 1890s.[2] Though Harlem Renaissance scholar Louise Johnson claims that at this time, "the Tenderloin was a vague area,"[3] as opposed to its uptown complement, San Juan Hill, Johnson marks out a clearly definable site—along Sixth Avenue from Twenty-third Street to Thirty-third, crossing one block west. Outlining concrete physical parameters, he constructs the Tenderloin as a marginal district within the larger city, both spatially and culturally.

Johnson visited Dunbar there in 1899, while the latter was producing his hit Broadway musical *Clorindy; or, The Origin of the Cake-Walk*. Johnson's Tenderloin experience informed the New York chapters of his only novel, *The Autobiography of an Ex-Colored Man* (1912), and he includes discussions of it in his history, *Black Manhattan* (1930), and his autobiography, *Along This Way* (1933). In *Along This Way*, he explains that, for him, the district was a revelation:

> Up to this time, outside of polemical essays on the race question, I had not written a single line that had any relation to the Negro. I now began to

grope toward a realization of the importance of the American Negro's cultural background and his creative folk-art, and *to speculate on the superstructure of conscious art that might be reared upon them.* (italics mine)[4]

The New York chapters of *The Autobiography* buttress the African American "superstructure of conscious art" by adjoining it to the emergent metropolitan modernist aesthetic. The novel delivers a unique understanding of the New York life espoused in the 1890s—the mosaic of cultures it contained, the transgressions of popular morality it actualized, the literary watersheds it signaled. Although *The Autobiography* is fiction, Johnson toggles between fictional narrative and documentary discourse, and his New York chapters are deliberately written in a self-contained documentary style. His unnamed narrator alludes to this, remarking, "More that I learned [in the Tenderloin] would be better suited to a book on social phenomena than to a narrative of my life."[5] H. L. Mencken concurred, suggesting that the novel "is not, at bottom, a novel at all, but a sort of mixture of actual biography and fantasy, with overtones of sociology."[6] Remarkably, it includes a mere handful of New York chapters. But by only dipping into Tenderloin culture, the narrator, the author, and the audience are all consigned to an outsider status that illuminates the effect of New York City on the nation at large.

Both Johnson and his ex-colored man fit the profile of what Chicago sociologist Robert Park, in his 1928 study of moral and ethnic transience, termed a "marginal man," in that they enter a "moral region"—a marginal urban neighborhood with distinct cultural and spatial boundaries —experience a cathartic release of personal inhibition, adopt newfound cultural blueprints, and ultimately experience substantial personal transformations. Johnson recalls in *Along This Way* that while visiting Dunbar, he "took in something of the nightlife in Negro Bohemia, then flourishing in the old Tenderloin district. . . . These glimpses of life . . . showed me a new world—an alluring world, a tempting world, a world of greatly lessened restraints, a world of fascinating perils; but, above all, a world of tremendous artistic potentialities."[7] Despite the Tenderloin's reputation—Dunbar once wrote that there was "no defense to be made for it"[8]—the Tenderloin's black bohemia provided the mise en scène of the modern artistic urban landscape that could perform as a model for Harlem's New Negro Renaissance a generation later. For Johnson, the Tenderloin was a singular "atmosphere in which artistic ideas were born and developed."[9]

Park suggests that the diverse body of "tastes and temperaments" located in urban neighborhoods interacts on both spatial and nonspatial landscapes, both in established urban districts like the Tenderloin and Harlem and in the minds of "marginal" individuals. More broadly speaking, he argues that these "marginal men" can experience a productive catharsis after having migrated and congregated in new moral regions. "This release," he writes, "is followed in the course of time by the reintegration of the individuals so released into a new special order."[10] One such "new special order" found its home in the cabaret culture of New York's Tenderloin. For the purposes of this essay, the "changes and fusions of culture" Park highlights punctuate recent assertions of Johnson's novel as a "slippery" text that "rejects the ontology of racial categories" and cultural definition.[11] They also inform and enliven our understanding of the Tenderloin's signature cultural forms—ragtime piano, for example. Post-bellum–pre-Harlem African American musicians invented a hybrid musical style known as "ragging the classics," or the application of classical music to freestyle piano. "Ragging the classics" is one trope of many Johnson employed to investigate the effects of urban marginality on migrant African Americans, and the success of this endeavor makes *The Autobiography* arguably the finest U.S. novel of the 1910s.

In his *Black Manhattan,* Johnson fully attempts to revise the popularly held image of a "black Sodom" to that of a "black Bohemia." In one passage, for example, he exalts the Tenderloin for stimulating an atmosphere of industry for professional black athletes—specifically jockeys, boxers, and baseball players—along with a host of enterprising and ambitious minstrel stage craftsmen:

> [T]he New York of the upper twenties and lower thirties . . . was the business and social centre of most of the colored men engaged in these professional sports, as it was also of the genuine black-face minstrels, the forerunners of the later colored performers; wherever their work might take them, they homed to New York. And because these men earned and spent large sums of money, there grew up in New York a flourishing black Bohemia.[12]

Johnson significantly omits gambling and prostitution, historically the district's most celebrated pastimes; he prefers instead to address the "artistic effort" that emerged there. "It is in the growth of this artistic effort that we are interested," he writes, "the rest of the manifestations were commonplaces. . . . The gambling clubs need not be explained."[13] This revision is consistent with the whole of Johnson's life, which was openly dedicated to elevating the status of black cultural forms rather than consigning them to sensationalistic notoriety.

The "flourishing black Bohemia" he describes in *Black Manhattan* was a later interpretation of the area, more defensible in 1930 after the enormously popular reception of the New Negro Renaissance. In contrast, *The Autobiography*'s New York chapters willfully revolve around African American drinking and gambling habits, cross-racial assignations, and the general pursuit of vice. But if Dunbar's earlier Tenderloin novel, *The Sport of the Gods* (1902), tracks the naturalistic slippery slope of a guileless country boy who evolves from well-meaning son and brother to gambling addict, violent drunk, and murderer, *The Autobiography* catenates the steps of a talented vagabond who stumbles into Tenderloin life and is able to take something productive from his experience—the ability to play ragtime piano, for one thing—and move on.

Like *The Sport of the Gods*, *The Autobiography* provides a fictional treatment of this black bohemia of the 1890s and the marginalization process that occurs there. Johnson acknowledges the dissipating effects the region has on his characters—who drink, gamble, and play ragtime as vehemently as Dunbar's—but the Tenderloin provides his ex-colored man with an enlightened understanding of U.S. citizenship. Johnson demonstrates how "low life" experiences cannot be reduced to good or bad; they add to our cultural identities in simultaneously jarring and stimulating ways. Vice and creativity are no longer portrayed as mutually exclusive. Moral experimentation, Johnson argues, is a social necessity, the means by which cultural acclivity might be attained; and as such, again, the "black Bohemia" that Johnson's ex-colored man encounters is a vital precursor for its illustrious successor, Harlem in the 1920s.

Johnson's anonymous ex-colored man is born in Georgia around 1870 to a fair-skinned mulatto woman and a white southern gentleman. He is raised by his mother and passes as a white child in Connecticut, where his father sends them to clear the way for a respectable marriage. Since the ex-colored man spends his most formative period relatively affluent and unaware of his blackness, he is ill prepared for the realities faced by African Americans at the end of the nineteenth century. Achieving this sense of preparedness seems to necessitate a certain level of personal dissipation. For more than a year he negotiates the pitfalls of the Tenderloin, which within weeks had subsumed his fictional predecessor Joe Hamilton in *The Sport of the Gods*. Having been trained as a cigar manufacturer during a brief stay in Florida, the ex-colored man supports himself in New York by the same trade. Over time, however, his rapturous outings in the gambling clubs and cabarets take precedence. He inevitably revokes his respectable status as a skilled worker, and "at last realized that making cigars for a living and gambling for a living could not be carried on at the same time, and [thus] . . . resolved to give up the cigar making."[14]

During this time, which he regards as his "dark period,"[15] the ex-colored man's New York consists of ten city blocks: again, along Sixth Avenue from Twenty-third Street to Thirty-third, with the blocks crossing one block west,[16] a remote outpost where "Central Park was a distant forest, and the lower part of the city a foreign land."[17] Although the ex-colored man is a mulatto and later refers to some white strangers in the Tenderloin's milieu as "slummers" (presumably as distinct from himself), it seems as if no one in the culture of the Tenderloin really "belongs." Over the course of his dark period, he acquaints himself with "a score of bright, intelligent young fellows who had come up to the great city with high hopes and ambitions and who had fallen under the spell of this under life, a spell they could never throw off."[18] One Tenderloin habitué is given the nickname "the doctor" for having spent two years at Harvard Medical School. "But here he was," the ex-colored man intones, "living this gaslight life, his will and moral sense so enervated and deadened that it was impossible for him to break away."[19] As Harvard Medical School had begun matriculating African Americans in 1865,[20] "the doctor" defies racial categorization. Regardless, when the ex-colored man refers to the Tenderloin as a "lower world" later in the narrative, it can be construed as racially motivated condescension,[21] but its dissipating effects have equal-opportunity status.

The ex-colored man tells us that along with musicians, minstrels, thespians, and athletes, the cabaret was also a place where whites would come during a night of "sight-seeing, or slumming."[22] Though it is a refuge from the greater Tenderloin, it also "enjoyed a large patronage of white sightseers and slummers and of white theatrical performers on the lookout for 'Negro stuff,' and, moreover, a considerable clientele of white women who had or sought to have colored lovers."[23] Their presence is not wholly intrusive, a fact that in some ways foreshadows Johnson's later encouragement of Carl Van Vechten's slumming escapades in Harlem. In fact, there is a distinction made between whites with apparent "insider" status and "outsiders" who found the situation alienating. Some would only peer in for a minute or two to satisfy a minor curiosity; others would stay all night, including a number of single white women:

> They were all good-looking and well-dressed, and seemed to be women of some education. One of these in particular attracted my attention; she was an exceedingly beautiful woman of about thirty-five. . . . When I came to know her, I found that she was a woman of considerable culture; she had traveled in Europe, spoke French, and played the piano well. She was always dressed elegantly, but in absolutely good taste.[24]

To the ex-colored man's surprise, rather than appearing as an outsider in the predominantly black setting, she exemplifies the marginal characteristics of the Tenderloin's cultural milieu. But for the ex-colored man (and, needless to say, an early-twentieth-century, white, middle-class audience), the most alarming revelation is her open, sexually charged relationship with a black "sport" at the cabaret. He learns that the woman, whom he refers to as "the widow," bestows jewelry on her escort and pays for his clothes to be form-fitted at the most expensive New York tailors. He also ascertains that the man is not alone; indeed, there were many like him. Johnson does not conclude that the widow's companion is being reduced to a (perhaps racially motivated) object of sexuality (even prostitution) but rather that this well-heeled white woman is an insider in the vortex of the club's social matrix.

Even the scene of her own murder makes it appear as if she belongs in the purview of the club as much as the ex-colored man, who by this time is something of a celebrity there. She is shot in the throat by her companion, who catches her sharing a bottle of champagne with the ex-colored man. The ex-colored man had been warned that "the pair had lately quarreled and had not been together at the 'Club' for some nights," and had worried that the escort, "generally known as a 'bad man,'" might fly into a jealous rage, which he does.[25] Regarding this as a jealousy killing complicates the escort's motives. If it is money he is after, why cut off the supply? Or, if he believes the ex-colored man might replace him, why not kill *him*?

Johnson frustrates other deterministic class associations in the Tenderloin. Tenderloin gamblers, for example, are not themselves intrinsically associated with poverty or the slums per se. Their standing in the Tenderloin is determined by the Tenderloin. Upon first entering one of the gambling clubs, the ex-colored man recalls "aristocrats of the place" who posed elegantly at the tables and "seemed to be practicing a sort of Chesterfieldian politeness towards each other."[26] Startled, he soon observes seedy men in linen dusters begging for fifty cents to get back in the game; these latter have literally lost the clothes off their backs and are graciously provided dusters by the management. He has trouble reading this bizarre medley of urban types, since up to that point he had experienced rigidly delineated boundaries of caste. It then becomes apparent that those same patrons exhibiting "Chesterfieldian politeness" might (and most likely will) themselves don linen dusters in a night or two. As the ex-colored man explains, "In my gambling experiences I passed through all states and conditions that a gambler is heir to. Some days found me able to peel ten- and twenty-dollar bills from a roll, and others found me clad in a linen duster and carpet slippers."[27] We are invited to witness a powerful act of citizenship here: in this novel, immoral action becomes socioeconomic wisdom.

The ex-colored man does not take his artistic strides in Tenderloin gambling establishments, however, but in the Tenderloin's cabarets or "professional clubs." Both *The Autobiography* and *Black Manhattan* refer to the cabaret's importance for cultivating a new ethos of African American professionalism. In *Black Manhattan,* Johnson differentiates between "honky-tonks" and "professional clubs": honky-tonks were nightclubs with black and white patrons that sold alcohol and provided both professional and amateur entertainment; professional clubs, in contrast, did not hold liquor licenses and were frequented almost exclusively by professional entertainers, athletes, and their "satellites and admirers."[28] One of the professional clubs the ex-colored man discovers, which he generically refers to as the "Club" (modeled after a Tenderloin cabaret on West Twenty-seventh Street called Ike Hine's), educates him in ragtime piano. He also ascertains a model for the future of African American cultural production there. The parlor walls are adorned with photographs and lithographs of Frederick Douglass, the prize fighter Peter Jackson, and "every colored man in American who had ever 'done anything.'"[29] A back room is stripped of any furniture, to free space for rehearsals during which "song and dance teams practiced their steps, acrobatic teams practiced their tumbles, and many other kinds of 'acts' rehearsed their 'turns.'"[30] The presence of prize fighters, jockeys, and professional entertainers of all sorts draws an audience that is male and female, established and transient, black and white. Newcomers on the scene, though at first disdained for being "green," are encouraged to contribute their talents. A piano prodigy in his own right, the ex-colored man is naturally drawn to the unique musical experiments ennobled by this time and place.

The ex-colored man had been trained in classical piano early in life and to him, ragtime is a revelation. The music he finds in the Tenderloin is so original and raw that the first ragtime musician he encounters had received no formal training and played piano "by ear alone."[31] The acquisition of ragtime is one more addition to the ex-colored man's inductive process of knowledge formation; it is his latest payment from a continuous process of cultural annuity, informed by his exposure to varying regional cultures—New England, the South, Europe, and so forth. Exposure and influence, the ex-colored man himself admits, is the wellspring of his talents: "The fact is, nothing great or enduring, especially in music, has ever sprung full-fledged and unprecedented from the brain of any master; the best that he gives to the world he gathers from the hearts of the people, and runs it through the alembic of his genius."[32]

Johnson's ragtime "Club" officially prohibited drinking and gambling. We are told, however, that the ex-colored man could not afford a night at the "Club" without first winning money at the gambling tables. The two institutions, gambling clubs and cabarets, were a part of one culture, but the cabarets were the points of convergence for those "creative efforts" Johnson brings to light in his history. Stressing here the early professionalization of black cultural production, Johnson attests that "it was in such places that early Negro theatrical talent created for itself a congenial atmosphere, an atmosphere of emulation and guildship."[33] The ex-colored man does, in fact, update his already well-developed musical talents by combining a preexisting knowledge of classical music with ragtime, a form strictly associated with African American artists. Self-taught over long nights of exploring the Tenderloin, the ex-colored man discovers a highly marketable commodity in this way, and therefore the apparatus to improve his condition.

Ragtime was the most popular music in the United States from the late 1890s to World War I. It combined the European tradition of crafted composition with signature African American syncopated rhythms, often starkly coopting Mozart or Mendelssohn for irreverent effect. The fictional ex-colored man takes full credit for inventing the hybrid of classical and ragtime: "I brought all my knowledge of classical music to bear and, in so doing, achieved some novelties which pleased and even astonished my listeners. It was I who first made ragtime transcriptions of familiar classic selections."[34] Critics widely considered ragtime piano in the United States both musically and morally corrupt. Coopting classical and nationalistic music for popular forms is hardly unique in U.S. history, but there can be no doubt that the hybrid form was popularly associated with immoral social action. "We have musical unions in many of our cities," Edward Baxter Perry extolled in a 1918 review entitled "Ragging Good Music," "and one of the first rules they should pass is that any member found guilty of what is called 'ragging' a classic should be dismissed from the organization in disgrace, and never again permitted to appear in any reputable organization."[35] As Edward A. Berlin laconically sums up the attack: "The main lines of the [critics'] offensive were: (1) ridicule; (2) appeals to racial bias; (3) prophecies of doom; (4) attempts at repression; and (5) suggestions of moral, intellectual, and physical dangers."[36] The music was compared with malaria, alcohol, and "a dog with rabies."[37]

Kathleen Pfeiffer has powerfully argued that rather than simply whitening a black form, as others have claimed, the ex-colored man was blackening a white form as well.[38] Though by twenty-first-century standards the sounds and lyrics seem quite tame, ragtime's reception resembles the present-day controversy surrounding hip hop—Berlin writes that "whites [disapproved of the music] because they feared [its] effects on impressionable white youth, and many African Americans did because they feared that their own youths would be corrupted by a music associated with brothels and cabarets, and because they found the texts of ragtime songs to be racially demeaning."[39] Subsequently, there was a strong move to censor piano rags: in New York City, ragtime was banned from a free pier concert in the summer of 1902 and by 1914, prohibited in public schools citywide. In Johnson's representation of the Tenderloin, then, there exist glimmerings of cultural ascendancy that naturally ignite a reactionary backlash.

Ironically, members of the establishment became ravenous consumers of the new form. The ex-colored man performs at the Club nightly and boasts that "it was no secret that the great increase in slumming visitors was due to my playing."[40] "Among other white 'slummers,'" he meets the wealthy white man to whom he later gives the appellation "my millionaire." His millionaire bears "the indefinable but unmistakable stamp of culture"[41] and provides the ex-colored man with a means to recommence his temporarily stagnated pattern of mobility: "Through [ragtime] I . . . gained a friend who was the means by which I escaped from this lower world. And, finally, I secured a wedge which has opened to me more doors and made me a welcome guest than my playing of Beethoven and Chopin could ever have done."[42] But the workload was severe at times, and it has been argued that this "wedge" was a self-serving one, rather than a means to uplift the African American community. "Just like the stereotype of the happy darky," Robert H. Cataliotti argues, "driven 'mercilessly to exhaustion' by a white 'tyrant,' the ex-colored man is content with his pay, looks upon his subjugation as a 'familiar and warm relationship,' and finds in that tyrant an assimilationist model."[43] But this cultural interaction between audience and entertainer serves the musical hybrid the ex-colored man invents, as much as it entertains the millionaire and his modish acquaintances. Indeed, if white forums for "ragging the classics" should be considered tyrannically assimilationist, then we would, by disallowing mutually beneficial influence, significantly hinder both black and white cultural production.

True, the ex-colored man cashes in on an older manifestation of radical chic, and his millionaire has access to an inexhaustible fortune. His money, along with a degree of cultural acceptance, enables him, like Van Vechten or his fictional prototype, Prince Rodolphe in Eugène Sue's seminal urban mystery *Les Mystères de Paris* (1842), to wander freely in the underworld and discover its most entertaining talents. The millionaire propositions the ex-colored man to play at a fashionable New York soirée, for those who would never have the opportunity to appreciate ragtime if it remained within the restricted confines of the Tenderloin. Though the guests in this upper-class parlor party are "all decidedly blasé,"[44] the ex-colored man begins his session with one of his "liveliest ragtime pieces," and observes, almost instantaneously, a "surprising" effect. All talking, eating, and cynical repartee cease—the audience is entranced.[45] The millionaire has successfully delivered the Tenderloin to the Fifth Avenue salon.

This form of salon slumming is not restricted to imported musical talents from morally marginalized spaces, as the very act of reading about the Tenderloin no doubt provoked a sense of cultural "release." Johnson illustrates chic New Yorkers enjoying ragtime in an upscale parlor as one avatar of the readers themselves: "These were people—and they represented a large class—who were expecting to find happiness in novelty, each day restlessly exploring and exhausting every resource of this great city that might possibly furnish a new sensation or awaken a fresh emotion, and who were always grateful to anyone who aided them in their quest."[46] One reason Johnson designed his short novel to reflect the first-person autobiography was that, as Eugene D. Levy attests, "For whites, reading a black man's autobiography often served as a vicarious substitute for personal contact with blacks."[47] This is particularly true at a time when whites had so little contact with blacks, as in the case of New York in the prewar period. Taking up a narrative such as this one supplanted the vicarious experience of engaging in the illicit nightlife of the Tenderloin, or laboring in the close atmosphere of a cigar factory. The millionaire voices his satisfaction, and perhaps Johnson's, when he informs our narrator at the conclusion of his first parlor performance, "Well, I have given them something they've never had before."[48] So it was a form of slumming in three ways: (1) the ex-colored man was once again exposing himself to a significantly alien culture; (2) the modish New York socialites tasted African American culture without actually having to enter into it; and (3) for readers unfamiliar with the Tenderloin, white or black, the experience of reading *The Autobiography* was itself a secondary form of slumming.

Given that *The Autobiography* is in part a novel about passing (at the end of the tale, we find the ex-colored man back in New York passing as, of all things, a prosperous white landlord), and that *Black Manhattan's* purpose is largely to actualize a feeling of cultural uplift and legitimacy for African Americans, Johnson betrays a sense of personal uncertainty regarding the Tenderloin's legacy. A character who contributes significantly to black cultural production but soon disposes of his cultural past is hardly a poster child for the elevation of African American art implicit in the *Black Manhattan* project. A brief look at Johnson's actual autobiography, *Along This Way* (1933), helps resolve the seeming contradiction between the ex-colored man's perceptions of the Tenderloin in *The Autobiography* and Johnson's morally innocuous, though culturally uplifting, Tenderloin in *Black Manhattan*.

Alfred A. Knopf published the second edition of *The Autobiography* in 1927, at which time Johnson was given credit as the author and received numerous letters from a confused public inquiring about various periods of his life. "That is, probably," he admits in *Along This Way*, "one of the reasons why I am writing the present book."[49] By the time he moved to New York to write for Broadway with Cole and his brother Rosamond, the Tenderloin he describes in *The Autobiography* existed only residually. Cole and the Johnson Brothers, as they were known, rented rooms at the Marshall Club at 260 West Fifty-third Street, where African American New Yorkers enjoyed "a fashionable sort of life that hitherto had not existed."[50] The Marshall boasted "excellent food," a welcome setting, and an "unprecedented" parlor atmosphere with "crowds of well-dressed colored men and women lounging and chatting . . . [and] loitering over their coffee and cigarettes while they talked or listened to the music."[51] Its habitués were hard-working and highly professional musicians, composers, performers, and managers, there to make a name for themselves on Broadway.

"As the Marshall gained popularity," Johnson writes, "the more noted theatrical stars and the better-paid vaudevillians deserted the down-town clubs and made the hotel their professional and social rendezvous."[52] And his description of Ike Hine's in *Along This Way*, the model for the "Club" in *The Autobiography*, corresponds with that of the Marshall, though his choice of words is revealing: "It was principally a club for Negroes connected with the theater, but it drew the best elements from the various circles of Bohemia—except the gamblers."[53] Both Ike Hine's and the Marshall were sanctuaries of professionalism where the "guildship" of musicians and artists flourished. During his time at the Marshall, Johnson writes that he and his collaborators "worked according to a schedule. . . . When we didn't go to the theater, our working period approximated ten hours a day."[54] Although transgressive activities such as gambling, drinking, cross-racial sexuality, and ragtime piano are intertwined with transcultural production, Ike Hine's "was in every respect surprisingly orderly" and the Marshall was a "professional and social rendezvous" for black entertainers.[55]

A brief meeting between Johnson and Mencken, as Johnson recalls it in *Along This Way*, retrospectively accounts for the intentions underpinning the New York chapters in *The Autobiography*. Johnson reveals that Mencken was an author who had "made a sharper impression" on him "than any other American then writing." For nearly forty-five minutes they talked in Mencken's office at the magazine *The Smart Set*, where Mencken was an editor: "I [Johnson] had never been so fascinated at hearing anyone talk. He talked about literature, about Negro literature, the Negro problem, and Negro music." He informed Johnson that African American authors were making a mistake "when they indulged in pleas for justice and mercy, when they prayed indulgence for shortcomings, when they based their protests against unjust treatment on the Christian moral or ethical code, when they argued to prove that they were as good as anybody else." Instead, Mencken argued, "'What they should do . . . is to single out the strong points of the race and emphasize them over and over and over; asserting, at least on these points, that they are better than anybody else.'" Johnson's response to Mencken's speech brings together all of the

ambiguous threads: "I called to his attention that I had attempted something of that sort in *The Autobiography of an Ex-Colored Man.*"[56]

By the 1920s, the Tenderloin's black bohemia existed as a dated precursor for young New York blacks and a fond memory for older activists like
Johnson. But its legacy was this usable past on which to build a legitimized
future. In the struggle to establish a cultural continuum between slave narratives and New Negro modernism, we must retrieve the Tenderloin's
black bohemia, and the marginal men and women who inhabited it, from
its obscured position in the African American tradition. Harlem, with its
far greater numbers after the Great Migration of the 1910s and 1920s, was
enormously important for black and white cultural production. But those
ten short blocks in the Tenderloin enabled African American artists to
invent new reasons, as Johnson reminisced in 1933, "to grope toward a
realization of the importance of the American Negro's cultural background and his creative folk-art, and to speculate on the superstructure of
conscious art that might be reared upon them."[57]

NOTES

1. Timothy J. Gilfoyle, *City of Eros: New York City, Prostitution, and the Commercialization of Sex, 1790–1920* (New York: Norton, 1992), 204.

2. James Weldon Johnson, *The Autobiography of an Ex-Colored Man* (1912; repr.
New York: Penguin, 1990), 82; and James Weldon Johnson, *Black Manhattan* (1930;
repr. New York: Da Capo Press, 1991), 73.

3. Louise Johnson, *Rediscovering the Harlem Renaissance: The Politics of Exclu-
sion* (New York: Garland Press, 1997), 10.

4. *Along This Way: The Autobiography of James Weldon Johnson* (1933; repr. New
York: Viking, 1973), 152.

5. Johnson, *Autobiography,* 79.

6. H. L. Mencken, "The Negro as Author," in *H. L. Mencken's Smart Set Criticism,* ed. William H. Nolte (1920; repr. Washington, DC: Regnery, 1987), 320.

7. Johnson, *Along This Way,* 151, 152.

8. Paul Laurence Dunbar, *The Sport of the Gods,* with an introduction by
William L. Andrews (1902; repr. New York: Signet Classics, 1999), 67.

9. Johnson, *Black Manhattan,* 78.

10. Robert E. Park, "Human Migration and the Marginal Man," in *Theories of
Ethnicity: A Classical Reader,* ed. Werner Sollors (1928; repr. New York: New York
University Press, 1996), 161.

11. Kathleen Pfeiffer, "Individualism, Success, and American Identity in *The
Autobiography of an Ex-Colored Man,*" *African American Review* 30.3 (1996): 406.

12. Johnson, *Black Manhattan,* 73.

13. Ibid., 74.

14. Johnson, *Autobiography,* 82.

15. Ibid., 82.

16. Ibid., 82.

17. Ibid., 82–83.

18. Ibid., 83.

19. Ibid., 83.

20. Randall Kennedy, Introduction, *Blacks at Harvard: A Documentary History of African-American Experience at Harvard and Radcliffe,* ed. Werner Sollors, Caldwell Titcomb, and Thomas A. Underwood (New York: New York University Press, 1993), xix–xx.

21. Robert H. Cataliotti, *The Music in African American Fiction* (New York: Garland Press, 1995), 67.

22. Johnson, *Autobiography,* 78.

23. Johnson, *Along This Way,* 176.

24. Johnson, *Autobiography,* 79.

25. Ibid., 89.

26. Ibid., 67–68.

27. Ibid., 83.

28. Johnson, *Black Manhattan,* 74.

29. Johnson, *Autobiography,* 76.

30. Ibid., 76.

31. Ibid., 74.

32. Ibid., 73.

33. Johnson, *Black Manhattan,* 78.

34. Johnson, *Autobiography,* 84.

35. Edward A. Berlin, *Ragtime: A Musical and Cultural History* (Berkeley: University of California Press, 1980), 70.

36. Ibid., 40.

37. Ibid., 44.

38. Pfeiffer, "Individualism," 410.

39. See Berlin's entry on "Ragtime" in *The Encyclopedia of New York City,* ed. Kenneth T. Jackson (New Haven, CT: Yale University Press, 1995), 976.

40. Johnson, *Autobiography,* 84.

41. Ibid., 84.

42. Ibid., 84.

43. Cataliotti, *Music,* 56.

44. Johnson, *Autobiography,* 86.

45. Ibid., 87.

46. Ibid., 87.

47. Eugene D. Levy, *James Weldon Johnson: Black Leader, Black Voice* (Chicago: University of Chicago Press, 1973), 130.

48. Johnson, *Autobiography,* 87.

49. Johnson, *Along This Way,* 239.

50. Ibid., 171.

51. Ibid., 171.

52. Ibid., 176.

53. Ibid., 176.

54. Ibid., 172.

55. Ibid., 176.

56. Ibid., 305.

57. Ibid., 152.

Chapter 8

Jamming with Julius

Charles Chesnutt and the
Post-Bellum–Pre-Harlem Blues

Barbara A. Baker

While few would dispute the fact that blues music is among the United States's most original and enduring artistic contributions to the world, less often acknowledged is that the aesthetic strategies that undergird the music, taken in sum, add up to much more than any individual element of which it is comprised. The strategies at the heart of the blues make up a unique aesthetic of their own—the blues aesthetic—that speaks across disciplines and genres to an American style that emerged before Louis Armstrong became the musical goodwill ambassador to the world, before the phonograph record was invented, and before Bessie Smith stomped a plaintive complaint that made her the Empress of the Blues, an internationally recognized figure, and one of the first martyrs for the desegregation cause.[1]

Valuing the blues aesthetic as the significant American artistic creation that it is requires recognizing that its transcendent strategies straddle art forms, that the black and southern creative resilience expressed in blues music is also inherent in American literature such as that written by Charles Waddell Chesnutt. Although he would not have referred to himself as such and, to date, he has not been discussed as such, Chesnutt must be counted among American blues writers. Coining the term "post-bellum–pre-Harlem" to define the artistic milieu through which he stealthily maneuvered, Chesnutt relied on the same sophisticated blues strategies, culled and refined from within the southern black community with which he was intimately familiar, to speak beyond the particulars of his circum-

stance and to deliver to the mainstream reading population a timely message of enduring significance akin to the blues. Thinking of Chesnutt's art
in terms of the broader context of the blues aesthetic provides the reader
with access to a synthesis of strategies that is isolated neither in literature
nor in the political undercurrent of much of his work but developed in
concert along with America's best loved music before the turn of the twentieth century. Chesnutt's literary reliance on key elements of the blues aesthetic makes his work part and parcel of the blues tradition.

Chesnutt, whose most lasting testament is *The Conjure Woman* (1899),
manipulates many of the same techniques in use by the great blues innovators who were his contemporaries. While Chesnutt's conjure tales vary
in quality and purpose, "Mars Jeems's Nightmare," published in the original collection, is representative of his best work. In this discussion, I will
show how this story serves especially well to illuminate four key elements
that are fundamental to the emerging blues aesthetic in nineteenth-century American art.

First, the story relies on cultural knowledge specific to the southern
black community. Most of the creators of the blues were unnamed bards
who extended the African-derived, southern black improvisational styles
already at work in earlier African American vernacular forms like the spirituals, sermons, tall tales, and work songs. It is not coincidental that the
South bred the blues nor that the art form was molded by black creators.
Chesnutt expresses the resilience of the southern black community
through a playfully masked subversion, a surreptitious means of truth
telling necessitated by the circumstances of slavery and neoslavery in the
American South.

These truth-telling techniques make up a second element that Chesnutt's story shares with blues. Both seemingly improvise a stylized signifying that creates the opportunity for subversion by "jamming" on
established and accepted themes. Third, Chesnutt's fiction shares with
music an expression of the cultural, and ultimately the artistic, fusion of
blackness and whiteness in American art, a creolization of African and
European elements undeniably at work in blues music and its derivatives.
Chesnutt's story shows that, while black and white aesthetic strategies
often retain their distinctiveness in American literature and music, more
often they meld together, forming a new aesthetic that is creolized in a
uniquely American way. In the new American art, African and European
ways of knowing and interpreting the world come together, often in an
interplay that embodies a fourth characteristic of the blues, the dialectical

negotiation of contrary emotions as represented by the laughter and tears of blues music.

It is important to note that these are only four elements associated with a complex, much discussed nexus of strategies at work within the blues aesthetic. While scholars often recognize the blues in literature, rarely is the burgeoning blues in post-bellum–pre-Harlem fiction discussed. Doing so, however, emphasizes the influential role of southern African American culture as an agent of empowerment and expressivity that fed the innovations of writers like Chesnutt long before the Harlem Renaissance and before the term "blues" was common parlance used to describe America's new music.

Much has been said about the blues' influence on writers of the Harlem Renaissance and beyond. Eric J. Sundquist, for example, argues in "'The Drum with the Man Skin'" that Renaissance writers like Zora Neale Hurston began to recognize and make use of the "fluidity and capacity for improvisation" that had long been a part of "black vocal and instrumental music."[2] Writers as far ranging as Hurston, Richard Wright, Sterling Brown, Ralph Ellison, James Baldwin, LeRoi Jones (Amiri Baraka), Alice Walker, and Toni Morrison purposefully engage the blues as a means symbolically to represent a diversity of experiences in African American cultural life. The same factors that gave rise to the blues in the first place also inspired aesthetic techniques used by writers who produced their most significant works before W. C. Handy published the first blues song, "Memphis Blues," in 1912.

Ralph Ellison and Albert Murray, among others, have elegantly made the case that the blues embodies aesthetic systems that afford all who listen to it entry into the idea that most truly American art is fundamentally black. Yet, both also tend to look toward the blues' most sophisticated offspring, such as the jazz renderings of Louis Armstrong, Charlie Christian, and Duke Ellington. For his part, Murray distinguishes and elevates the jazzed-up elaborations on the original art form as the superior goods and generally undervalues the nascent folk creations from which they were spawned. Murray has applied the blues aesthetic to nearly every conceivable American art, from the paintings of Romare Bearden to the stories of Ernest Hemingway, so long as the artist accomplishes the highly learned "vernacular imperative," which is to gather up all that can be known and forge a sword with which to slay the blue feeling common to the human condition through improvisation, extension, and elaboration on the motifs or riffs established by the greatest modern artists, including the inventors and improvisers who elaborated on the antics of Brer Rabbit and Brer Fox.

While lauding Ellison's and Murray's "breathtaking act of cultural chutzpah"[3] in bringing to the forefront, through the blues, the idea that the distinctive part of the American national character is aesthetically and culturally black, Henry Louis Gates Jr. claims that Ellison's and Murray's joint enterprise, which focuses more on black-derived American artistic strategies than on traditional blues music, nonetheless acknowledges the improvisatory prehistory of the blues. It is this prehistory, however, to which we must turn if we are to come to a more complete understanding of the complex, charged, and fertile southern atmosphere that generated the American blues aesthetic in the period between the end of radical Reconstruction and the beginning of World War I. The blues lends insight into the aesthetic milieu that produced American art that emerged in a particular time and place out of a particular set of circumstances in the American South. The United States is the only place touched by the African diaspora where blues music emerged, just as blues and blues-derived music, in turn, are perhaps the most widely recognized authentic American art, yet the music itself is not the only artistic product that this particular time, place, and circumstance produced. Southern literature is also drenched with blues-oriented maneuvers.

Through the blues it becomes clear that the circumstances of slavery, as well as those of the post-Emancipation neoslavery that followed it, gave rise to specific ways of knowing and negotiating the difficulty of a coming together of cultures in the South. The blues aesthetic appropriately illustrates a set of artistic strategies that this coming together produced, and it helps us to understand that the vernacular and musical underpinnings of blues speak much more broadly to the way African Americans in the American South came to author and to compose the most original of American art that came to speak to and for an entire nation.

That the blues is an African American creation goes without saying, although it is ironic that the citizenry of the country embraced the music long before acknowledging the humanity of and granting constitutionally guaranteed civil liberties to its creators. Intellectuals like W. E. B. Du Bois, ardently pursuing these liberties for his people, pointed up the irony in the fact that African Americans had generated America's only original music. In "The Sorrow Songs" (1903), Du Bois writes, for example, "so by fateful chance the Negro folk-song—the rhythmic cry of the slave—stands today not simply as the sole American music, but as the most beautiful expression of human experience born this side the seas." The music "remains as the singular spiritual heritage of the nation and the greatest gift of the Negro people."[4] Suggesting that African American religious songs, folk tales, dancing, secular music, and literature come from the same source, James Weldon Johnson claims "that the Negro was the creator of the only things artistic that have sprung from the soil and been universally acknowledged as distinctive American products."[5] Black secular music such as blues "has been developed into the distinct musical idiom by which America expresses itself popularly and by which it is best known."[6]

Although many of the techniques employed in African American musical forms—the blue note, the pentatonic scale, and the art of signifying—are generally considered to be African derived, the stifling oppression of slavery in the southern United States produced a climate in which the musical elements that became blues incubated. In the South, African Americans were particularly challenged to find means not just to survive but to preserve a sense of humanity, with creativity, even humor, in the face of the most devastating and often destructive adversity. Humiliating dehumanizing efforts on the part of slave masters could be countered by slaves in songs. The praise meetings were often the only arena in which the slaves could express themselves freely; so in public, as the songs became more secular, they took on more double entendres to mask their true meanings, which were often stylized complaints about regrettable or deplorable situations. This strategy of resilience in the face of adversity seemed to throw off the heaviest loads through dark stories told in rhythmic tunes that countered the blues feeling common to all people, and it undoubtedly owed its creative energy to the collective will of a people languishing in bondage and hoping for freedom.

Flight from the racially hostile atmosphere of the blues' southern birthplace fueled both the development and the dispersion of the music. The desire, need, and possibility for both geographical mobility and upward mobility experienced by the African American creators of the blues were primary catalysts for the fact that the aesthetic possibilities that contributed to blues congealed when they did. When freedom came, the blues exploded. In the several decades between the end of the Civil War and the beginning of World War I, African Americans were "free to sing whatever they pleased. . . . [T]hey were free to play any instrument they wished . . . and they gave full range to their propensity for improvisation in whatever they sang or played."[7] In fashioning the improvisational new music, free

African Americans drew on "the repertory already in their possession—that is the slave songs."[8]

The southern experience was integral to the idioms in which this new generation of African Americans continued to express themselves, even as a cultural whirlwind spread them in a thousand directions. Murray notes that the blues not only "speak about downhome experience . . . but they speak also in the terms, including the onomatopoeia, of downhome phenomena."[9] Chesnutt, too, in creating Uncle Julius's authentic-sounding southern voice, echoed the strains of downhome onomatopoeia that added to the appeal and popularity of early blues music. Like other blues innovators, Chesnutt shared a vantage point from inside southern black culture, and he was well aware of the significance of his intimate knowledge of the people to his art. Commenting in his journal in 1880 on Albion Tourgée's *A Fool's Errand: By One of the Fools* (1879), for instance, Chesnutt remarked that he could write a far better book because he was "a colored man who [had] lived among colored people all his life." He was familiar "with their habits, their ruling passions, their prejudices, their condition, their public and private ambitions." Besides, he added, he also "possessed such opportunities for observation and conversation with the better class of white men in the South as to understand their modes of thinking," too.[10] Chesnutt clearly recognized that his special circumstances as an observer of the interactions among black and white southerners had supplied him with a wealth of resources with promising artistic possibilities.

Chesnutt recognized and intentionally capitalized on the seemingly exotic nature of the post-bellum–pre-Harlem South. Although his keen observation and recreation of black dialect are well documented, his attention to musical idioms and their continuity with vernacular forms has rarely been acknowledged. Always in search of material that would be palatable to the northern literary marketplace and still allow him flexibility to exercise his politically motivated voice, Chesnutt began to record black vernacular culture, "things . . . which are peculiar [to southern blacks] . . . and would be doubly interesting to people who know little about them."[11] He went "to work as a kind of ethnographic collector . . . becoming a pupil . . . of black popular culture."[12] By May 1880, he specifically noted black musical expression as a possible subject of interest to the northern literary markets. He wrote that the ballads and hymns that "the colored people sing with such fervor, might be acceptable" to the literary people of the North: "They have certain elements of originality which make them interesting to a student of literature."[13] Chesnutt was a self-taught musician who observed in black music, among other things, the call-and-response patterns and "good-time effect" that would later take shape more explicitly in blues.[14] The same strains that informed the music contributed to his emerging aesthetic sensibility, and the dialect story, to which he eventually turned, shares black, southern aesthetic strategies with blues.

African American musical forms entered the mainstream in much the same way that, popularized in the 1880s by writers like Joel Chandler Harris and Thomas Nelson Page, the dialect stories did. Both forms began as imitative retellings of black and southern cultural events intended not to offend the largely white mainstream audiences who indulged in them. They both contained fictionalized racial history, even when the speakers were native informants from the southern black community. As the editor of *The Century*, R. W. Gilder, put it, for instance, "the Negro" was permitted "to speak on the race question" if he recounted "the correct experience of the African American community, one that did not upset the white folks' comfort in their sense of self and that self's relation to people of color."[15] In order to take advantage of the opportunity to write that was created by the market's desire for dialect stories, Chesnutt signified "on the racist figures of popular culture in order to seize and invert their cultural power."[16] As Ellison suggests, it is through this signifying strategy of seizing and inverting cultural power that African Americans also changed the joke of minstrelsy into the blues.[17]

This kind of signifying had most likely been at work in African American vernacular forms as far back as the first days of contact between Africans and Europeans in this country. Sundquist suggests that the signifying strategy was African derived and nurtured in the climate of southern slavery, where African American speech was "in a constant condition of signifying on the linguistic power of the masters, appropriating and depleting the power . . . by subverting its authority."[18] In blues, the strategy is seen, for instance, in the riffing and jamming on established themes. To jam or to riff is to extend or alter the meaning of the established material, to create an inspired allusion to that material by alluding to a frame of reference only to modify the connotation of the original. Jamming in this way is central to the blues and reflects the continuity of expression within the African American vernacular tradition, but it also suggests the manner in which authentic African American vernacular expressions often comment beyond the community and speak across the multidimensional facets of Americanness.

The jamming, riffing, signifying strategy is at work in Chesnutt's *Conjure Woman,* in which he deliberately recasts Uncle Julius in the image of Uncle Remus in order to establish continuity with an accepted means of southern storytelling, appropriating its power and subverting its message. He deliberately casts Uncle Julius as the stereotypical plantation "old-time darky" in an effort to liberate the image from its original connotation. In so doing, his signifying mask takes up with it the other two elements that I have argued are essential to the blues aesthetic, the fusion of blackness and whiteness and contrary emotions working in a dialectical interplay.

It must be remembered that Chesnutt inherited, along with the perplexing dilemma of his mixed racial heritage, a sense of movement and freedom away from the South. His parents, free persons of color, after all, had met on a northbound wagon train while fleeing a racially hostile Fayetteville, North Carolina, in 1856, and they had instilled in their son a desire for education as well as his life's ambition to free himself through his art from the curse of the one-drop laws and the invisible but rigid color line.

While he overtly made his message clear in countless essays and speeches written later in his career, Chesnutt surreptitiously accomplishes the same objective through Julius, by jamming on the established tradition and subverting the preconceived notions of his readers. We are told in "The Goophered Grapevine" at the outset of *The Conjure Woman* that Julius, unlike Remus, is "not entirely black, and this fact . . . suggested a slight strain of other than negro blood. There was a shrewdness in his eyes, too, which was not altogether African."[19] R. V. Burnette points out that Chesnutt had not depicted Julius as a person of mixed racial heritage in the original 1887 publication of "The Goophered Grapevine" but had revised the character to inject "the fact of miscegenation" into the story.[20] Chesnutt's purposeful interjection of miscegenation into the creation of his best-known character, Julius, is reminiscent of Murray's claim that the American cultural configuration, with blues as its primary metaphor, is incontestably mulatto. While both terms, "miscegenation" and "mulatto," force a recognition of the blackness and whiteness of American culture and art, both terms are also more polarizing than "blues," which is indicative of the blending of racial heritage and epistemologies that can be thought of as a creolization of cultures because something beyond the individual contributions of either culture is expressed. The blues aesthetic illustrates how American art is often a creole creation representing the emergence of a new American identity, much like Julius's, which often adds up to more than the sum of the elements that contribute to its making.

Chesnutt's characterization of Julius also prefigures the suggestion that Ellison would later articulate: African American experience is an experience that all Americans must identify with and recognize as intertwined in the very texture of American experience.[21] The blending of blackness and whiteness in American aesthetic systems would come to fruition in blues music, and by the time of Chesnutt's death in 1932, the African American sensibility underlying the texture of most American music would be acknowledged. Chesnutt's concerns went further than Ellison's, however, because Chesnutt's work implies that African American blood, not just African American experience, is blended with so-called white American identity. Working at a point in southern history when African Americans actively exerted a self-defining force, Chesnutt constructed an image of whiteness designed to include blackness, a concept strongly resembling the suggestion that Ellison would later make in the definitive American blues novel, *Invisible Man* (1953), in which he illustrates that the whitest white is made by adding a drop of black. Consider, for example, the invisible man's job at the paint factory, where he is charged with stirring the dark black dope into the white paint, a scene symbolically suggesting a blended cultural configuration.

In his best stories, Chesnutt returns again and again to the blending of cultures, or more specifically, to the coming together of African and European ways of knowing and negotiating the world, and through the temporal shifts executed through the frame narratives and the tales within the tales, he suggests the long history of this coming together, which was well in motion during slavery. "Mars Jeems's Nightmare" is a telling example because in the story, the conjure woman, Aun' Peggy, transforms the white slave owner, Mars Jeems, into the black slave, "The Noo Nigger." As in the other stories in the collection, in "Mars Jeems's Nightmare," Julius is the trickster, accomplishing his signifying jamming through several layers of masking that permit him cleverly to manipulate the northern newcomers, John and Annie. To secure employment for his grandson Tom, Julius tells the tale that conflates slavery times and the post-bellum–pre-Harlem era at the same time it blurs distinctions between black people and white people. The term "noo nigger," for instance, signifies both on the New Negro of the post-Reconstruction years, a term used by Booker T. Washington, among others, to distinguish African Americans from the mythic slave of historical fiction, and the "the lazy, degenerate, or criminal postbellum blacks, the 'new Negro' of the late nineteenth century."[22]

In "Mars Jeems's Nightmare," however, the "noo nigger" is a white slave owner who, through the African-derived art of conjure, becomes a black slave, and thereby experiences southern plantation slavery from both sides of the color line, from the perspective of both the master and the slave, the European and the African American. This conflated identity provides Mars Jeems with the experiences of slavery; he is beaten and starved by the cruel overseer Nick Johnson for impertinence and for his inability to hold a hoe properly, as any black slave surely should know how to do. While the story seems to suggest Mars Jeems's transformation from white to black and then back again, in fact, once he has experienced slavery, he cannot go back again. Chesnutt's deeper meaning is that Mars Jeems's identity, like that of all Americans, has been transformed to include both African and European ways of knowing the world; he becomes something more than either individual identity in much the same way that the blues and its derivatives are inclusive of and expressive of a creolized American identity.

Because the tale within the tale that Julius tells John and Annie also "conjures" them into granting employment to Julius's grandson Tom, it illustrates the fact that the circumstance of slavery was not unlike the situation for many African Americans in the post-Emancipation period. While John and Annie want to fire Tom because he seems lazy and ignorant, Julius cleverly convinces them that they, like Mars Jeems, must learn to make allowances for "po' ign'ant niggers w'at ain' had no chanst ter l'arn,"[23] because if they do not, they cannot prosper, according to Julius, in the New South with the New Negro whose identity and destiny are clearly wrapped up with their own.

In teaching this lesson, Chesnutt also relies on the blues strategy of wringing humor out of unfortunate circumstances. For instance, the reason Solomon has Mars Jeems conjured in the first place is because he is a hard, cruel man, works his slaves from daylight to dark instead of from sun to sun, and will not allow the slaves to court one another because Mars Jeems says he "wuzn' raisin' niggers, but wuz raisin' cotton."[24] At every turn, Chesnutt plays on the stereotypical racial fictions presumably held by his largely white and northern readership. He masks the truth in order not to upset his readership's comfort by implying that the slaves in Julius's tale accept their status as slaves and want nothing more than to work until the sun sets so that they can use the evening hours to sing, dance, and play the banjo. They want only the opportunity to be the "happy darkies" they will become via conjure by the end of the tale. Chesnutt is able to subvert racist images by simultaneously supplying comforting "darky" humor at the same time he surreptitiously suggests dark injustice. In this way, the conjure tales prefigure the tragic/comic nature of the blues, which often seem to laugh just to keep from crying. Ellison's often-cited definition of blues in "Richard Wright's Blues" explains that the blues "fingers the jagged grain" of a painful situation in order to transcend it through an expression that is both tragic and comic.[25]

In "Mars Jeems's Nightmare," we have the far from humorous situation in which Mars Jeems, transformed into "the noo nigger," has been thrown into jail for impudence. Chesnutt does not miss the opportunity to add some comforting "darky" humor to Mars Jeems's uncomfortable situation. Aun' Peggy sends Solomon to the jail with a conjured sweet potato to change the slave back into Mars Jeems. But first Aun' Peggy has to rub a special potion in Solomon's eyes because the slave is so black, Solomon will not be able to see him in the dark. Then, when Solomon finally does find "the noo nigger" asleep in the corner, "Solomon des slip' up ter 'im, en hilt dat sweet'n' 'tater 'fo' de nigger's nose, en he des nach'ly retch' up wid his han', en tuk de 'tater en eat it in his sleep, widout knowin' it."[26] The reader is meant to laugh at this incarcerated slave's unfortunate circumstance. The irony is that this stereotypical "darky," who is so black that he cannot be seen in the dark, and so gluttonous that he eats a sweet potato in his sleep, is not a slave at all; he is the conjured Mars Jeems.

Laughing at pain, specifically at the hardships endured by African Americans, is a strategy of resilience that entered American humor through the minstrel tradition and the technique of masking, and came to fruition in blues music. Plantation fiction, like the Uncle Remus tales, often relied on this kind of masking to create humor out of tragedy. Chesnutt, however, creates the illusion of the minstrel "darky" while turning the mask on its head. The reader is meant to experience the southern situations from both sides of the mask, and from both sides of the color line, until it is impossible to distinguish the fool from the foil. It may seem in "Mars Jeems's Nightmare," for instance, that the well-spoken white homeowner, John, is to be admired for his command of his property and his hired help. As in all the tales in the collection, though, Julius outwits him and has his own way. So, the question arises: With whom is the reader meant to identify? The reader is meant to experience the blackness of whiteness and the whiteness of blackness expressed so well in the tragic/comic nature of the blues.

To his readers, Chesnutt's conjure tales might have seemed like fantastical humor drawn from the sometimes extravagant beliefs of the southern black community, but the tales that Chesnutt produced at the same time that blues music was emerging in the South were also blues, speaking beyond themselves and at many different levels. Chesnutt must be counted among the many blues artists because, like them, he gathered up the raw material of the southern black community, and using the same means as the great blues improvisers, shaped those materials into American fine art that gives voice to the yearnings of a nation in search of itself and its own uniquely complicated identity.

NOTES

1. Smith became better known for allegedly bleeding to death outside a white-only hospital "than for what she had done in life," according to her biographer Chris Albertson. See his *Bessie* (New York: Stein and Day, 1992), 32. For the facts of her fatal car crash see Frederick Spencer, *Jazz and Death: Medical Profiles of Jazz Greats* (Jackson: University Press of Mississippi, 2002), 208.

2. Eric J. Sundquist, "'The Drum with the Man Skin': Jonah's Gourd Vine," in *Zora Neale Hurston: Critical Perspectives Past and Present,* ed. Henry Louis Gates Jr. and Kwame Anthony Appiah (New York: Amistad, 1993), 47.

3. Henry Louis Gates Jr., "King of Cats," *The New Yorker* 8 (April 8, 1996): 76.

4. W. E. B. Du Bois, *The Souls of Black Folk,* ed. Henry Louis Gates Jr. and Terri Hume (1903; repr. New York: Norton, 1999), 155.

5. James Weldon Johnson, "Now We Have the Blues," in *The Selected Writings of James Weldon Johnson: Social, Political, and Literary Essays,* ed. Sondra Kathryn Wilson, vol. 2 (New York: Oxford University Press, 1995), 388.

6. Ibid., 389.

7. Eileen Southern, *The Music of Black Americans: A History,* 3rd ed. (New York: Norton, 1997), 358.

8. Ibid., 358.

9. Albert Murray, *Stomping the Blues* (New York: Da Capo Press, 1976), 188.

10. Charles Waddell Chesnutt, *The Journals of Charles W. Chesnutt,* ed. Richard H. Broadhead (Durham, NC: Duke University Press, 1993), 125.

11. Chesnutt, *Journals,* 125–26.

12. Richard H. Brodhead, introduction to Chesnutt, *Journals,* 24.

13. Chesnutt, *Journals,* 121.

14. Chesnutt, *Journals,* 122.

15. Quoted in Stephen P. Knadler, "Untragic Mulatto: Charles Chesnutt and the Discourse of Whiteness," *American Literary History* 8.3 (1996): 431.

16. Eric J. Sundquist, *To Wake the Nations: Race in the Making of American Literature* (Cambridge, MA: Harvard University Press, 1993), 285.

17. Ralph Ellison, "Change the Joke," in his *Shadow and Act* (New York: Random House, 1953), 53.

18. Sundquist, "'Drum,'" 44.

19. Charles Waddell Chesnutt, *The Conjure Woman and Other Conjure Tales,* with an introduction by Richard H. Brodhead (1899; repr. Durham, NC: Duke University Press, 1993), 34.

20. R. V. Burnette, "Charles W. Chesnutt's *The Conjure Woman* Revisited," *CLA Journal* 30.4 (1987): 439.

21. Ralph Ellison, "The Art of Fiction," in his *Shadow and* Act, 172.

22. Sundquist, *To Wake the Nations,* 277.

23. Chesnutt, *Conjure Woman,* 68.

24. Ibid., 58.

25. Ralph Ellison, "Richard Wright's Blues," in his *Shadow and Act,* 78.

26. Chesnutt, *Conjure Woman,* 64.

Chapter 9

Rewriting Dunbar

Realism, Black Women Poets, and the Genteel

Paula Bernat Bennett

The complete assimilation of American culture will equip the Negro with the "refinement" and "taste" requisite to writing in a tradition utterly alien to his temperament.[1]

In 1924, Allen Tate, Southern Fugitive and New Critic-to-be, reviewed *An Anthology of Negro Poetry,* edited by Newman Ivey White and Walter Clinton Jackson. Although Tate called the volume "useful," he did not, in fact, have much use for it. On the contrary, if the anthology is representative of the bulk of African American poetry "from its beginning in Phyllis [*sic*] Wheatley down to Countee P. Cullen," Tate wrote, "[I]t is just as well that the entirety of poetry in this field . . . isn't generally available, for . . . it is on the whole . . . worthless, and the good would . . . be submerged in the . . . bad."[2] The only black writer whom Tate fully exempts from this condemnation is Jean Toomer, author of the widely hailed, experimental *Cane* (1923) and to Tate "the finest Negro literary artist that has yet appeared in the American scene."[3] Of Clinton and Jackson's many sins, Tate views Toomer's omission as among the most egregious.

Tate's admiration for Toomer may be token; but his praise has a credible ring. Anticipating by a year one of Alain Locke's key arguments in *The New Negro* (1925), Tate is disturbed by the anthologists' privileging of an aesthetic that he views as a whitening of the black man's soul. Tate asserts that Toomer "is interested in the interior of Negro life, not in the pressure of American [sic] culture on the Negro." In favoring poets like William Braithwaite, the editors chose authors "only Negro by an accident of blood, [having] as little of the Negro temperament as Longfellow."[4] Black writers who failed to embrace what Tate calls "the interior of Negro life" but that he defines only in terms of what Toomer was not (i.e., not Longfellow) were, quite simply, not black.

Because of the implosion of identity politics in the early 1980s, the essentialist approach in Tate's review to race, not to mention literature, no longer seems as self-evident as it was in 1924. Flawed or not, however, his argument cuts to issues that were roiling in the black literary community in his day. By 1924, modernism was well underway, and, like their white counterparts, African American writers were increasingly engaged, as Henry Louis Gates Jr. puts it, with "matters of language and voice." Behind their focus lay the question of "the absence or presence of the black voice in the text" that had plagued African American poetry from Wheatley on, and that the publication of Paul Laurence Dunbar's internally divided work only made more urgent.[5] Increasingly sensitized to the gulf between their strivings toward gentility and post-Emancipation realities, black writers between Dunbar and Hurston sought, Gates argues, to fashion a language more directly expressive of the varieties of African American experience as they knew them.[6]

Gates's observations represent a fundamental insight into the way black poetry evolved in the post-bellum–pre-Harlem years. This essay will expand upon his comments in relation to the writing of four black women poets, all of whom chose to challenge the genteel aesthetic governing Clinton and Jackson's anthology as a standard for measuring black social and cultural progress. Through most of the nineteenth century, the genteel was the dominant style, used by all authors, whatever their class, ethnic, or racial backgrounds, with relatively few exceptions. To suggest, as Tate and Locke do, that black writers' adoption of this style was imitation or mimicry, where white writers' use of it was not, is consequently misleading.[7] Unless employing dialect or writing satire, a nineteenth-century poet was expected to write this way. At the same time, performatively and culturally, the genteel was a highly problematic discourse for African Americans to employ.

Tate to the contrary, the real difficulty with the genteel was not its "whiteness," however, but its self-conscious poetical-ness. Almost another language, it announced itself not only by romantic vagueness and idealism but also by anachronistic turns of phrase (such as "doth" and "thee"), exclamations and apostrophes, and frequently inverted syntax. Given how embedded these devices were in the middle-class American literary imaginary—an imaginary shaped by Shakespeare, Milton, and other writers of the elite British tradition—even the most black-identified poet could not use them without sounding white, and middle-class to boot. In reaching towards a more specifically black voice and content, the poetry written by the four women I discuss here—Lizelia Augusta Jenkins Moorer, Maggie Pogue Johnson, and the sisters Priscilla Jane and Clara Ann Thompson— reflects their efforts to find ways of writing more compatible with their experience than was the genteel—a shift in priorities for which Dunbar's intervention was crucial. In this way, they helped move black poetry toward a language of its own—one that, in the standard or in the vernacular, was Other and American at once, sometimes in surprisingly powerful ways.

Paul Laurence Dunbar

Viewed by many as the most talented black poet between Wheatley and Hughes, Dunbar is a puzzle without a solution. Nor will this essay offer one, not only because I am skeptical that one exists but also, far more importantly, because it was precisely his contradictions that made him such a generative figure for other poets. An extraordinarily prolific and versatile writer, Dunbar published eleven volumes of poetry, four short story collections, and four novels in thirteen years. Blessed with a lyric gift that could spin gold from straw, he earned his reputation during the post-bellum–pre-Harlem years largely by writing dialect poetry wherein, some claim, he exploited the racist conventions of minstrelsy and of white Plantation School authors—Thomas Nelson Page, Joel Chandler Harris, James Whitcomb Riley—for commercial gain.[8]

Although elsewhere in his writing Dunbar denounced slavery passionately, he undeniably wrote many dialect poems that romanticize it, such as "The News," "The Deserted Plantation," "Chrismus on the Plantation," and "A Banjo Song," in which black speakers lament their masters' deaths, fondly recall their lives in slavery, and tout their fidelity and banjo playing.[9] Of such poems, William Dean Howells, the highly influential critic and father of realism, said, "Paul Dunbar was the only man of pure African blood and of American civilization to feel the Negro life aesthetically and express it lyrically. . . . [H]is . . . achievement was to have studied the American negro objectively, and to have represented him . . . with . . . entire truthfulness."[10] In a mean-spirited mood one could translate this as, "Dunbar's unique achievement was to take slavery's victims, and by aestheticizing them, turn them into *objets d'art* for white, middle-class readers like myself to learn from and enjoy."

As is well established, Dunbar was far more ambivalent about his vernacular poetry than were Howells and other white magazine editors. Viewing it as a narrowing of his talent, he resented the pressure they put on him to write it. His opinion was certainly true, but when Dunbar blames editors for his writing dialect poetry, his complaint begs some important questions, including what led him to write it in the first place, and, no less striking, why he wrote it so well. If Dunbar really devalued dialect poetry so much, how could he bring such sympathy, wit, and wisdom to his writing of it? And coming right down to it, why do so many of his dialect poems—such as "Accountability," "An Ante-Bellum Sermon," "When Malindy Sings," "Little Brown Baby," "In the Morning," and "A Negro Love Song"[11]—seem alive in ways that his standard verse, which he valued more, does not? If, as I believe, the strengths of Dunbar's dialect poetry and the weaknesses of his standard verse share a single root—his unswerving loyalty to a genteel aesthetic—then Howells was right: Dunbar's most important literary contribution lay in his vernacular verse.

When Dunbar began writing, the problem that Howells and other white editors confronted was that which Tate and Locke both identify: the genteel's inability to incorporate the real. By the 1880s, the push toward realism, spearheaded by Howells, had already started to undermine the genteel's dominance as a literary practice—no surprise, since it had been in use for rather too long anyway. Tired of repeating their precursors and themselves, fiction writers and poets began to reinvigorate their writing by turning to more realist modes such as local color and regionalism. In these works, dialect served as the real's linguistic signature, no matter how faked it actually was. Taking dialect from whatever cultures they could find it in —Chinese, southern, black, Jewish, rural, urban, or Native American— poets and storytellers alike used it to bring verbal novelty and seeming touches of reality to their work.

To judge by the contradictions embedded in Howells's praise for Dunbar's dialect poetry (Can something that is aestheticized also be "objective" and "true"?), it would seem that what realism's father really saw in the young black poet was not the truth of black lives, of which he had little or no direct knowledge, but the answer to his own aesthetic dilemma.

Dunbar's vernacular verse, which was neither strictly realist nor strictly genteel but partook of both styles at once, allowed Howells, who only gave up writing genteel poetry himself in the 1890s, to have his cake and eat it too.[12] By taking poetry down from the heights where the genteel had imprisoned it and giving it over to black speakers, Dunbar had succeeded where Howells himself had failed. He had revitalized the aesthetically oriented lyric and filled it with the wonder and beauty of everyday life—moves he effectively allegorizes in "When Malindy Sings," when he gives his unschooled black singer the advantage over her genteel white competitor, Miss Lucy. This was no mean achievement; and its influence on Dunbar's contemporaries and on his successors was, as Gates suggests, immense.[13]

At the same time, because Dunbar never abandoned genteel aesthetics wholly in his lyric verse, he did not carry the realism of his vernacular poetry to its logical conclusion, either in the dialect poems themselves or in his standard verse. His dialect poems have black speakers and settings, but, faithful to genteel aesthetic principles, they avoid anything close to a realistic representation of the painful, ugly sides of pre- and post-Emancipation life. On those occasions when his standard poems do confront the latter, as in "To the South on Its New Slavery," "The Haunted Oak," and "Douglass," their claim to authenticity—that is, to being the expressions of an African American voice—is subverted by their use of the genteel's signature rhetorical gambits: in particular, verbal and syntactic archaisms such as "pinions foul," "I trow," and "with amaze."[14] Poems such as "We Wear the Mask," "Sympathy," and "The Poet,"[15] where Dunbar brings together a black speaker, black reality, and contemporary standard speech patterns, are simply too rare to challenge the general impression of out-of-dateness and derivativeness that his continued reliance on genteel rhetorical strategies creates.

As I see it, these are the contradictions that Dunbar left unresolved at his premature death in 1906. As such contradictions often are, they were a boon to later writers, who struggled to cohere what Dunbar could not: a distinctively black voice speaking of distinctively black experience in the vernacular and the standard alike. If Gates is right that this desire was not fully satisfied until Hurston's *Their Eyes Were Watching God* (1937),[16] then the four post-bellum–pre-Harlem women poets I discuss here, none of whom possessed one-tenth of Dunbar's or Hurston's talent, nevertheless represent significant steps along the way to this conclusion.

Lizelia Augusta Jenkins Moorer, Maggie Pogue Johnson, and the Thompson Sisters

Neither of the first two women, Lizelia Augusta Jenkins Moorer and Maggie Pogue Johnson, remotely qualifies as a professional poet. By her own account, Moorer, a teacher at Claflin University, South Carolina's first black college, decided to publish because she was frustrated with the way both northern and southern writers misrepresented southern blacks; and she wanted to tell "the unvarnished truth." "Seeing that the one cannot get at the facts, while the other will not, I reach the conclusion that the story must be told by a Negro—one who is a victim to the inconveniences of prejudice."[17] Most of *Prejudice Unveiled: and Other Poems* (1907) is dedicated to this mission. Much less is known of Maggie Pogue Johnson. However, based on the subtitle to her sole volume, *Virginia Dreams* (1910)— "Lyrics for the Idle Hour, Tales of the Time Told in Rhyme"—and her brief statement that she published at the request of friends,[18] it seems she was a coterie poet, producing entertaining verse, half of which consisted of dialect poems, for her own crowd.

To realize just how seriously Moorer took her mission to tell "the unvarnished truth," one only need look at the titles of her poems: for example, "Prejudice," "Jim Crow Cars," "The Peonage System," "Injustice in the Courts," "Lynching," "The Truth Suppressed."[19] Item by item, each offers a searing indictment of a society whose glut of post-bellum–pre-Harlem evils, as Dunbar asserted, made the Old South seem relatively benign by comparison. But this is also where the cutting difference between Dunbar and Moorer lies. Ever the genteel poet, Dunbar frames his appeal to the South in the high-minded rhetoric of an earlier time, even as he tactfully implies, but does not detail, its new cruelties, and he further weakens his poem's edge by loading his comparison to chattel slavery with "homely joys" and "chubby children."[20] On the other hand, Moorer utterly strips away any hint of "the mask that grins and lies,"[21] as in the following lines from "The Peonage System":

> Oft we find an overseer with a gun and club and whip,
> Who at night within the stockade locks the Negroes, lest they skip,
> If they offer a resistance for their treatment in this cage,
> They are clubbed into submission in the overseer's rage.[22]

To be sure, there are moments of light among Moorer's jeremiads, and she praises Lincoln, Theodore Roosevelt, and two southern-born educators—who, by supporting blacks, jeopardized their careers. Overall, however, she paints a grim picture, sacrificing beauty repeatedly to truth, and the ideal to the real. Of the Jim Crow car, she writes, "Legalized humiliation is the Negro Jim Crow car" (8);[23] of what goes on in lynching, "Then the flesh is cut in pieces and the souvenirs begin; / Each must have the piece allotted for the friends at home to see."[24] Of jury trials, she says, "When a mob has forced a jury to a stand against the right, / All the waters of the ocean cannot make the conscience white."[25] One would have to return to the antebellum period to find poetry this saturated with anger, this ruthless in expression. Confronting everything from separate and (un)equal schooling to corrupt politicians and courts, Moorer, whose nonpolitical poetry more or less conforms to genteel standards, avoids it here by using unadorned language to tell the truth, and letting the chips (including the very prosey quality of her verse) fall where they may.

Speaking from her subject position as a black woman educator, Moorer uses truth to undo the genteel, by this means recapturing something of the fierce energy and uncompromising anger of abolitionist poetry. Johnson, on the other hand, modeled herself on Dunbar, to whom she dedicated a worshipful poem, and her poetry might, therefore, seem a step backward from the real. Yet, by drawing her vernacular vignettes from the lives of post-bellum–pre-Harlem African Americans whose attitudes and speech patterns were close to their slave roots, she managed to avoid the nostalgic romanticization of slavery that mars so many of Dunbar's vernacular poems. Instead, she creates space for a more faithful social real.

What gives Johnson's poetry special interest is her speakers. These blacks are neither objects of sympathy nor exotics, as the genteel tradition would have them, nor are they the Plantation School's carefree "darkies" of bygone days. Rather, they are hard-working, somewhat frazzled men and women, who revel in nothing more than a table groaning with food (in the poem "What's Mo' Temptin' to de Palate?" the speaker recites her favorite edibles dish by dish),[26] good company, and swapping stories— and, of course, active participation in church services. Alongside the local minister, their hero is "Booker T.," but they are equally voluble on the virtues of "Brudder Wright's mule."[27] They are curious about new fashions for women and men, but slyly mocking of them as well; they look back on slavery with equanimity, not nostalgia; they look forward with hope and pride. They love their children even when scolding them, and each other, as long as each pulls his or her own weight.

Johnson's poems are too long to quote in full, but the following lines from "Krismas Dinner"—partially based on Dunbar's "The Party"—will illustrate these points, and the way in which the speakers' reality emerges through the thicket of mauled speech. This reality is that of free men and women who briefly gather to enjoy the fruits of their labor in the way they love best—by eating. Where Dunbar's "Party," even if meant as parody,[28] is improbable in the extreme, Johnson's poem, while teasing, is sufficiently similar to family gatherings this writer has attended to possess the ring of truth:

> Parson Reuben Jones was called,
> To say de blessed wuds,
> En as he 'gin to cle'r his throat,
> His inmos' soul was stirred:—
>
> "Heabenly Fodder look down on us,
> En dis earfly blessin',
> We thanks De fer dis possum roas',
> All brown wid ash-cake dressin,
>
> "We thanks De fer dis sausage,
> En squirrel cooked wid beans,
> En all dis nice fried chicken,
> Dese onions en dese greens;—
>
> "En as we goes to eat it,
> Wilt Dou be our frien',
> To keep us all from dyin',
> We ax dis, en amen." . . .
>
> Den we 'menced to eatin'.
> Dat was a stuffin' time,
> Case no one said a wud
> To pass away de time.
>
> Jis' 'cept to ax fer eatin's,
> Den in a quiet way,

> Dey w'ud cle'r der throats
> En hab a wud to say.
>
> You talk about folks eatin'!
> But neber in my rouns'
> Has I eber eat up so much grub
> As I did at brudder Browns.
>
> De wimmen dey was near de stove,
> En I tho't dat dey wud melt,
> But dey jis kept on a' eatin'
> 'Till dey had to loose dey belts.
>
> En when dem folks did git up,
> Dat table was cleaned up right,
> Possum carcass, chicken bones,
> Was all dat's lef in sight.[29]

As gentle in tone and ambiance as Moorer's poems are tense with outrage and frustration, Johnson's dialect vignettes register the other side of post-bellum–pre-Harlem black life, the side that, one suspects, made survival possible through all the horrors that Moorer describes.

What distinguishes the Thompson sisters is that, unlike Dunbar, Moorer, and Johnson, who are primarily interested in describing events, they are more concerned to expose the causes behind them. Whether Priscilla Jane and Clara Ann Thompson decided to rewrite Dunbar's material out of disgust with the way in which Howells misread him, or with the way in which Dunbar lent himself to misreading, their poems on slavery and the post-bellum–pre-Harlem African American experience offer the most explicit critiques of his work that I have found by the period's women poets. Like Dunbar, the Thompsons largely avoid the kinds of physical brutalities that made enslavement hell for its victims. However, in a small number of poems they explore with raw truthfulness the skewed personal interactions between blacks and whites, and the various ways in which slaveholders made not just their slaves' but also their own lives miserable—subjects that Dunbar deals with elsewhere but not in his poetry.

Like Johnson, the Thompsons self-published, and therefore were not burdened with white patronage or its constraints. Acute students of slaveholder psychology, they portray the "masters" of men and women as destroyed by the very power they cherish. Indeed, like early abolitionists, the Thompsons appear to view slaveholding as an addiction, making victims not just of slaves but of slaveholders as well, who became uncontrollably dependent on those they feared, hated, and abused. As the Thompsons depict this dynamic, slaveholders needed slaves not only to pick cotton, serve dinner, or swat flies but also emotionally, in ways that give a bitterly ironic twist to the trope of the faithful slave.

In "Freedom at McNealy's," Priscilla Thompson, writing in the standard, turns this overexploited trope—used by Dunbar, among others—ugly side out. The war lost and his plantation in ruins, McNealy assembles his two hundred slaves to tell them they are free. As Thompson describes McNealy's slaves, they are "[m]en of middle age all palsied," "blighted youths and orphaned infants," and women to whose skirts cling children "[t]hrough whose veins his own blood runs." "Void of learning, inexperienced," they are "[l]aunched upon the crafty world" by their erstwhile owner, but not before McNealy tries to obtain their pity. "[W]ith quivering voice and husky, / [He] Tells them of his heavy losses, / Meanly seeking sympathy." Having "soft hearts," Thompson tells us, the newly emancipated slaves oblige, pushing lifelong cruelties aside to shake "his tyrant hand." Then, except for two, they leave. Aunt Jude and Uncle Simon, old, helpless, and frightened, beg McNealy to let them stay: "Told him, all their days remaining, / They would gladly give to him,"

> And McNealy, pleased and flattered,
> With no feeling of remorse,
> Takes them back into his service,
> As you would a faithful horse.[30]

To appreciate the full power of this last stanza, one must consider conventional treatments of the faithful slave trope such as Dunbar's "The Deserted Plantation" (in which the speaker revisits the abandoned site of his bondage and, awash in nostalgia, vows to "stay an' watch de deah ole place an' tend it / Ez I used to in de happy days gone by")[31]—or his even more egregious "Chrismus on the Plantation," whose similar "farewell" scene ends not with one slave remaining but all, voluntarily, after their erstwhile master tearfully tells them that he cannot pay them wages:

> All de women was a-cryin', an' de men, too, on de sly,
> An' I noticed somep'n shinin' even in ol' Mastah's eye.
> But we all stood still to listen ez ol' Ben come f'om de crowd
> An' spoke up, a-try'n' to steady down his voice and mek it loud.[32]

Perhaps both "ol' Ben," who initiates the slaves' self-sacrificial gesture in this poem, and the speaker of "The Deserted Plantation" are also Uncle Simons, so broken they could not survive elsewhere. However, Dunbar presents it as slaveholders saw it. In their version, they could perpetrate obscene crimes, including selling their own children, and still be forgiven; they could rape and still be loved; they could burn, mutilate, and torture, and still be served willingly. Finally, when their own arrogance lost them everything, they could still expect those whom they abused to pity them. In "Freedom at McNealy's," Thompson exposes the narcissistic foundation of a thought process that allowed men like McNealy to do unforgivable evil and never know it. In Dunbar's poems, on the other hand, the (former) slaves who freely volunteer their services enable slaveholders and their apologists, past, present, and future, to retain their ignorance.

In such instances, the genteel's inability to confront evil made it evil's unwitting accomplice. The coarse final stanza of "Freedom at McNealy's" contains all the brutal clout the situation deserves. Does this degrade the former slaves, taking away a dignity and decency that, as some argue,[33] Dunbar restored to them? Possibly, but to this writer, at least, that seems preferable to letting slaveholders off the hook, especially given that apologists for slaveholding, if not the slaveholders themselves, are still with us.

In "The Favorite Slave's Story," Priscilla Thompson again pinpoints the narcissistic foundation of slaveholder neediness. In this poem we learn of its impact on a single slave family: the mother, Maria, and her three children, Peter, Susan, and Simon, "the favorite slave" who narrates the poem. Speaking in the vernacular, Simon, now a family man himself, tells his daughter's fiancé about his life under slavery. As in the narratives of Olaudah Equiano and Harriet Jacobs, what emerges is not a tale of consistent brutality but of irrational inconsistencies, where periods of "spoiling" and abuse alternate at the slaveholders' whim. One minute, Miss Nancy, having caught her husband abusing Maria, threatens to leave him; the next, she joins him in the abuse. No "Angel in the House," Miss Nancy eventually allows her husband, both a profligate and an alcoholic, to sell all her slaves with the exception of Simon, her "pet." Whites, Simon learns, even in the best of times were not to be trusted, and he relays this message:

> I tell you son de good white-folks,
>> Wus good in times uv ease;
> But soon as hawd times cummed tha' way,
>> Dey'd change, quick as you please.[34]

And Simon transmits other, equally depressing insights. Before selling the faithful Maria down the river, for example, Miss Nancy manipulates circumstances so as to justify her criminal intent: "One mawnin', jest to pick a fuss, / She said she missed a pie; / . . . / An' ef [Maria] didn't bring it back, / She'd have her whooped an' sold."[35]

The consequence of this sort of behavior is constant emotional mayhem. Those with power scream, weep, and lie; those without it live in terror, one that finally overwhelms the white family as much as it does the slaves—if not more so. The husband dies, a raving madman, of alcohol poisoning; and, as the war begins, Miss Nancy is left to wring her hands, "cryin' day an' night, / An' beggin' [Simon] to stay" as other slaves begin "a-walkin' off, / To suit their own free mind."[36] Contrary to her expectations and to the myth of the faithful slave, Miss Nancy's "favorite" leaves too, taking wife and children. At poem's end, we see Simon not nostalgically mourning for "de happy days gone by," but contentedly ensconced in his own home, patriarch of his household.

Like spoiled children who know nothing of limits, Priscilla Thompson's slaveholders cannot appreciate why those on the giving end might hate them. Rather, they remain fixed in their immaturity, possessing the power of gods and the temperaments of two-year-olds. The irony—one ubiquitously present in the literature on slavery—is that, as with children, this spoiling makes the slaveholders miserable. Never possessing enough, they cannot achieve the closure that freedom from desire would bring. In this sense, they are even more trapped by slavery than their slaves. Though their slaves never satisfy them, they make slavery their god.

In a canny move, Clara Thompson extends her sister's insights on the relationship under slavery among excessive power, narcissism, and immaturity to the relationships during the post-bellum–pre-Harlem era between whites and blacks. In "Uncle Rube and the Race Problem," whites ask the poem's narrator, the garrulous Rube, to tell them how he would "solve de Negro Problum," and Rube gives them answers they do not much care for, beginning with the suggestion that whites change the way they talk to blacks:

> 'How'd I solve de Negro Problem?'
>   Gentlemen, don't like dat wo'd!
> 'Mind me too much uv ol' slave times,
>   When de white man wus de lo'd.
>
> Spoutin' roun' about 'My niggahs',
>   Knockin' us fum lef' to right,
> Sellin' us, like we wus cattle,
>   Drivin' us fum mawn till night—[37]

Whites, Rube says, only know how to give orders, and they blame African Americans for everything and praise them for nothing: indeed, they tear down any black who does manage to "mak[e] a mawk."[38] Furthermore, where whites are quick to see blacks' faults, they never see their own; they worry about nonconcerns like amalgamation, and they refuse to "play faiah."[39] Twice, Rube points to the success of European immigrants in fitting into American mainstream society. Adopting genteel attributes worked for them, he argues, but not for blacks, because whites do not permit it:

> 'Don't know whaur to place de black man?'
>   He will fin' his place; —You'll see!
> Like de foreign whites is doin'
>   When you learn to let him be.[40]

Rube's "solution"—to leave a black man like him alone instead of "git[ing] into his way"[41]—is sound, but the whites who seek his advice do not hear a word he says. What they want from him (or, better, need) is not the truth but his absolution. As with McNealy and Miss Nancy, the hand-wringing whites in this poem expect blacks to redeem them from the situation they themselves created. If these whites would accept responsibility for what they have done, Rube says, then they would now know what to do without his telling them; but this is not what they want, insuring that the "Negro Problum" will persist indefinitely into the future, which, of course, it has.

In "Uncle Rube and the Race Problem," Clara Thompson deliberately uses an ungenteel speaker (a "rube") to stress both the gulf between blacks and whites and the need for plain talk over that divide. The main point that emerges from this unsuccessful interchange is that becoming genteel (or "uplift," as it was known) failed as an answer to the "Race Problem," not because gentility was incompatible with African Americans (Tate's view) but because, in focusing only on elevating the black community, it tacitly ceded to white racism the power to dictate the grounds. This is precisely what Rube is challenging when he insists that the problem will not be resolved until whites change. There was just so much even the most genteel of blacks could do. The rest was in the hands and hearts of those who had set the conditions and who alone had the power to change them.

In this poetry, one can, I think, hear the door shutting on black optimism, especially the belief that the acquisition of gentility in itself could bridge the gap racism made. To this day, African Americans remain the single minority for whom cultural assimilation, not to mention an enormous contribution to American culture in all its branches, has not been enough. At the same time, however, one can also hear another door opening—that which made space for African American women poets to write their lives as they knew them, free of genteel restraints, in voices recognizably their own, whether in the standard or in the vernacular—the very great gift that Dunbar, more than any other single figure, gave them.

NOTES

1. Allen Tate, "Negro Poetry," in *The Poetry Reviews of Allen Tate, 1924–1944,* ed. Ashley Brown and Frances Neel Cheney (Baton Rouge: Louisiana State University Press), 21–22.

2. Ibid., 21.

3. Ibid., 22.

4. Ibid., 22.

5. Henry Louis Gates Jr., *The Signifying Monkey: A Theory of African-American Literary Criticism* (Oxford: Oxford University Press, 1988), 174.

6. Ibid., 178–79. Although I have "translated" Gates's language into my own terminology, I have tried to be true to his basic intention in this seminal passage, and throughout his discussion of the role Dunbar played in the birthing of a black literary voice. In this sense, Gates's comment that Dunbar "drew upon dialect as the medium through which to posit this mode of realism" (176)—by which he

means a realism designed to refute Plantation School stereotypes of African Americans—is the starting point of my essay.

7. See Tate, "Negro Poetry," 21–22; and Alain Locke, "The New Negro" in *The Norton Anthology of African American Literature,* ed. Henry Louis Gates Jr. and Nellie Y. McKay (1925; repr. New York: Norton, 1997), 961.

8. See Joan R. Sherman's introduction to *African-American Poetry of the Nineteenth Century: An Anthology* (Urbana: University of Illinois Press, 1992), 12–14; and William M. Ramsey, "Dunbar's Dixie," *Southern Literary Journal* 32 (1999): 30–34.

9. Joanne M. Braxton, ed., *The Collected Poetry of Laurence Dunbar* (Charlottesville: University of Virginia Press, 1993), 136–37, 67–68, 137–38, 20–21.

10. William Dean Howells, introduction to *Lyrics of Lowly Life,* in *The Complete Poems of Paul Laurence Dunbar,* ed. Howells (New York: Dodd, Mead, 1944), viii–x.

11. Braxton, *Collected Poetry,* 5–6, 13–15, 82–83, 134–35, 190–91, 49.

12. Julie Bates Dock, "William Dean Howells," in *Encyclopedia of American Poetry: The Nineteenth Century,* ed. Eric L. Haralson (Chicago: Fitzroy Dearborn Publishers, 1998), 224–29.

13. Gates and McKay, eds., *Norton Anthology,* 961.

14. Braxton, *Collected Poetry,* 216, 219, 208. The Dunbar poems in this essay are quoted with permission of the University of Virginia Press. For an illuminating and sympathetic discussion of "black-white-ness" in Dunbar's poetry, see Shirley Eversley's entry "Paul Laurence Dunbar" in Haralson, ed., *Encyclopedia of American Poetry,* 138–40.

15. Ibid., 71, 314, 191.

16. Gates, *Signifying Monkey,* 173–74.

17. Lizelia Augusta Jenkins Moorer, *Prejudice Unveiled: and Other Poems* (1907; repr. Boston: Roxburgh, 2004), 5. American Verse Project, University of Michigan, http://www.Hti.Umich.Edu/cgi/t/text/text-idx?

18. Maggie Pogue Johnson, *Virginia Dreams: Lyrics for the Idle Hour, Tales of the Time Told in Rhyme* (n.p.: John M. Leonard, 1910), 5. New York Public Library. Digital Schomburg: African American Women Writers of the Nineteenth Century. http://digilib.nypl.org/dynaweb/digs/wwm9712/@Generic__BookView.

19. Moorer, *Prejudice Unveiled,* 7, 14, 17, 42, 31, 62.

20. Dunbar, "To the South," in Braxton, *Collected Poetry,* 218.

21. Dunbar, "We Wear the Mask," in Braxton, *Collected Poetry,* 71.

22. Moorer, *Prejudice Unveiled,* 18.

23. Ibid., 14.

24. Ibid., 32.

25. Ibid., 43.

26. Johnson, *Virginia Dreams,* 31.

27. Johnson, "Dat Mule ob Brudder Wright's," in *Virginia Dreams,* 32–33. All of

Johnson's poems in this essay are quoted with permission of the New York Public Library.

28. Braxton, *Collected Poetry,* xxv.

29. Johnson, *Virginia Dreams,* 12, 13, 14.

30. Priscilla Jane Thompson, *Gleanings of Quiet Hours,* in *Collected Black Women's Poetry,* ed. Joan R. Sherman, vol. 2 (1907; repr. New York: Oxford University Press, 1988), 66–69. All of Thompson's poems in this essay are quoted with permission of the New York Public Library.

31. Braxton, *Collected Poetry,* 68.

32. Ibid., 137.

33. Ibid., xxvi–xxviii.

34. Thompson, *Gleanings,* 55.

35. Ibid., 56.

36. Ibid., 61.

37. Clara Ann Thompson, *Songs from the Wayside,* in *Collected Black Women's Poetry,* ed. Joan R. Sherman, vol. 2 (1908; repr. New York: Oxford University Press, 1988), 33. Thompson's poems in this essay are quoted with permission of the New York Public Library.

38. Ibid., 35.

39. Ibid., 37.

40. Ibid., 38 (see also 36).

41. Ibid., 36.

Chapter 10

Inventing a "Negro Literature"

Race, Dialect, and Gender in the Early Work of Paul Laurence Dunbar, James Weldon Johnson, and Alice Dunbar-Nelson

Caroline Gebhard

"There is now a negro literature," *The Tuskegee Student* declared in 1900.[1] That year, a single issue of *The Southern Workman* (November 1900) featured three black writers with national reputations: Paul Laurence Dunbar (1872–1906), Alice Dunbar (1875–1935) (later Dunbar-Nelson), and Charles W. Chesnutt (1858–1932). Dunbar's contribution, "De Critters' Dance," is a whimsical satire of religiosity. His spouse's contribution, "Esteve, the Soldier Boy," explores a major theme in her work, the murky politics of racial identity. Chesnutt's piece, "Tobe's Tribulations," contains "virtually the whole of Chesnutt's folk aesthetic."[2] By 1900 Paul Dunbar was the most famous black writer in America, yet he knew he had competition. Upon hearing Chesnutt was writing a novel, he wrote Alice, "As long as the Negro literary field held me above I could afford to take it pretty easily, but now that another Richmond has come on—a Richmond so worthy of my mettle, too,—'a horse, a horse!'"[3]

White literary America began to take notice: critic and poetaster Richard Henry Stoddard seconded the *Tuskegee Student*'s pronouncement on the new "Negro literature." Nevertheless, he claimed that "this negro literature has thus far been furnished practically exclusively by writers of the white race, almost the only exception being Mr. Paul Laurence Dunbar."[4] *The Tuskegee Student,* however, rejected his claim that blacks were not the authors of this new literature; it pointed to the "brainy Du Bois," "Mrs. Harper," and "our own Principal Washington." Furthermore, the

Student wrote, Daniel Murray, the assistant librarian of Congress who had assembled the black literature exhibit for the Paris Exposition of 1900, "will gladly send Mr. Stoddard a list of Negro authors."[5] The exhibit, widely covered in the press, was selected from over one thousand titles of "real literary merit" by black Americans uncovered by Murray.[6]

The conviction was widespread in African American circles that blacks had begun to make their mark in literature, notwithstanding white America's slowness in recognizing it. "It will not be easy to convince the American people that the negro has made even a beginning as an author and contributor to American literature," Fannie Barrier Williams admitted. Nevertheless, she argued that Murray's labors proved it. Although she paid tribute to a long history of black writing, Williams emphasized the literary striving of her own contemporaries. She praised work by Washington, Du Bois, Dunbar, and Chesnutt as "representative of the best things contributed to American literature by negro authors."[7]

Yet the self-conscious creation of a "Negro literature"—distinct from antebellum black writing that had been pervaded by antislavery politics and dominated by nonfictional genres—has often been thought to have begun only with the Harlem Renaissance in the 1920s.[8] The commentary of Williams and others shows, however, that in 1900 black critics recognized the birth of a new literature that reflected the postbellum aspirations and lives of black Americans and at the same time brooked no special pleading on the question of literary merit. Yet this birth was far from easy. In his essay, "Post-Bellum–Pre-Harlem," Chesnutt recollected that Thomas Dixon and Thomas Nelson Page were widely appreciated while "at that time a literary work by an American of acknowledged color was a doubtful experiment both for the writer and the publisher."[9]

What Chesnutt and his fellow writers achieved has been obscured, in part because of the low artistic valuation of the earlier period by influential critics like William Stanley Braithwaite (1878–1962). Identifying with the later "New Negro" movement, he dismissed Dunbar and earlier writers as "negligible, and of historical interest only."[10] Yet the term "New Negro" dates back to 1895, even though it is most often associated with Alain Locke's celebrated 1925 anthology.[11] Eager to claim the mantle of the "new," the heralds of the Harlem Renaissance elided the fact that twenty years before, black writers had also aspired to make a great "Negro" literature that would be "racial" yet "universal."

But what would the hallmarks of this new "Negro" literature be? How would writers themselves only one generation removed from slavery handle themes like the plantation, or should they treat such subjects at all? Should the African American writer see himself as engaged in a project of educating white audiences about black experience? And what was the place of the "New Negro" woman? Above all, what language would or should this new literature be written in—literary English or the vernacular English spoken by most blacks in America? These questions cannot be fully addressed here; however, this essay will grapple with the one that implicates them all: language. Comparing the early work of Dunbar and James Weldon Johnson sheds new light on the vexed question of black dialect, especially in view of Johnson's well-known later condemnation of this mode as limited to "only two stops: pathos and humor."[12] However, Dunbar-Nelson's early work suggests alternative choices in the linguistic palette of the new black artist. Considering these three writers together reveals how dialect and gender are intertwined in the emerging domain of "Negro literature." This approach also illuminates the role of mastery of "literary English" in its founding. Finally, framing these writers' early works as a literary field demonstrates that black literature is not the creation of a single artist nor one era alone—that the brilliant work of the Harlem Renaissance is thoroughly rooted in the post-bellum–pre-Harlem experiments of Dunbar and his fellow artists.

First, it is crucial to recall what literary success meant to the children and grandchildren of former slaves. Chesnutt put most plainly literature's advantages to literate African Americans who otherwise had little access to capital: "I want fame; I want money; I want to raise my children in a different rank of life from that I sprang from."[13] For this generation, literary achievement promised, then, "cultural capital," conferring not just material but also social benefit. John Guillory, extending Pierre Bourdieu's seminal concept, identifies several forms of "cultural capital"; the most critical here is "linguistic capital"—"the means by which one attains to a socially credentialed and therefore valued speech, otherwise known as 'Standard English.'"[14] In the literary arena, Guillory explains, "Authors confront a monumentalized textual tradition already immersed as speakers and writers in the social condition of linguistic stratification that betrays at every level the struggle among social groups over the resources of language, over cultural capital in its linguistic form."[15]

Circa 1900, African American writers, on the one hand, confronted the "monumental" tradition of English letters, and on the other, competed with other social groups, in Guillory's terms, for "the resources of language." However, as Gavin Jones observes, the hottest linguistic commodity in late-nineteenth-century America was dialect; moreover, while dialects from Maine to Louisiana could be parodied or invoked to assert the cultural superiority of the white middle class, they also registered "an anxious, constantly collapsing attempt to control the fragmentation and change that characterize any national tongue."[16] Because dialect was both wildly popular and a peculiarly charged site of cultural anxiety, African American dialects presented a critical opportunity for the black writer. Yet tapping this black linguistic resource has too often been viewed as an illegitimate form of cultural capital—crass exploitation or racist collusion. Yet the fact that white writers capitalized on "black" characters—i.e., characters who speak in dialect—did not mean that black writers of the era gave up their right to this material or believed they could not do it better. Moreover, black dialect offered the black writer "cultural capital" in another sense: it stood for the value of a cultural heritage in a society that denied that blacks had any culture of their own. Henry Louis Gates Jr. argues that dialect is the black poet's "only key" to the African past, functioning as "a verbal dialectic" between "English" and the lost African mother tongue.[17] Dunbar, Gates concludes, wrote his best poetry when he mined the resources of dialect.[18] Even Gates, though, charges Dunbar with "opportunism."[19]

But Dunbar understandably viewed black dialect as his patrimony. In it, he saw far more than a way to reach white audiences: the true inheritors of this speech—just like the best interpreters of the slave past—were African Americans like himself. The World's Columbian Exposition in 1893, where he encountered the Dahomeyans, proved pivotal. When Dunbar heard the music of this West African people at the Chicago fair, he had an epiphany: "Instantly the idea flashed into my mind: 'It is a heritage.'"[20] The black American, he wrote, should "seize upon these songs, preserve them and make them distinctively his own."[21] Although he had experimented in a variety of dialects, from then on black dialect became one of Dunbar's signature modes. Already concerned that "others" were stealing the black's true heritage, he questioned his future wife in terms that argued the "Negro" writer should claim his linguistic heritage:

> I want to know whether or not you believe in preserving by Afro-American
> ... writers those quaint old tales and songs of our fathers which have made
> the fame of Joel Chandler Harris, Thomas Nelson Page, Ruth McEnery Stu-
> art and others? or whether you like so many others think we should ignore
> the past and all its capital literary material.[22]

However, black writers were more likely to be seen as imitative, or at least not sufficiently distinctive, by white and even some black critics when they wrote in so-called pure English. Significantly, then, Dunbar, and Chesnutt and Johnson as well, not only staked their claim to black dialect but refused to relinquish their rights to "literary" English as well. Chesnutt, for example, recalls that the framing narratives in *The Conjure Woman* "were written in the best English I could command."[23] Although Negro literature was thus from the outset a fractured linguistic field, such fracturing should not be read as a sign of schizoid cultural inferiority on the part of the artist. Too many critics have viewed this double claim as compromised ambivalence rather than artful strategy; Dickson Bruce Jr., for example, asserts that because of his "assimilationist ideals,"[24] Dunbar was torn between black dialect as a "basis for molding a distinctive black identity" and standard English poetic forms. But this is to read literary history backwards; as Gates suggests, "we tend to forget how startling was Dunbar's use of black dialect as the basis of poetic diction."[25] Later, writers did come to see black dialect as emblematic of the black artist's tragic double bind in white America. Circa 1900, however, this strategy—which also appears in W. E. B. Du Bois's writings—of valuing Negro dialect as the language of black American cultural transmission enabled writers to defy the color line by simultaneously affirming black forms and the black artist's freedom to move between language registers: while Dunbar and his fellow black writers felt they must reclaim black dialect and black themes for the black artist, they also could not afford—nor did they wish—to abandon their equal claim upon the language of American high culture.

Two early poems show Dunbar's originality in employing this double stratagem: one in literary English, the other addressing a similar theme, only this time in black dialect. The first, with the deceptively simple title "Song" (1895), was published in *Majors and Minors*.[26] Later, it was included in *African Romances,* with music by S. Coleridge-Taylor, under the title, "An African Love Song" (1897).[27] This brief lyric evokes English ballads going back to "The Nut-Brown Maid" (c. 1503). Dunbar may have had this poem in mind because of its popularity; not only was it collected as a Child Ballad, but also a number of poets of the 1890s, including his bride-to-be, made use of the image of the "lissome nut-brown maid."[28] In any case, "Song's" archaic language ("thy," "thine"), the reference to wine, and the setting all conjure up pastoral tradition dating back to the English Renaissance, which elevated the rural subject by casting him as a lovesick "swain" smitten with a country maid. Dunbar, however, boldly inserts an

"African" maid into the pastoral mix, thus consciously racializing this traditional mode:

> My heart to thy heart,
> My hand to thine;
> My lip to thy lips,
> Kisses are wine
> Brewed for the lover in sunshine and shade;
> Let me drink deep, then, my African maid.[29]

In the second stanza, Dunbar subtly connects the quintessential emblem of perfect love, the rose, with the ardent black lover: "Lily to lily, / Rose to Rose; My love to thy love / Tenderly grows."[30] The implication is that this bloom is not only *not* inferior to the white one; in some respects, it surpasses it. That the lily implicitly stands in for the white pastoral couple of English poetry is suggested by the next lines calling for black lovers not to be separated: "Rend not the oak and the ivy in twain, / Nor the swart maid from her swarthier swain."[31] The logic of separation by race may seem troubling now, but the poem's thrust is to declare the black beloved worthy of the highest forms and symbols of romantic poetry.

To put black lovers on the same poetic ground as white ones seems hardly revolutionary now, but this was far from true then. The media was permeated by racist characterizations of black people as bestial or ridiculous: blacks were hardly serious subjects of romance or courtship. For example, *Leslie's Weekly,* a magazine akin to *Life Magazine* in capturing its time in photographic images, ran a popular series of photographs called "The Blackville Gallery." In one photo, captioned "The Blackville Wedding," a poor African American couple taking their vows is held up to ridicule: the solemnity of the occasion is burlesqued by the caption, "Honey, does you' lub yo' man?" and the prominently placed sign on the wall, "Lebe you razzer At de Do, Deakin Jonez."[32] The way the Jim Crow social contract was routinely underwritten by white derision is suggested by the popularity of this series with white readers.[33]

Still, the antiracist message of black love poems in literary English, like "Song," did not resonate with readers until the mid-twentieth century: although this poem was always included in editions of Dunbar's poetry printed during his life and in the 1913 posthumous edition, it was not otherwise reprinted until 1950.[34] However, another Dunbar love poem, "Negro Love Song," written in dialect, has been widely and continuously reprinted. First published in *Century Magazine*,[35] it later became part of the pathbreaking musical *Clorindy; or, The Origin of the Cakewalk* (1898), with music by Will Marion Cook and lyrics by Dunbar, under the title, "Jump Back Honey." Its original title, "A Negro Love Song," points to Dunbar's attempt to control discourse about African Americans of the time. Words like "African" and "Negro" register the writer's desire to dignify blackness. Yet Dunbar refused to write as if formal English were the superior tongue: dialect, this poem asserts, is as capable of expressing a lyrical tenderness as the most proper English diction. The playful refrain of this poem mimics the delicate dance of Eros—a one-step-closer, one-step-backward process. The lover both asks and demands, "Love me, honey, love me true? / Love me well ez I love you?"[36] One can imagine why it was so popular when set to music: like a classic Beatles lyric, it captures both the innocence and sensuousness of the first stages of love.

> Seen my lady home las' night,
> > Jump back, honey, jump back.
> Hel' huh han' an' sque'z it tight,
> > Jump back, honey, jump back.[37]

"Jump back" works as a paradoxical, braking figure of speech playing against the urgent desire the poem plots—the poet escorts his lady home, holds her hand, feels his heart beating, hesitates at her door, then puts his arm around her waist, and, finally, kisses her. The repeated refrain, "jump back," literally tells her to back off as he pulls her closer: this mock warning intensifies the erotic tension, yet suggests the playfulness of an artful lover:

> Put my ahm aroun' huh wais',
> > Jump back, honey, jump back.
> Raised huh lips an' took a tase,
> > Jump back, honey, jump back.[38]

Dunbar's masterly refrain reveals his recognition of dialect's potential to voice complex emotion: nothing about the poem capitulates to minstrel notions of black inferiority. Alice, who saw *Clorindy* on a roof-top theater in New York, told her husband, "Jump back, honey, jump back goes like a flash," adding, "The audience went wild and demanded an encore."[39]

James Weldon Johnson saw himself in 1900 as similarly engaged in bringing "a higher degree of artistry to Negro songs."[40] Reappropriating dialect for black art was central not only to Dunbar's but also to Johnson's rediscovery of what Johnson called "the importance of the American Negro's cultural background."[41] Yet because of dialect's strong association with minstrelsy, employing it was, as Kevin K. Gaines has argued, equivalent to walking a tightrope "between minstrelsy and uplift."[42] We must retrace Johnson's own fraught relationship with black dialect because despite his early experimentation with this form and his admiration of Dunbar, he later almost categorically rejected it. Yet this fact has too often been divorced from his early work, which was more deserving than anything Dunbar wrote of the criticisms he later leveled at dialect in general. Like many writers, Johnson became a harsh judge of his early efforts; moreover, the new race militancy after World War I led him, as well as many others, to turn against a mode that had begun to seem craven in the face of white power. Ironically, even as he sought to preserve Dunbar's reputation as "the first American Negro poet of real literary distinction,"[43] his attack on black dialect helped consign his friend in many critics' eyes to the dust bin of minstrelsy.

It has become commonplace to attribute the dichotomy in Dunbar's work between standard English and black dialect to the poet's own supposed racial schizophrenia.[44] Yet Johnson follows Dunbar's same practice of grouping poems according to their language registers. In *Fifty Years and Other Poems* (1917), he separates his poems in literary English from his "jingles and croons," as he labeled his dialect poems. Nevertheless, few critics have viewed this division as a sign of Johnson's own racial confusion, even though his poetry freely employs terms that Dunbar uses far more sparingly: "pickaninnny," "darkies," "mammy," and "coons." Johnson takes many more risks in conjuring minstrel stereotypes than Dunbar. Indeed, although he culled a group of poems from his popular turn-of-the-century stage work in *Fifty Years,* he was already having misgivings about his dialect creations; some work he chose not to republish at all and at least one poem, "Run Brudder Possum," was revised to eliminate the word "coon."[45] Indeed, Johnson's oeuvre suggests he always viewed dialect as best suited to comedy and not appropriate for serious poetry. For example, the subject of love elicits race-neutral language, even on occasion imagery suggesting whiteness: "How fair and slender was your throat, how / white the promise of your breast," the poet sings to his "princess" in

"Vashti."[46] There is nothing to compare to Dunbar's "African maid" in *Fifty Years and Other Poems,* and Johnson's own "Negro Love Song," "Ma Lady's Lips Am Like De Honey," is not only derivative of Dunbar's "Jump back, Honey," but done with a much cruder touch that pushes the poem toward buffoonery: "Honey on her lips to waste; / 'Speck I'm gwine to steal a taste."[47]

Still other dialect poems in this volume cross the line into full-fledged clowning. The last of the "Jingles and Croons," "The Rivals," tells how a suitor bests his competitor, causing him to be thrown from his mule, splitting his store-bought pants wide open: "W'en dat darky riz, well raly, I felt kinder bad fu' him; / He had bust dem cheap sto' britches f'om de center to de rim."[48] Johnson's most distinctive dialect poems do mine folk material for comic pathos. However, this side of Johnson is rarely on display; instead it is "Sence You Went Away" (1900) that always exemplifies his dialect poetry. Significantly, this is the poem Johnson himself chose to anthologize; ironically, it is also the poem where Dunbar's influence is at its strongest—and where the dialect, less bound to folk type, expresses a universal emotion, loneliness.

Johnson is far more at home addressing serious race themes in high poetic diction. The noble sentiments of his Negro national anthem, "Lift Every Voice and Sing," are perfectly in harmony with the title poem, "Fifty Years," and poems such as "To America," "O Black and Unknown Bards," and "O Southland!" In these, the collective struggle is commemorated in formal English, as if the poetry of racial striving must be strictly segregated from the vernacular. This bifurcation is not surprising, given Johnson's conviction that "the first step" in writing poetry is mastering standard English: "The English language is the material . . . to be moulded and chiseled and polished into thought forms of beauty."[49] That Johnson means standard English is unmistakable: he also calls for poets-in-training to learn correct usage for such words as prepositions. Yet in contrast to the high oratorical style of Johnson's public race poetry—and in sharp contrast to Dunbar—the only moment where race and Eros meet in Johnson's early poetry in literary English is in "The White Witch." This poem warns black men against white women, their erotic appeal likened to a lynching, the body burning "like a living coal,"[50] the victim powerless to resist.

Johnson's own best poetry is not written in dialect; indeed, rejecting it to represent the rhetorical effects of black preachers in *God's Trombones* (1927) marked the culmination of a long artistic evolution. In his 1922 preface to *The Book of American Negro Poetry*, he defends spirituals and ragtime but is far more skeptical of the value of the black vernacular: "Naturally, not as much can be said for the words of these songs as for the music."[51] Although he credited Dunbar for being "the first to use it [Negro dialect] as a medium for the true interpretation of Negro character and psychology,"[52] he nevertheless believed dialect defunct because of its close association with minstrel and plantation traditions: black writers should transcend dialect through "a form that is freer and larger than dialect, but which will still hold the racial flavor."[53] Certainly, this is his goal in *God's Trombones*—to render black speech rhythms in more or less standard English.

Late in life he even suggested that Dunbar shared his distaste for dialect. In *Along This Way* (1933), he remembers Dunbar saying, "I have never gotten to the things I really wanted to do"; yet admitting that "Paul never told me definitely what the things were that he really wanted to do," he hazards the guess that Dunbar planned to write epics in "straight English that would relate to the Negro."[54] Despite Johnson's assertion that he and Dunbar often discussed the limitations of dialect, Dunbar's letters paint quite a different picture. To Alice, Dunbar wrote that Johnson wanted him "to join the quadruple alliance, Cole—R. Johnson, J. Johnson & me."[55] Was the young Johnson, soon to go to New York to become a professional songwriter specializing in black dialect, really such a keen critic of it circa 1900? Johnson himself confesses that it was only much later that his ideas about poetry were "thoroughly clarified."[56] It is hard not to conclude that, looking back on conversations that had taken place thirty years earlier, now convinced of a new artistic creed, Johnson would interpret Dunbar's remarks in the light of his present views. Nor should critics underestimate the literary rivalry here. Although it was important to Johnson, personally, to discard black dialect, unfortunately his bias against it has been rarely taken into account. Instead, his pronouncements about dialect have become "more or less canonical."[57]

Like Johnson, as an anthologist and polemicist during the Harlem Renaissance, Dunbar-Nelson helped to define the modern canon of African American literature. In 1922 she called for a "Negro Literature for Negro Pupils," pointing to the damaging effects of being given only a "a milk-white literature to assimilate."[58] Unlike Johnson, however, she did not turn away from black dialect; rather, she worried that Dunbar would be remembered only as a dialect poet. Her first anthology, *The Dunbar Speaker and Entertainer* (1916), devotes two sections to dialect, one "humorous" and the other "serious." Nevertheless, Dunbar-Nelson's view early in her career suggests that the black woman writer in 1900 inevitably approached the issue differently than her male peers.

Circa 1900 black dialect work, like twentieth-century rap, was largely a masculine preserve. For African American male performers like Bob Cole, Rosamond Johnson, Ernest Hogan, Bert Williams, and George Walker, such work offered opportunities in all-black musical theatrical shows or in traveling vaudeville acts.[59] Poets such as Daniel Webster Davis and James D. Corrothers, who wrote primarily in dialect, also made money performing their work at readings, and again, like today's hip-hop artists, found a market for their work with black as well as white audiences. Conversely, for the kind of woman that Alice Ruth Moore was before she married Dunbar—young, aspiring to a literary career, active in the black women's club movement—public performances for money, especially dialect poems, would have called into question her refinement and taste.[60]

This gendering of black dialect is further supported by Dunbar's script for *Jes Lak White Fo'ks* (1900), an "operetta." In it, the poet puts heavy black dialect into the mouth of the patriarch, Pompous Johnsing: "But I an goin' get no bargain counter duke for my daughter, huh-uh, honey. . . . I has been engaged in diplomatic regotiations wid an Af'ican King."[61] But Dunbar makes Johnsing's daughter, Mandy, speak very proper English: "Father you're only mocking / Such levity is shocking."[62] Even Harper's "Aunt Chloe" poems featuring a former slave woman tend toward standard English, only sketchily suggesting black speech."[63] Black women writers—perhaps until Zora Neale Hurston—felt more constrained than men in the way they could develop their linguistic inheritance—their "cultural capital" from slavery. As partners in racial uplift, black women could ill afford to dispense with the prerogatives of genteel femininity. For black women, so often caricatured as hypersexual and ignorant, language associated with a lack of proper decorum or education carried a double risk.

From the outset, Dunbar-Nelson resisted the idea that black writers had to use dialect: "But if one should be like me—absolutely devoid of the ability to manage dialect—I don't see the necessity of cramming and forcing oneself into that plane because one is a Negro or a Southerner."[64] Instead, she took an individualist stand, adding, "I frankly believe in everyone following his bent. If it be so that one has a special aptitude for dialect work, why it is only right that dialect work should be made a specialty." These statements comprise her answer to Dunbar's rhetorical question about whether African American writers should draw upon the slave past.[65] Although in her reply to Dunbar, she appears to reject dialect for herself, it is not true that she could or did not write it. Instead of the "Negro dialect" associated with the plantation, however, she skillfully renders contemporary "hybrid" dialects of Creoles of color.

Dunbar-Nelson's "The Praline Woman," first published in *The Goodness of St. Rocque and Other Tales* (1899) but also included in her anthology under "serious" dialect pieces, consists almost entirely of the enterprising flow of talk by a woman who sells her pralines on Royal Street in New Orleans. Her speech is represented as a true Creole, a mix of Black English and Gallic speech patterns:

> "Praline? Pralines? Ah, ma'amzelle, you buy? S'il vous plait, ma'amzelle, dey be fine, ver' fresh. Sho chile, ma bébé, ma petite she put dese up hissef. . . . You tak' none? No husban' fo' you den!"[66]

Through her monologue to prospective customers, we learn her story; we also learn that she resents patronizing comments about her speech. Recalling an Irishman's question to her—"Auntie, what fo' you talk so?"—she includes her rejoinder, "An' I jes' say back, 'What fo' you say faith an bejabers?' Non, I don' lak I'ishman, me!"[67]

Another early story making use of black Creole dialect also explores the tension between the Irish immigrants and African Americans in New Orleans. In "Mr. Baptiste," the Irish longshoremen strike to oppose the hiring of any black workers, but the blacks resist by breaking the strike. When Mr. Baptiste, an indigent, elderly Creole who discourages inquiry into his personal history, has the temerity to cheer for the blacks, he becomes the first victim of the white mob's violence. Here, too, Mr. Baptiste speaks a mixture of French- and southern black-influenced dialect: "Yaas, dose cotton-yardmans, dose 'longsho'mans, dey . . . t'row down dey tool an' say dey work no mo' wid niggers."[68] Dunbar-Nelson's early Creole stories demonstrate that America vainly tries to reduce everything to black and white, whereas the reality is often not so simple. Her Mr. Baptiste appears to be a "gigi"—a special sort of Creole of African descent who "abhors everything American" yet keeps "negroes at bay for fear of familiarity" as well as keeping "whites from knowing him too well."[69] Still, she does not permit us to judge him too harshly when his one expression of solidarity with the blacks of his native city costs him his life.

What emerges in Dunbar-Nelson's early work is an individualist and feminist ethos, leading to alternative forms of linguistic experimentation for the new Negro literature. From the beginning, she strikes a feminist note; in *Violets and Other Tales* (1895), she celebrates the independence of the working woman, frankly wondering whether women should give up their liberty for marriage.[70] She also expresses the spirit of the "brave new woman" in her deft use of what her husband-to-be called her "bowery slang," that is, the laconic, tough-talking style of the stories of Edward W. Townsend.[71] In one story, "A Carnival Jangle," a young girl is tempted during Mardi Gras to don a male mask: " 'You'd better come with us, Flo, you're wasting time in that tame gang. Slip off, they'll never miss you; we'll get you a rig, and show you what life is.' "[72] For Alice Ruth Moore, "bowery slang," not black or even black Creole dialect, represented artistic and social freedom. This proto–jazz age style appealed to a young woman who liked to take walks down "Anarchy Alley."[73] However, "bowery slang" did not turn out to be the "cultural capital" she needed to launch a successful career as a mainstream writer, though she continued to publish in the black press.

The question of language—especially dialect—has continued to be central to definitions of African American literature. The question of how to tap the resources of the black vernacular without calling up pernicious stereotypes, however, is an issue that did not end with Dunbar and other writers of the post-bellum–pre-Harlem era. Later writers such as Hurston faced accusations that in representing black speech they merely reintroduced the stereotype of the "happy darky." More recently, the furor over "Ebonics" reveals how the question of black dialect remains loaded. Yet the work at the turn of the twentieth century by Dunbar, Johnson, Dunbar-Nelson, and others marks a critical chapter in the history of black cultural production in the United States. If the Renaissance of the twenties was a rebirth, the birth of "Negro literature" came more than twenty years earlier. Those writers like Braithwaite and Johnson who lived to take part in Harlem's Renaissance benefited from a long apprenticeship in mastering their craft. And those who did not—for example, Dunbar, who died in 1906, or Chesnutt, who stopped writing literature about the same time, or Pauline Hopkins, who died in obscurity—nevertheless deserve to be recognized for daring to invent the field of "Negro literature." In so doing, they showed the way for all their successors.

NOTES

1. My source for this *Tuskegee Student* editorial is Richard Henry Stoddard, "Literary Notes," *New York Mail and Express* (February 26, 1900), Paul Laurence Dunbar Papers, Manuscript (MS) 114, Box 18, Ohio Historical Society. Despite its name, the paper, edited by Emmett J. Scott, was not a student production; however, Charles Alexander, associate editor, probably wrote the literary editorials; see Booker T. Washington, vol. 4 of *The Booker T. Washington Papers,* ed. Louis R. Harlan et al. (Urbana: University of Illinois Press, 1972–89).

2. Eric J. Sundquist, *To Wake the Nations: Race in the Making of American Literature* (Cambridge, MA: Harvard University Press, 1993), 314.

3. Paul Laurence Dunbar to Alice Dunbar, 13 September 1898, in "The Letters of Paul and Alice Dunbar: A Private History," ed. Eugene Wesley Metcalf Jr. (Ph.D. diss., University of California, Irvine, 1973), 681–82; Metcalf, ed., "Letters," 683, footnotes the allusion to Shakespeare's *King Richard III* 5.4.7.

4. Stoddard, "Literary Notes," Dunbar Papers.

5. *The Tuskegee Student* (March 17, 1900), Dunbar Papers, MS 114, Box 18.

6. *Ideas* (Feb. 3, 1900), Dunbar Papers, MS 114, Box 18.

7. Fanny Barrier Williams, "The Colored Man Is Making His Mark in the Literary Field of To-day," *Chicago Times Herald* (April 29, 1900), Dunbar Papers, MS. 114, Box 18.

8. See Henry Louis Gates Jr., "The Trope of a New Negro and the Reconstruction of the Image of the Black," *Representations* 24 (Fall 1988): 143–44.

9. Charles Waddell Chesnutt, "Post-Bellum–Pre-Harlem," in *Breaking into Print,* ed. Elmo Adler (1931; repr. New York: Simon and Schuster, 1937), 53.

10. William Stanley Braithwaite, "The Negro in American Literature," in *The New Negro,* ed. Alain Locke (1925; repr. New York: Atheneum, 1968), 36.

11. See Amritjit Singh's "New Negro" in *The Oxford Companion to African American Literature,* ed. William L. Andrews et al. (New York: Oxford University Press, 1997), 536.

12. James Weldon Johnson, ed., *The Book of American Negro Poetry,* rev. ed. (New York: Harcourt, Brace, 1931), 4.

13. William L. Andrews, *The Literary Career of Charles W. Chesnutt* (Baton Rouge: Louisiana State University Press, 1980), 9–10.

14. John Guillory, *Cultural Capital: The Problem of Literary Canon Formation* (Chicago: University of Chicago Press, 1993), ix.

15. Ibid., 63.

16. Gavin Jones, *Strange Talk: The Politics of Dialect Literature in Gilded Age America* (Berkeley: University of California Press, 1999), 11.

17. Henry Louis Gates Jr., *Figures in Black: Words, Signs, and the "Racial" Self* (New York: Oxford University Press, 1987), 172.

18. Ibid., 179.

19. Henry Louis Gates Jr., *The Signifying Monkey: A Theory of African-American Literary Criticism* (New York: Oxford University Press), 1988, 176.

20. Paul Laurence Dunbar, "Negro Music," in *In His Own Voice: The Dramatic and Other Uncollected Works of Paul Laurence Dunbar*, ed. Herbert Woodward Martin and Ronald Primeau (Athens: Ohio University Press, 2002), 184. They date this important essay, which escaped previous bibliographers, 1899; however, my examination of the original in the Dunbar Papers, MS 114, Box 17, indicates that it more likely appeared in 1893 when Dunbar was writing for the *Chicago Record*.

21. Ibid., 184.

22. Dunbar to Alice Ruth Moore (17 April 1895) in Metcalf, ed., "Letters," 34.

23. Chesnutt, "Post-Bellum–Pre-Harlem," 49.

24. Dickson D. Bruce Jr., *Black American Writing from the Nadir: The Evolution of a Literary Tradition, 1877–1913* (Baton Rouge: Louisiana University Press, 1989), 71, 61.

25. Gates, *Signifying Monkey*, 176.

26. See "Song" in *The Collected Poetry of Paul Laurence Dunbar*, ed. Joanne M. Braxton (Charlottesville: University Press of Virginia, 1993), 13. The Dunbar poems here are reprinted with the permission of the University of Virginia Press.

27. Eugene Wesley Metcalf Jr., ed., *Paul Laurence Dunbar: A Bibliography* (Metuchen, NJ: Scarecrow Press, 1975), 92.

28. Alice Dunbar-Nelson, "At Bay St. Louis," in *The Works of Alice Dunbar-Nelson*, ed. Gloria T. Hull, vol. 1 (New York: Oxford University Press, 1988), 106–7.

29. Braxton, ed., *Collected Poetry*, 13.

30. Ibid., 13.

31. Ibid., 13.

32. "A Blackville Wedding," The Blackville Gallery No. 11, *Leslie's Illustrated Weekly* 86.2208 (January 6, 1898), 8–9.

33. Editorial column, "Features of *Leslie's Weekly*," *Leslie's Illustrated Weekly* 86.2210 (January 20, 1898), 34.

34. Metcalf, ed., *Dunbar: A Bibliography*, 164.

35. Paul Laurence Dunbar, "Negro Love Song," *Century Magazine* 49 (April 1895): 960.

36. Braxton, ed., *Collected Poetry*, 49.

37. Ibid., 49.

38. Ibid., 49.

39. Alice Dunbar to Dunbar [Summer 1898], in Metcalf, ed., "Letters," 601.

40. James Weldon Johnson, *Along This Way: The Autobiography of James Weldon Johnson* (1933; New York: Viking, 1973), 152.

41. Ibid., 152.

42. Kevin K. Gaines, *Uplifting the Race: Black Leadership, Politics, and Culture in the Twentieth Century* (Chapel Hill: University of North Carolina Press, 1996), 184.

43. Johnson, ed., *Book of American Negro Poetry,* rev. ed., 50.

44. See, for example, Michael Flusche, "Paul Laurence Dunbar and the Burden of Race," *Southern Humanities Review* 11.1 (Winter 1977): 49–50, and, more recently, Eleanor Alexander, *Lyrics of Sunshine and Shadow* (New York: New York University Press, 2001).

45. Bruce, *Black American Writing,* 247.

46. James Weldon Johnson, *Fifty Years and Other Poems,* with an introduction by Brander Matthews (Boston: Cornhill Company, 1917), 58.

47. Ibid., 64.

48. Ibid., 91.

49. Johnson, "Poetry Corner," in *The Selected Writings of James Weldon Johnson,* ed. Sondra Kathryn Wilson, vol. 1 (New York: Oxford University Press, 1995), 253.

50. Johnson, *Fifty Years,* 20.

51. Johnson, ed., *Book of American Negro Poetry,* 1st ed., 18.

52. Ibid., 35.

53. Ibid., 41.

54. Johnson, *Along This Way,* 161.

55. Paul Laurence Dunbar to Alice Dunbar, 31 March 1901, in Metcalf, ed., "Letters," 833.

56. Johnson, *Along This Way,* 161.

57. Johnson, ed., *Book of American Negro Poetry,* rev. ed., 3.

58. Alice Dunbar-Nelson, "Negro Literature for Negro Pupils," *The Southern Workman* (February 1922): 60.

59. See Thomas L. Morgan and William Barlow, *From Cakewalks to Concert Halls: An Illustrated History of African American Popular Music* (Washington, DC: Elliott and Clark, 1992).

60. Later Dunbar-Nelson gave many readings of her late husband's work, including his dialect poetry.

61. Martin and Primeau, eds., *In His Own Voice,* 136.

62. Ibid., 143.

63. Melba Joyce Boyd argues that Harper's use of "aural association and syntax" instead of phonetic spelling to represent black speech is an important innovation. Andrews et al., eds., *Oxford Companion,* 32.

64. Alice Ruth Moore [Dunbar-Nelson] to Paul Laurence Dunbar, 7 May 1896, in Metcalf, ed., "Letters," 37–38.

65. In fact, she interprets his question to be essentially about dialect: "You ask my opinion about Negro dialect in literature." Ibid., 37.

66. Alice Dunbar-Nelson, "The Praline Woman," in *The Dunbar Speaker and Entertainer,* with an introduction by Akasha (Gloria) Hull (New York: G. K. Hall, 1996), 66. She made minor changes to the original; I quote the later version as reflecting her final intention.

67. Ibid., 66.

68. Alice Dunbar-Nelson, *The Goodness of St. Rocque and Other Stories,* in Hull, ed., *Works,* 1:115.

69. Alice Dunbar-Nelson, "A Creole Anomaly," *Leslie's Weekly* (15 July 1897): 43.

70. Alice Dunbar-Nelson, "The Woman," in Hull, ed., *Works,* 1:25.

71. Paul Laurence Dunbar to Alice Ruth Moore [Dunbar-Nelson], 23 March 1896, in Metcalf, ed., "Letters," 87.

72. Alice Dunbar-Nelson, "A Carnival Jangle," in Hull, ed., *Works,* 1:77–78.

73. Ibid., 56–62.

Part IV

Turning the Century
New Political, Cultural, and Personal Aesthetics
(1900–1917)

Chapter 11

No Excuses for Our Dirt
Booker T. Washington and a "New Negro" Middle Class

Philip J. Kowalski

> In the home where there is system, you do not find the
> broom left standing on the wrong end. I hope all of you
> know which the right end of the broom is in this respect.
> —Booker T. Washington, "The Value of System in
> Home Life" (1902)

Knowing the right end of the broom "in this respect"[1] provides Washington with ample evidence that his students at Tuskegee have become indoctrinated into the system of hygiene and order. His concern with this issue reflects his oft-noted obsession with dirt and uncleanliness in *Up from Slavery* (1901)—an obsession that also tirelessly fuels his attempt to create, represent, and valorize a "New Negro" middle class in the South. As detailed in his most famous autobiography, Washington coopts the domestic values of those nineteenth-century white women reformers— the literary and historical heirs of Harriet Beecher Stowe's Miss Ophelia— whose insistence on a pristine and ordered household he adopts and adapts to the sociopolitical ideology of the New South's toned-down version of white supremacy. The "New Negro" was thus a clean, respectable quasi citizen who contributed to the community through hard work and a tacit acceptance of the caste system; yet daily baths, lack of grease spots, toothbrushes, and table settings also betrayed pretensions to middle-class respectability that Washington believed would result in a gradual enfranchisement effected in a nonresistant and nonthreatening way. Though perennially marked as conflicted cultural hero, dubious accommodation-ist, and benevolent despot of the Tuskegee Machine, Washington really figures as the leader of an underclass that politicizes a seemingly innocuous domesticity in order to exercise political and personal control in a subversive approach to gaining the franchise for southern blacks around 1900.[2]

In her reading of Stowe's *Uncle Tom's Cabin* (1852), Gillian Brown underscores the "intimacy between domestic and political issues," or the implicit connection between the system of slavery and Dinah's chaotic kitchen in the St. Clare household. "The time-honored inconvenience to which Dinah is attached," Brown explains, "is not merely backward kitchen technology but the political economy that enslaves her."[3] Washington's childhood memories echo this equation of dirt, disorder, and "shift-lessness" with slavery as a self-defeating political economy, yet his discussions of dirt and uncleanliness imply that while filth keeps one enslaved, slavery itself can be recuperated as a moderately edifying experience. "My life had its beginning in the midst of the most miserable, desolate, and discouraging surroundings,"[4] he says. Somewhat akin to his rehabilitation of slavery, Washington also transforms dirt from filth and rags into the bounty and richness of the Black Belt, and his fondness for "the potato-hole" initially intimates that dirt in its proper sphere—out of the house and in the earth—can benefit blacks considerably when tilled for agriculture.

Washington's celebration of middle-class manners and mores peppers his narrative, and his insistence on the British spelling of "labour," "colour," etc., subliminally signals his Anglicization for his white audience. These subtle spelling variations remind his white readers of his middle-class membership, and they function as an attempt to write against what Edward L. Ayers describes as "the sense of pollution whites associated with blacks, no matter how clean, how well-dressed, how well-mannered they might be."[5] Washington evokes the absence among slaves of bourgeois values such as attending to genealogical records, sleeping in beds, enjoying leisure time and sports, and, most significantly, participating in education and domestic manners: "I cannot remember a single instance . . . when our entire family sat down to the table together, and God's blessing was asked, and the family ate a meal in a civilized manner."[6] Washington tempers any seeming class ambitions, however, and portrays the pinnacle of middle-class respectability as a rather innocuous one. He confesses that his greatest ambition upon being freed consisted of no more than the polite taking of ginger cakes at teatime: "I then and there resolved that, if I ever got free, the height of my ambition would be reached if I could get to the point where I could secure and eat ginger-cakes in the way that I saw those ladies doing."[7] The taking of tea and cakes sanitizes and gentrifies former slaves while keeping them safely in the parlor and out of the political sphere.

Washington's aspiration to the middle-class rituals of these ladies bespeaks "the feminization of the African American male" as described by Donald Gibson in his reading of the first chapter of *Up from Slavery.* Specifically, Gibson notes, "the assertion that Washington implicitly makes" is that "black males neither are nor desire to be 'men' in the nineteenth- and twentieth-century traditional sense of that term: to have power, to choose their own destiny, to be equal to others in the society (especially other males), to vote."[8] The apparent satisfaction with the status quo in Washington's autobiography poses no sociopolitical threat and implies to an audience of white readers that black men "who do not aspire to such power" are "content to accept as their own the status then currently belonging to women."[9] Of course, Gibson's trope of a feminized black man is merely a complicated extension of the conventional nineteenth-century analogy between the woman and the slave; yet this feminization of Washington grows increasingly complex along entrenched yet subterranean political lines once he begins to associate with Yankee women who demand northern standards of cleanliness that offer implicit social, economic, and personal power.

Washington's political agenda requires an obligatory nod to the benefits of slavery—part of his overarching process of rehabilitating the black past —since it provides lessons in thrift and industry and supplies Washington with a rhetoric that offsets his seeming capitulation to class mobility. Next to the Atlanta Compromise speech, Washington's characterization of "the school of slavery" is perhaps the most controversial statement in the autobiography, and it functions as a precursor to the Hampton-Tuskegee ideal of black education that deemphasizes high academic standards and celebrates hard work and community contribution. "Notwithstanding the cruel wrongs inflicted upon us," Washington says, "the black man got nearly as much out of slavery as the white man did": "When freedom came, the slaves were almost as well fitted to begin life anew as the master," since "the slave owner and his sons had mastered no special industry." Slaves, on the other hand, "had mastered some handicraft, and none were ashamed, and few unwilling, to labour."[10] Washington's precarious extolling of "the school of slavery" that juxtaposes unskilled whites with skilled blacks implies a black work ethic that must be perceived as admirable by middle-class white readers, especially given the fact that Washington's discussion of "white trash" throughout the autobiography is a subtle but conscious attempt to advance an alternative or substitute Other associated with filth and ignorance, and in possession of no desire to improve.

After moving to West Virginia with his family, Washington describes how "some of our neighbours . . . were the poorest and most ignorant and degraded white people"; and "drinking, gambling, quarrels, fights, and shocking immoral practices were frequent."[11] Patricia Yaeger explains that dirt in southern literature is "a signpost that allows southern citizens to recognize a middle-class macrocosm and its underclass boundaries," but "it also serves as a disrupter of systems."[12] The very designation of "white trash" indicates this disruption or threat to the calm complacency of bourgeois ideals, and, most significantly, "dirt signals white trash origins."[13] Although Washington consistently calls for the amelioration of social conditions for both blacks and poor whites, his juxtaposition of both groups in this passage tends to equalize the differences between black residents and white trash. Furthermore, African Americans dedicated to self-improvement and civic service thus implicitly have more to offer than these self-indulgent and self-serving poor whites involved in "shocking immoral practices" who contribute nothing but iniquity to the community. During his "struggle for an education" in West Virginia, Washington thus tends to align and associate himself neither with the old southern aristocracy nor with white trash but with northern women, the ideological heirs of Vermont's Miss Ophelia, who inculcate in him the Yankee domestic economy of cleanliness, thrift, and industry with its inherent but hidden power base.

Stowe's representation of Miss Ophelia's attempt to impose order in the St. Clare household contrasts "the New England States" where "nothing [is] lost, or out of order; not a picket loose in the fence, not a particle of litter in the turfy yard" with Dinah's southern kitchen, which "generally looked as if it had been arranged by a hurricane blowing through it."[14] Much of Washington's rhetoric echoes Stowe's description of the virtues of New England and Miss Ophelia's condemnation of "shiftlessness" as "the sum of all evils," and these lessons he learns from Mrs. Viola Ruffner and Miss Mary F. Mackie. Stowe's description of Miss Ophelia could easily be applied to the work ethic Washington advocates: "People who did nothing, or who did not know exactly what they were going to do, or who did not take the most direct way to accomplish what they set their hands to, were objects of her entire contempt."[15] Washington's identification with northern women somewhat reinforces Gibson's thesis on "the feminization of the African American male," yet this argument neglects the politicization of the middle-class home in nineteenth-century America. In this sense, Washington's attention to the political ramifications of the "good housekeeping" of Stowe and of her sister, Catharine Beecher, although partaking of the maternal and operating behind the scenes, has profound consequences for the creation of a New Negro middle class that can reclaim those civil rights recently denied them.

Washington's position as houseboy to Mrs. Ruffner facilitates his escape from the dirt of the coal mines, and her textual introduction significantly follows the miners' conversation he overhears about the Hampton Normal and Agricultural Institute in Virginia. He describes her as a "Yankee" woman from Miss Ophelia's own Vermont, with "a reputation all through the vicinity for being very strict with her servants, and especially with the boys who tried to serve her."[16] Louis R. Harlan characterizes Mrs. Ruffner as "ostracized by the general's family because of her alien background and sharp tongue." Because of her relative social isolation, Mrs. Ruffner "threw all the frustrated energies of the New England do-gooder" into Washington's training, and he proved to be as much a godsend to her as she was to him.[17] Washington quickly learned that "she wanted everything kept clean about her, that she wanted things done promptly and systematically," and his descriptions of the ideal domestic sphere, as well as the "valuable lessons" he learns, sound remarkably similar to life in Stowe's "New England States":

> Nothing must be sloven or slipshod; every door, every fence, must be kept in repair. . . . Even to this day I never see bits of paper scattered around a house or in the street that I do not want to pick them up at once. I never see a filthy yard that I do not want to clean it, a paling off a fence that I do not want to put it on, an unpainted or unwhitewashed house that I do not want to paint or whitewash it, or a button off one's clothes, or a grease-spot on them or on a floor, that I do not want to call attention to it.[18]

Suellen Hoy notes how "confrontation with racial and cultural outsiders" during Washington's time "transformed cleanliness from a public health concern into a moral and patriotic one,"[19] as the concurrent work of Jane

Addams and the settlement houses particularly demonstrates. Washington's curious admissions test as administered by Miss Mary F. Mackie embodies this kind of confrontational and racial condescension that served as the foundation for the Hampton Institute, and aptly demonstrates just how conflicted this assimilation could be at times.

James D. Anderson explains that the "Hampton Idea" developed by General Armstrong "essentially called for the effective removal of black voters and politicians from southern political life, the relegation of black workers to the lowest forms of labor in the southern economy, and the establishment of a general southern racial hierarchy."[20] Armstrong further maintained that although blacks were "low," they were "not degraded," since "the Negro has one source of strength," namely, "the habit of industry acquired in the time of slavery."[21] Washington's championing of "some handicraft" developed during slavery clearly replicates the mildly racist pedagogy of Hampton, where manual labor as opposed to academic pursuits signified scholastic success. His eventual and categorical adoption of Armstrong's philosophy further complicated the already conflicted site he occupied as Hampton disciple and willing accommodationist, but his gradual and subtle manipulation of the system guaranteed him a great degree of personal power and, perhaps according to some distorted, trickle-down theory, general improvement to southern blacks.[22] Washington's admissions test to Hampton typifies the institute's emphasis on the willingness to work hard and question little, but in other ways Miss Mackie's sweeping and dusting of the recitation room is somewhat of a Yankee imposition or a belated act of northern aggression: "I swept the recitation-room three times. Then I got a dusting-cloth and I dusted it four times. All the woodwork around the walls, every bench, table, and desk, I went over four times with my dusting-cloth. . . . I had the feeling that in a large measure my future depended upon the impression I made upon the teacher in the cleaning of that room."[23] Washington describes Miss Mackie as "a 'Yankee' woman who knew just where to look for dirt," and her thorough and literal handkerchief inspection of the room satisfies her that Washington is worthy of admission: "I guess you will do to enter this institution," she informs him.[24]

Miss Mackie can be seen as a representative of what Hoy describes as one of those Yankee women who "shared a view of the freed population 'as culturally backward but not inherently deficient,'"[25] and whose improvement partially stemmed from their ability to keep clean. Despite this assertion, Miss Mackie exhibits an initial distrust of Washington, and this stems partially from his unkempt condition—starving, dirty, tired, and poor, he must have presented a rather startling appearance. "I felt that I could hardly blame her," he says, "if she got the idea that I was a worthless loafer or tramp."[26] Miss Mackie's recitation-room test smacks of Miss Ophelia's "getting in the kitchen with Dinah": an unwanted, aggressive, and ideological carpetbag of an act that betrays both Miss Mackie's condescension to and her distrust of this black man. Dinah's complaint in Stowe's novel captures this blurring of gender and class distinctions that Miss Mackie typifies as a "Yankee": "Lor, now! if dat ar de way dem northern ladies do, dey an't ladies, nohow."[27] Miss Mackie's ability to assume some small measure of power, despite traditional barriers she would have faced, perhaps prompts Washington's admiration of her confident independence.

Washington readily acknowledges "the part that the Yankee teachers played in the education of the Negroes immediately after the war,"[28] and Hampton emerges in his narrative as a kind of training ground for the newly gentrified. Hoy explains that the correlation between terms such as "clean" and "classy" arose in antebellum America as the bourgeoisie began to define itself in opposition to impoverished rural inhabitants,[29] and Washington's starry-eyed first days at Hampton attest to the civilizing influences of numerous and genuine gentilities that contrast starkly with the meretricious tokens of middle-class respectability he enumerates in Negro cabins throughout the South: "Life at Hampton was a constant revelation to me; was constantly taking me into a new world. The matter of having meals at regular hours, of eating on a tablecloth, using a napkin, the use of the bathtub and of the tooth-brush, as well as the use of sheets upon the bed, were all new to me."[30] Washington's praise of Hampton also presents him with another opportunity to contrast the willingness of white, educated northern women to work with the implicit shiftlessness of the old southern aristocracy and white trash, who either refuse to work or have not been taught "the dignity of labour."[31]

After Miss Mackie asks him to return to school earlier than usual, Washington, in the appropriate role as janitor, assists his now "good friend" in preparing Hampton for the first day of school:

Miss Mackie was a member of one of the oldest and most cultured families of the North, and yet for two weeks she worked by my side cleaning windows, dusting rooms, putting beds in order, and what not. . . . It was hard for me at this time to understand how a woman of her education and social standing could take such delight in performing such service, in order to assist in the elevation of an unfortunate race. Ever since then I have had no patience with any school for my race in the South which did not teach its students the dignity of labour.[32]

Mary Douglas comments that cleaning rituals such as this function "as an attempt to create and maintain a particular culture, a particular set of assumptions by which experience is controlled." Furthermore, "the rituals enact the form of social relations, and in giving these relations visible expression they enable people to know their own society." Washington's gospel of the toothbrush is thus a supreme example of one of these rituals that "work[s] upon the body politic through the symbolic medium of the physical body."[33] The Miss Mackies and Miss Ophelias thus represent a new kind of class to Washington—i.e., educated white (northern) women who value work for its own sake—and because she is female, Miss Mackie impresses Washington as an exemplar of an underclass who has nonetheless managed some degree of professional and personal satisfaction. The significance of this similarity between Yankee women and Washington lies in what Henry Louis Gates Jr. identifies as "the trope of a New Negro," an image that Washington, Fannie Barrier Williams, and N. B. Wood began aggressively to advance at least a year before the appearance of *Up from Slavery* with the publication of *A New Negro for a New Century* (1900), a kaleidoscopic anthology of African American writing that ranged from slave narratives to eyewitness accounts of black soldiers in the Spanish-American War. In addition to the obvious cultural work of gentrification that Washington's autobiography does, *A New Negro* also "clearly intended to 'turn' the new century's image of the black away from the stereotypes scattered throughout plantation fictions, blackface minstrelsy, vaudeville, racist pseudo-science, and vulgar Social Darwinism. . . . Accordingly, to manipulate the image of the black was, in a sense, to manipulate reality. The Public Negro Self, therefore, was an entity to be crafted."[34] The trope of the "New Negro" also functions as a metaphoric shorthand for Washington, since "this sort of self-willed beginning is that its 'success' depends fundamentally upon self-negation, a turning away from the 'Old Negro' and the labyrinthine memory of black enslavement and toward the register of a 'New Negro,' an irresistible, spontaneously generated black and sufficient self."[35]

The diluted racism of General Armstrong and the Hampton model, as well as the ideals of "education, industry, and property" rather than "political preferment," serve as the foundation upon which Washington establishes Tuskegee. He readily invests in a system that uneasily equates good housekeeping with model citizenship, and his subsequent insistence on "tools of civilization," such as the toothbrush, functions as a hallmark to perpetuate amicable town-and-gown relations in Tuskegee generated by useful industriousness and community service. This emphasis on community service that extends to all African Americans in the South is primarily directed at obviating white suspicion in the surrounding town of Tuskegee, and Washington consistently blurs the demarcation between town and institute, since, in the early days, white residents were afraid that the presence of Tuskegee would stir up hostility between the races. Washington explains how "we wanted to make the school of real service to all the people," and as a result "their attitude toward the school became favourable."[36] Washington's statement is belittled by the fact that students' character was assessed not merely by their moral behavior but also by how clean they appeared to the white community as they performed good or ill: "Over and over again the students were reminded in those first years— and are reminded now—that people would excuse us for our poverty, for our lack of comforts and conveniences, but that they would not excuse us for our dirt."[37] As Harlan notes, Washington's adamant insistence on "no excuses for our dirt" seems to have rendered Tuskegee a tense place at times: "Every evidence of student waste or neglect," he says of Washington's ceaseless monitoring of the campus, "all went into his little red notebook, from which flowed a thousand memoranda reminding errant faculty members of their high duty to make of Tuskegee a black utopia, a proof that Negroes were capable of the petit bourgeois life."[38] Or perhaps "the petit bourgeois life" that Washington deemed fit, as his initial tour of Alabama demonstrates.

Washington's curious use of dialect minstrelizes the very people he allegedly wishes to deminstrelize, and he painstakingly crafts a class of "black trash" that cleanliness, industry, and political reticence will supposedly uplift. Washington's cast of reminstrelized characters ranges from the political to the pathetic,[39] but they suddenly appear as a newly alternative Other constructed in direct contrast to the studied and factual rhetoric of his autobiography. He expresses impatience with the distorted desire to gain civil rights at any cost, and the figure of the man "designated by the others to look after my political destiny" is ridiculed for the rationale behind his voting practices: "We wants you to be sure to vote jes' like we votes," he informs Washington. "When we finds out which way de white man's gwine to vote, den we votes 'xactly de other way. Den we know's we's right."[40] Several other caricatures embody Washington's impatience with the shiftlessness inherent in the call to preach ("O Lawd, de cotton am so grassy, de work am so hard, and the sun am so hot dat I b'lieve dis darky am called to preach!") as well as a neosentimental use of pathos to underscore the implicit class advantages of staying clean in the form of the "old coloured woman" who was "clad in rags; but they were clean. She said . . . 'I ain't got no money, but I wants you to take dese six eggs, what's I's been savin' up, an' I wants you to put dese six eggs into de eddication of dese boys an' gals.' "[41]

Washington's class pretensions for African Americans are heavily qualified, and this, perhaps more than any other aspect, contributes to the conflicted site that he occupies, or that makes him difficult to define despite the simplicity and lucidity of his rhetoric. Washington's ideal position for African Americans on the socioeconomic spectrum hovers precariously between "white trash" and respectable bourgeoisie, or perhaps a kind of independent working class of blacks that does not trade in the sham of spurious commodities that signal economic success. On the other hand, the photographic images that appeared in *A New Negro for a New Century* compose a collection of well-dressed African American men and women, Mr. and Mrs. Booker T. Washington most notable among them, singled out for their accomplishments and dignity. As J. E. MacBrady notes in the introduction, "The photographs contained in this book make a most pleasing gallery of intelligent and progressive men, and strong, intellectual and charming women."[42] Washington's exploration of "the real, everyday life of the people"[43] thus consists of a series of observations that register his mild disgust with the confused class pretensions of rural African Americans. He initially mentions that "rarely was there any place provided in the cabin where one could bathe even the face and hands," but he is most astonished by the debt that poor blacks will accrue merely for the poorly constructed items that function as signs of membership in the middle class. "In these cabin homes," he says, "I often found sewing-machines which had been bought, or were being bought, on instalments, frequently at a cost of as much as sixty dollars, or showy clocks for which the occupants of the cabins had paid twelve or fourteen dollars." These commodities are more than figurative trappings—they are empty signifiers of a faux gentility since "in most cases the sewing-machine was not used, the clocks were so worthless that they did not keep correct time—and if they had, in nine cases out of ten there would have been no one in the family who could have told the time of day—while the organ, of course, was rarely used for want of a person who could play upon it."[44] The important and essential marks of Victorian domesticity should be the use of silverware and the practice of sitting down together at table to have a civilized meal, since these intermediaries between base appetite and polite etiquette indicate the control that Washington habitually exerts. The belief in the petit bourgeois life that Harlan notes is thus an exercise in patience and control, and even a kind of dissembling that does not disclose the manipulative political and social power that Washington worked tirelessly behind the scenes to accomplish for himself and his people.

Somewhat akin to this line of reasoning is Ann Douglas's argument about early-nineteenth-century clerical and feminine exploitation of the sentimental for the purpose of gaining political and social clout in the masculinized world of industry and finance that had culturally disempowered them.[45] This sentimentalized preoccupation with the domestic sphere that translates naturally to hygiene and etiquette casts Washington's insistence on cleanliness and order as a later and extended instance of the disenfranchised politicizing the domestic to gain social control. Washington advocates a quiet and unintimidating control based upon a utilitarian education and current complacency so as to avoid the stereotype of "an educated Negro" that "white people" find threatening. This somewhat minstrelized image appears "with a high hat, imitation gold eye-glasses, a showy walking-stick, kid gloves, fancy boots, and what not—in a word, a man who was determined to live by his wits."[46] Washington's own vision of impractical attempts by blacks to be liberally educated focuses upon "one of the saddest things" he witnessed while traveling throughout Alabama, namely, "a young man, who had attended some high school, sitting down in a one-room cabin, with grease on his clothing, filth all around him, and weeds in the yard and garden, engaged in studying a French grammar."[47] Although Washington previously confesses that he has "stated in such plain words what I saw" in order to "emphasize the encouraging changes that have taken place in the community," his tendency to blame the impoverished victims of history complicates the trickster status that Frederick L. McElroy facilely assigns him.[48] Washington's paradoxical rhetoric invests him with a slipperiness and unpredictability that permits the behind-the-scenes manipulation that, if foregrounded, would constitute a real threat to white hegemony. Washington's categorical condemnation of a love for "high-sounding things" among students encompasses their tendency "to be fond of memorizing long and complicated 'rules' in

grammar and mathematics," as well as the subject of "banking and dis-
count" though none has a bank account, and their inability "to locate the
proper places for the knives and forks on an actual dinner-table, or the
places on which the bread and meat should be set."[49]

This focus on domesticity naturally embraces "lessons which would
teach them how to care for their bodies";[50] and Washington seems reas-
sured by the fact that "they were all willing to learn the right thing as soon
as it was shown them what was right."[51] These rituals of cleansing that
establish and maintain the body politic are lessons in maintaining personal control, a kind of corporeal self-policing, with consequences that
will have far-ranging political and social effects. Washington thus firmly
installs the Hampton Idea in Tuskegee Institute, and he offers his pedagog-
ical philosophy that "if we were to make any permanent impression upon
those who had come to us for training, we must do something besides
teach them mere books"; for "we wanted to give them such a practical
knowledge of some one industry, together with the spirit of industry,
thrift, and economy, that they would be sure of knowing how to make a
living after they had left us."[52] The culmination of Washington's Hampton
and Tuskegee educational philosophy involves the recuperation of dirt, for
dirt can be respected and utilized in its appropriate context, and the geography of the Black Belt and the value of agriculture, as well as "the vestiges
of southern labor history, the association of Africans and African Americans with the soil that they tilled" and "the earth in which they were
buried,"[53] supply Washington with this convenient rehabilitation and
inversion. He says, "we wanted to be careful not to educate our students
out of sympathy with agricultural life, so that they would be attracted
from the country to the cities, and yield to the temptation of trying to live
by their wits," much like the condemned image of "an educated Negro."
Cities must be eschewed as the real centers of dirt and filth, and country
life should be celebrated so that graduates of Tuskegee will "return to the
plantation districts and show the people there how to put new energy and
new ideas into farming."[54]

Despite periodic student resistance, Washington adamantly adheres to
this philosophy in order to avoid allegations that somehow he and his students had "lost our heads," become "stuck up," or were trying to "show
off,"[55] and this accusation he particularly wants to dodge in connection to
his trip to Europe. "I had heard it said that too often," he says, "when people of my race reached any degree of success, they were inclined to unduly
exalt themselves; to try and ape the wealthy, and in so doing to lose their

heads. The fear that people might think this of us haunted me a good deal."[56] All of the trappings of Victorian respectability—a harmonious family life and the proper celebration of Christmas, bodily cleanliness and the Grand Tour—serve as avenues to a very guarded and heavily qualified bourgeois success for Washington. Ayers aptly observes that these avenues do provide a necessary means to a desired end, for "once black men and women owned their homes, farms, and thriving businesses, once they had their own schools and colleges, once they were willing to divide their votes along economic self-interest, then the vote would return."[57] Washington's curious belief that "those who have accomplished the greatest results are those who 'keep under the body,'" or "those who never grow excited or lose self-control, but are always calm, self-possessed, patient, and polite"[58] betrays this subversive approach to gaining political enfranchisement for southern blacks around 1900.

One of Washington's final and extended testimonies to the beneficial effects of good hygiene occurs in the "gospel of the tooth-brush" passage, which is notable since Washington's rhetoric—the words he writes and speaks—has been highly sanitized. Washington initiates this rather thorough examination by crediting General Armstrong with the phrase "the gospel of the tooth-brush," a clear and direct echo of Benjamin Franklin's emphasis on the razor and the proverbial American success story that accompanies it. "No student is permitted to remain who does not keep and use a tooth-brush," Washington explains. "Several times, in recent years, students have come to us who brought with them almost no other article except a tooth-brush. They had heard from the lips of older students about our insisting upon the use of this, and so, to make a good impression, they brought at least a tooth-brush with them."[59] While certainly part of a larger discourse about the importance of dental hygiene among urban, immigrant populations,[60] Washington's "instrument of civilization" is grounds for dismissal itself because it effects an essential indoctrination or socialization—a dirty desire for immediate equality will not issue from a clean mouth. Washington is particularly proud of this accomplishment. "It has been interesting to note," he explains, "the effect that the use of the tooth-brush has had in bringing about a higher degree of civilization among the students." Of course, this interesting observation buttresses his conviction that "absolute cleanliness of the body has been insisted upon from the first."[61] "Absolute cleanliness" is thus the sole criterion for being coopted and enfranchised, even having the possibility of a future, according to Washington.

Booker T. Washington's insistence upon hygiene and order really was not all that different from that of Jane Addams and countless other settlement workers, yet he has been criticized for being an accommodationist because, unlike Addams, his skin color and socioeconomic status identified him with the very race he was trying to uplift. Addams and the other settlement workers were almost invariably educated, middle-class whites who could come and go as they pleased, and whose association with an immigrant underclass could never taint their white skins. Washington's patient ability to make do with what the system did allow helped him to gain admiration from many, especially white southerners who saw him as reasonably harmless. The outspoken or implicit accusations of activists such as W. E. B. Du Bois and Ida B. Wells managed to sully and distort Washington's already complicated and sometimes indiscernible personal motives. Although Washington may have bathed, brushed, cleaned, scrubbed, and whitewashed everything and everyone, the charge of perennially capitulating is the one stain he could not obliterate.

NOTES

1. Booker T. Washington, "The Value of System in Home Life," in *Character Building: Being Addresses Delivered on Sunday Evenings to the Students of Tuskegee Institute* (New York: Doubleday, Page, 1902), 84.

2. This politicization of the domestic parallels Washington's more aggressive, though veiled, behind-the-scenes attempts to secure civil rights for blacks. As many historians have noted, Edward L. Ayers explains that even though "in the 1880s [Washington] had publicly attacked the segregation of railroad cars" and "in the year before his trip to Atlanta had encouraged blacks to boycott streetcar companies that would separate the races," it is important to understand that "Washington encouraged boycotts because such resistance fell in the economic rather than the political realm; it sought to use the leverage of blacks as paying customers to win their fair rights in the marketplace—blacks' best hope for justice, in his eyes. Washington believed in the market as a color-blind arbiter that would eventually award its benefits without concern for race." See Edward L. Ayers, *The Promise of the New South: Life after Reconstruction* (New York: Oxford University Press, 1992), 324.

3. Gillian Brown, *Domestic Individualism: Imagining Self in Nineteenth-Century America* (Berkeley: University of California Press, 1990), 14.

4. Booker T. Washington, *Up from Slavery: An Autobiography,* ed. William L. Andrews (1901; repr. New York: Norton, 1996), 7.

5. Ayers, *Promise,* 139.

6. Washington, *Up from Slavery*, 7–10.

7. Ibid., 11.

8. Donald Gibson, "Chapter One of Booker T. Washington's *Up from Slavery* and the Feminization of the African American Male," in *Representing Black Men,* ed. Marcellus Blount and George P. Cunningham (New York: Routledge, 1996), 96.

9. Ibid., 97.

10. Washington, *Up from Slavery*, 14.

11. Ibid., 17–18.

12. Patricia Yaeger, *Dirt and Desire: Reconstructing Southern Women's Writing, 1930–1990* (Chicago: University of Chicago Press, 2000), 265.

13. Ibid., 263.

14. Harriet Beecher Stowe, *Uncle Tom's Cabin; Authoritative Text, Background and Contexts, Criticism,* ed. Elizabeth Ammons (1852; repr. New York: Norton, 1994), 135, 180.

15. Ibid., 137.

16. Washington, *Up from Slavery*, 24.

17. Louis R. Harlan, "Booker T. Washington in Biographical Perspective," in *Booker T. Washington in Perspective: Essays of Louis R. Harlan,* ed. Raymond W. Smock (Jackson: University Press of Mississippi, 1988), 11.

18. Washington, *Up from Slavery*, 25.

19. Suellen Hoy, *Chasing Dirt: The American Pursuit of Cleanliness* (New York: Oxford University Press, 1995), 87.

20. James D. Anderson, *The Education of Blacks in the South* (Chapel Hill: University of North Carolina Press, 1988), 36.

21. Quoted in ibid., 42.

22. For an earlier and alternative view of the influence of Hampton upon Washington's program at Tuskegee that downplays the racism of Armstrong, see Robert G. Sherer, *Subordination or Liberation? The Development and Conflicting Theories of Black Education in Nineteenth-Century Alabama* (Tuscaloosa: University of Alabama Press, 1977), 46–54.

23. Washington, *Up from Slavery*, 28.

24. Ibid., 29.

25. Hoy, *Chasing Dirt,* 54.

26. Washington, *Up from Slavery*, 28.

27. Stowe, *Uncle Tom's Cabin,* 183.

28. Washington, *Up from Slavery*, 33.

29. Hoy, *Chasing Dirt,* 7.

30. Washington, *Up from Slavery*, 31.

31. Ibid., 37.

32. Ibid., 37.

33. Mary Douglas, *Purity and Danger: An Analysis of Concepts of Pollution and Taboo* (New York: Praeger, 1966), 128.

34. Henry Louis Gates Jr., "The Trope of a New Negro and the Reconstruction of the Image of the Black," in *The New American Studies: Essays from Representations,* ed. Philip Fisher (Berkeley: University of California Press, 1991), 326–27.

35. Ibid., 322.

36. Washington, *Up from Slavery,* 64.

37. Ibid., 80.

38. Harlan, "Booker T. Washington," 4–5.

39. Houston A. Baker Jr., *Modernism and the Harlem Renaissance* (Chicago: University of Chicago Press, 1987), 25–36.

40. Washington, *Up from Slavery,* 53.

41. Ibid., 61, 52.

42. J. E. MacBrady, Introduction, *A New Negro for a New Century,* ed. Booker T. Washington et al. (1900; repr. New York: Arno Press, 1969), 5.

43. Washington, *Up from Slavery,* 54.

44. Ibid., 54.

45. Ann Douglas, *The Feminization of American Culture* (New York: Noonday Press, 1998), 80–117.

46. Washington, *Up from Slavery,* 57.

47. Ibid., 58.

48. Frederick L. McElroy, "Booker T. Washington as Literary Trickster" *Southern Folklore* 49.2 (1992): 89–107.

49. Washington, *Up from Slavery,* 58–59.

50. Ibid., 60.

51. Ibid., 58.

52. Ibid., 60.

53. Yaeger, *Dirt and Desire,* 37.

54. Washington, *Up from Slavery,* 60.

55. Ibid., 75, 124.

56. Ibid., 124.

57. Ayers, *Promise,* 324.

58. Washington, *Up from Slavery,* 83.

59. Ibid., 80.

60. Hoy, *Chasing Dirt,* 125–26.

61. Washington, *Up from Slavery,* 81.

Chapter 12

War Work, Social Work, Community Work
Alice Dunbar-Nelson, Federal War Work Agencies, and Southern African American Women

Nikki L. Brown

In late January 1918 Alice Dunbar-Nelson sat amid a packed audience in Wilmington, Delaware, attending a colloquium on the preparedness of American forces during World War I. The town meeting piqued her personal and professional interests, since several of her friends and colleagues were participating in the basic training exercises at black base camps. However, the evening took an unpleasant turn when a local professor of science, chairing the discussion, announced that he had developed a test measuring and ranking the mental capacity of enlisted servicemen according to race. Proclaiming that the day "of sentimental consideration in education was past," the professor reported that African American soldiers scored the worst, lower than the "ignorant sturdy mountaineer" or the newly arrived immigrant, although the rural folk and the immigrants were "much below par."[1] Black men, charged the professor, were mentally unfit for battle. Not to his surprise, middle- and upper-class, college-educated, native-born white men scored best on the exam.

Dunbar-Nelson became indignant when the professor announced his findings, though she let him finish his presentation. But when he claimed that for the first time in history, human nature was being scientifically studied, Dunbar-Nelson had had enough. She rejoined immediately, "Good Lord, Professor, it has been studied since the world began!"[2] Launching her own critique, she disputed the test's methodology and hypotheses. The exam revealed little besides the professor's own racial bias, she declared. The professor responded that caste systems existed in all other countries, and that a racial caste system had become the United States's way of separating groups based on merit and ability. Dunbar-Nelson shot back, "[This] is nothing in the world but the old-time aristocratic landholding class trying to grab for power, and using this time, not theological argument, but the kind of science learned from German universities (where it has, as everyone knows, been a howling success on moral character)." If a racial caste system endured in the United States after the war, Dunbar-Nelson answered, "I'd rather take my chances in England."[3]

In challenging the claim of mental unfitness of African American men, Alice Dunbar-Nelson risked public condemnation, as her quest for civic equality could be interpreted as unpatriotic dissent. African American women faced the same difficulties as they undertook their war work—supporting African American servicemen *and* the goal of democracy—within a segregated society. African American women's groups often provided the sole means of financial and moral support of black servicemen and their immediate families. Yet, in their prominent contributions toward war work for African American troops, they risked a political backlash from national war work organizations. Many national agencies preferred to ignore the "race problem" in the American military for the duration of the war.

For American women generally, the immense selection of ways "to do one's bit" during World War I fell into roughly two categories: federal agencies or privately funded organizations. The Red Cross, the YWCA, and the YMCA, the most visible and best funded organizations, provided a laundry list of programs, including hospital assistance, canteen service, hostess houses, and financial contributions. Particularly important was the Woman's Committee, the Committee on Women's Defense Work of the Council of National Defense. This federal organization acted as a clearinghouse of programs for American women volunteering for war work. All national organizations registered with the Woman's Committee, and state representatives of the Woman's Committee connected local groups with larger regional organizations. For white women, the chief difficulty in war work was navigating the myriad local, state, and federal programs and finding one that best suited individual communities. For black women, a number of limitations impeded the effective engagement of African American communities in these national patriotic efforts. Most white organizations offered black women few work opportunities and vague plans for African American community involvement. Moreover, black women met stiff resistance because of institutional racism within white organizations that imposed a strict code of segregation. This discussion will focus on Alice Dunbar-Nelson, whose travels through the South led to a primary account of the war work of southern black women.

Indeed, African American women blazed their own trails and instituted their own programs for wartime community service, even among federal programs. Historian William J. Breen has argued that southern black women saw possibilities for social reform offered by the war, though their war aims differed significantly from the states' and the nation's objectives.[4] Like the suffrage movements, the antilynching movement, and the club movement, the war work movement among African American women grew out of a dense network of their political and social organizations. More often than not, African American women worked on their own, directing their efforts for predominantly black programs. Dunbar-Nelson's reporting provides a unique glimpse into the way black women, especially in the South, participated in the nation's war effort and strove to meet the special needs of their home communities.

Alice Dunbar-Nelson was well versed in the club work and community activity of black women in the United States. Since 1896 she had been a founding member of the National Association of Colored Women (NACW), and she remained active in the National Federation of Colored Women's Clubs. She had also cultivated a distinguished career as a journalist and author. In 1916 Alice Dunbar married Robert Nelson, and from Wilmington, she devoted herself to women's activities in the NACW, regional politics, the NAACP, and the women's suffrage movement. Dividing her time between progressive reform initiatives and the world war gathering momentum in Europe, Dunbar-Nelson lent a unique vision to wartime community service, as an African American woman who both supported the war and worried over its consequences for blacks in the United States.[5]

Soon after attending the colloquium on war preparedness, Dunbar-Nelson sought to join a professional organization that made use of her experience as a community activist. What she found was the Circle for Negro War Relief, Inc., which fit just the type of work she desired. As its name implied, the Circle dedicated its work to bringing material relief to African American soldiers and aiding their families, who, in the absence of a head of household, had fallen on hard times. "In all cases," the Circle's advertising pamphlet read, the negro soldier's absence will be felt more keenly than can possibly result from the service of any other soldiers in ranks, for it must be admitted that the colored troops represent the most impoverished class in the United States. . . . 'The Circle for Negro War Relief, Inc.' was formed out of the minds of its founders as a most needed war measure.[6]

Concerned that other national agencies overlooked the immediate needs of black soldiers, the Circle followed a proactive formula by contacting black base camps directly to ascertain what the soldiers needed most, then asking local African American churches and schools to send the materials.

The group's executive secretary, Caroline S. Bond, made a personal appeal to Alice Dunbar-Nelson at the end of January 1918. Hoping to establish a unit of the Circle in Wilmington, Bond wrote Dunbar-Nelson, "I am especially happy to have this offer coming from you because I know just what influence you have and what you can do. Won't you start a Unit there? We already have twenty Units started and are anxious for the work to spread over the country as rapidly as possible."[7] From the beginning, the Circle offered Dunbar-Nelson autonomy to conduct war work in Wilmington the way she thought best. Prominent club women, such as Margaret Murray Washington, Beverly K. Bruce, Madame C. J. Walker, and her daughter A'Lelia Walker Robinson, joined the list of volunteers.[8] "Colored women throughout the country are showing more than a casual interest in the work of the Circle for Negro War Relief," declared *The New York Age*, adding that units had been founded in New York, New Jersey, Connecticut, Pennsylvania, Ohio, and Washington, D.C. By mid-1918, the Circle counted among its members over fifty units in twenty-five states.[9] The Circle also filled a professional niche for Alice Dunbar-Nelson that had opened as a result of the war. She supplemented her work with writing fiction and war poems for the *A.M.E. Church Review* and *The Crisis*.[10] Dunbar-Nelson continued with the Circle until July 1918, when the Woman's Committee approached her about an investigative war work tour through the southeastern United States.

At a July 8, 1918, meeting of the Executive Board of the Woman's Committee of the Council of Nation Defense, Emmett J. Scott relayed his fear that African American women were in a state of unrest.[11] Appointed in October 1917 as a liaison between African Americans and the War Department, Scott oversaw all matters, military and domestic, relating to African American service during the Great War. Just six months into his administration, a bitter dispute between the Red Cross and African American nurses began to take shape. In spring 1918, the Red Cross issued a national call for twenty-five thousand experienced nurses to join the armed forces. However, the agency denied admittance to all African American registered and graduate nurses, on the grounds that building separate living facilities for them had stretched the Red Cross's budget beyond its limit.[12] The organization's flat rejection of the black nurses' offers caused a scandal; the depth of the institutional racism within the nation's largest charity was doubly disappointing. By summer 1918 the disenchantment among African American women had become acute. Scott recommended to his colleagues that "a woman be employed to organize the colored women in the States," to investigate the mood of southern black women, and to report her findings to the Woman's Committee.[13]

Hannah Patterson, resident director of the Woman's Committee, knew of Alice Dunbar-Nelson from her previous endeavors in war work, and wrote to her in Wilmington about the possibility of travel and research in the South.[14] Under the Woman's Committee plan, Dunbar-Nelson visited eight states to organize African American women under the direction of each State Council of Defense. The Committee also intended Dunbar-Nelson to monitor the level of anti-American sentiment in African American communities, determining that Dunbar-Nelson "will confer with the leaders among her own people and report to the Woman's Committee their opinion as to conditions among colored people."[15] On August 12, 1918, Patterson formally employed Dunbar-Nelson as a field representative of the Woman's Committee.[16]

The organization Alice Dunbar-Nelson joined was, in theory, a federal body overseeing the war work of all American women. The Woman's Committee aimed to get every American woman functionally performing in the American war machine. However, Dunbar-Nelson was often the first and only representative from the Woman's Committee to contact southern African American women about their war work. She alone was responsible for forming a cohesive narrative of southern African American women's work for the Woman's Committee. The selection of Dunbar-Nelson as a field representative created an awkward situation for the Woman's Committee and the NACW. By all contemporary accounts, black women's work typically fell within the province of the NACW. The group was, after all, the nation's largest black women's organization. The Woman's Committee hired Dunbar-Nelson when it could have consulted the NACW directly. Furthermore, Mary Burnett Talbert, president of the NACW from 1916 to 1920, heard of the investigation of southern black women's war work some six weeks *after* Dunbar-Nelson concluded her research.[17] Dunbar-Nelson was aware of the delicacy of her position, and she was eager to report on the good faith efforts made by black women who tried to work within the federal system. Alternatively, the Woman's Committee sought an African American woman who was knowledgeable about the South and who could work independently of other organizations.

The racial politics of World War I held that black and white women kept the appearance of unified patriotic activity, while the racial etiquette of the period demanded that black women and white women undertake their war work separately. Owing to the disconnection, one of the most serious problems Dunbar-Nelson encountered at the beginning of her trip was the lack of cooperation between white and African American women in Louisiana and Mississippi. She boarded a train in Washington, D.C., on August 12, bound for her home of New Orleans, the first stop in her tour. The Woman's Committee gave her vague instructions about the nature of her work, although it stressed she should interview African American women with their respective State Councils of National Defense. In New Orleans, Dunbar-Nelson found that twenty thousand African American women had registered with the Louisiana Council of National Defense. Infant weighing and baby measurement stations were the most popular programs, all guided by Mrs. William Porteour, the special city chairman of the Louisiana Council. "The colored women have been lovely and have co-operated in every way possible and the feeling between the races is ideal—no need of anxiety at all," wrote Dunbar-Nelson in her first letter to Hannah Patterson, her supervisor. All that was missing, Dunbar-Nelson felt, was a community spirit of war work for the nation. "There isn't any organization," she added, "just a lovely co-operation, and general foggy feeling of goodwill and sisterly love."[18]

Upon further investigation, however, Dunbar-Nelson discovered that in densely African American areas of Louisiana, there had been no organization whatever. No one from the Louisiana State Council had made a trip to Baton Rouge, Shreveport, or Alexandria, cities with at least a 50 percent African American population. In contrast, black women were organizing themselves. In New Orleans, Dunbar-Nelson encountered a thriving labor union movement among domestic workers. When she took a moment to speak with labor organizers, they told her that African American women in the area had distanced themselves from federal war work because of the policy of segregation in the Red Cross and the federal government. They attempted to gain employment with the government in its war work campaign, but, instead, were assigned to domestic and janitorial positions, even as "potential scrubwomen, no matter how educated or refined the girl may be."[19] Dunbar-Nelson offered that the best she could do was to listen and to write Hannah Patterson of the racial troubles.

Patterson rebuked Dunbar-Nelson's assessments, primarily on the issue of the domestic workers' union. The Woman's Committee would not recognize the efforts of the domestics' union, or any labor union, Patterson declared. The labor union represented highly suspicious activity during the war, since the Russian Bolshevik Revolution in the previous summer of 1917 had ignited American fears of labor unrest in the United States. Patterson added, "The New Orleans Unit of the Woman's Committee would be entirely right in . . . not giving [the domestics' union] any assistance." She directed Dunbar-Nelson to limit her survey to war work alone. She made no mention of the problem of racial discrimination, nor did she offer solutions to lessen the affront felt by the black domestic workers.[20] Just one week into her survey, Alice Dunbar-Nelson took note of the rising conflict among southern black women; she witnessed an increasingly problematic division between patriotic duty that called for cooperation with a national organization relying on segregated war work, on one hand, and on the other, the commitment to fight racism and focus on African American advancement.

The next state, Mississippi, manifested the same problem of no coordinated effort between the races. Dunbar-Nelson was greeted warmly in Como by Mrs. Edward McGehee, the white chairman of the Mississippi State Council of Defense, on 18 August. "The colored women are alive and anxious to work—Mrs. McGehee has seen to that," attested Dunbar-Nelson in a letter to Patterson.[21] McGehee vowed to assist her in her travels through Como, Sardis, Jackson, and Meridian. McGehee had splendidly organized the women of the state, even going as far as "financing the salary and expenses of the colored organizer out of her own pocket."[22]

Yet, she found also the same tense interaction in Mississippi as she had in Louisiana. From the African American perspective, segregated war work, combined with the neglect of the efforts of African Americans, pushed black Mississippians to their limits. Dunbar-Nelson remarked, "The colored people, even the most ignorant, are doing a lot better thinking. . . . It isn't German propaganda, either, it's American propaganda, that is working harm among the people."[23] In fact, widespread attacks and one near lynching had cost Mississippi its black patriotic constituency during the war. One terrible incident took place in Vicksburg, where a number of blacks from the city had been tarred and feathered, including two women, Ella Brooks and Ethel Barrett.[24] In response, the African American brass band of Vicksburg refused to accompany draftees marching to the station. The Mississippi chapter of the Red Cross had refused to allow black women to wear its canteen uniforms and denied them membership in the organization.[25] In a final insult, the Negro Patriotic League of Mississippi was denied membership in the Mississippi State Council of National Defense, and in response, the group launched a statewide protest. In the meantime, the League held its own meetings and clubs, and sent its representatives to organize the Vicksburg African American community.[26] Despite her suggestions that the Woman's Committee "work with [colored groups] . . . to co-ordinate and centralize effort," Dunbar-Nelson left Louisiana and Mississippi fully aware that African Americans had already embarked on war work independent of white agencies.[27]

Dunbar-Nelson was also concerned that national institutions were hedging their support for black women's efforts when she arrived in Selma, Alabama, on August 24. She found the same hopeful, but disconnected, work across the state. On August 25, she spoke before a crowd of African Americans in the largest black church in the city, and she asserted that World War I would improve the current social conditions and increase economic opportunities. But first, African Americans should cast their lots firmly for the Allied cause. Black soldiers must contribute their fullest to military service, while black wives and mothers must support their loved ones by conducting Red Cross work, conserving food, knitting, and sending comfort kits.[28] A German victory would crush white America, and along with it, black America, Dunbar-Nelson added. The address in Selma spurred an immediate response. She asked for anyone interested in war work to stay after, and a hundred African American women did so. The women informed Dunbar-Nelson that, in Selma, a war work organization of black women had failed to materialize. Some women had formed individual groups, selling war savings stamps and knitting scarves, but the Alabama State Council generally had not approached them, much less organized units for them. The hundred women decided to organize a unit immediately, and selected an executive committee "to familiarize itself with the activities of state work" and to call future meetings. Their newly formed group was known as the "Dallas County Unit," the first assembly of African American women officially associated with the Woman's Committee in Selma.[29]

The city of Birmingham and its industrial neighbor, Bessemer, evinced a closer partnership. Jefferson County, encompassing both Birmingham and

Bessemer, established a war work program "more thriving, active, and alert than any that I have come across anywhere thus far," Dunbar-Nelson wrote to Patterson.[30] Under the guidance of the Jefferson County chairman and Mrs. H. C. Davenport, African American women ran elevators in department stores and replaced men at the factory machines. At Acipco, an industrial plant in Birmingham, the welfare manager vowed to make the work space as pleasant for African American female workers as he had for the men, with "YWCA buildings, swimming pools, a woman director, etc."[31]

In the city of Bessemer, the African American residents took part in a thriving Council of National Defense Unit, one that worked in conjunction with the Colored Community House. The Bessemer unit was responsible for the ever popular comfort kits, filled with chocolate, cigarettes, magazines, and Bibles. The ladies made their own service flag, decorated with five hundred stars, and the wives of soldiers knitted layettes for expectant mothers. When Dunbar-Nelson visited, a food conservation drive was under way that eventually amassed over one thousand quarts of canned food. For the children of the area, the unit built its own playground and hired a teacher in the industrial arts to oversee it. The Bessemer unit reached such a high level of productivity that it spearheaded the development of a Council of National Defense Unit in Brighton, another industrial town a few miles away. Dunbar-Nelson happily reported that the "work of the Council of National Defense among colored women in Alabama is quite active."[32] War work in Jefferson County, Alabama, provided an exceptional model of cooperation and spirit between African American women and white women.

However, the success in Jefferson County carried less influence than the Woman's Committee had expected. The situation in Mobile, Alabama, typified Dunbar-Nelson's experience throughout the South.

> There is no Council of Defense, Woman's Committee, [or] so called for Mobile county for colored women, but a "War Service Club" operating in the same manner. . . . I talked with the chairman and the other members of the War Service Club, but was unable to elicit any definite information as to their activities. I fear their work is [yet] to be done, not [already] accomplished.[33]

Mrs. McGehee, of the Mississippi State Council, was the notable exception to the shaky state of affairs in southeastern war work. McGehee actively included African American women within the sphere of the Council of

National Defense, yet she also observed that much more had to be done to make the effort truly interracial.

By mid-October 1918, Alice Dunbar-Nelson had been traveling for nearly six weeks. At the end of October, she wrapped up the investigation of eight southern states, and returned to Wilmington. But upon her arrival, she was greeted with the news that the Woman's Committee had disbanded nearly a week earlier. The organization no longer existed as a federal body, nor did it retain any employees except the Executive Board members. Instead, a newly created Field Division of the Council of National Defense replaced the Woman's Committee, although the Woman's Committee maintained an advisory role to the Field Division to meet any emergencies that might arise regarding women's war work.[34] Dunbar-Nelson received a letter from Hannah Patterson further explaining the dissolution of the Woman's Committee, as well as informing Dunbar-Nelson abruptly that she had been laid off.[35] With an Allied victory secured by September 1918, the Field Division considered the situation "inadvisable to send out a representative from headquarters for work among Negro women" and laid aside all the past and future work among southern African American women. "We know that you will appreciate the conditions which make this change necessary," ended Patterson, who, in the course of the changeover, had been promoted to associate director of the Field Division.[36]

When the Woman's Committee disbanded at the end of the war, Alice Dunbar-Nelson's narrative might have ended as well, had she not been given an opportunity to reflect on her findings and publish them. Early in 1919, Emmett J. Scott approached her again, this time about writing an essay about black women and the world war. She set to work assembling her data, then submitted an article, "Negro Women in War Work," which appears in *Scott's Official History of the American Negro in the World War.* Her depiction of African American women during the conflict remains the most accessible account of black women's war work, though her description of interracial war work is not altogether positive. In contrast to the optimistic correspondence to the Woman's Committee, Dunbar-Nelson, in "Negro Women and War Work," describes the association between black and white women as uneven and lukewarm. "The problem of the woman of the Negro race was a peculiar one," Dunbar-Nelson acknowledges. "There were separate regiments of Negro soldiers; should there be separate organizations for relief work among Negro women? Could she be sure that when she offered her services she would be understood as desiring to be a help, and not wishing to be an associate?"[37] In fact, a tenuous partnership was the best association African American women and white women could expect. Dunbar-Nelson concludes, "To the everlasting eternal credit of the colored woman it could be said that, in spite of what might have been absolute deterrents, she persisted in her service and was not downcast in the face of difficulties."[38]

Dunbar-Nelson's investigation and essay illustrate the thriving culture of social and political activism among southern African American women during the war. Like Dunbar-Nelson's investigation for the Woman's Committee, African American women's war work manifested two specific identities. One demonstrated genuine loyalty to the United States, expressed by an eagerness to work with established organizations for the Allied cause. An alternate identity, committed to African American uplift and advancement, embodied a dedication to black soldiers, families, and communities. The war work of Dunbar-Nelson, as well as the southern black women she interviewed, operated with several interdependent positionalities at once: African American and white, institutional and public, middle class and working class, secular and religious, and marginalized and patriotic. These women manifested the spirit of double consciousness, a notion described by W. E. B. Du Bois in his *Souls of Black Folk* (1903). They wore one facade for their white employers and another for the white southerners with whom they attempted to cooperate, while trying to remain faithful to the core objective of aiding African American soldiers and families. Despite the rigid structures of institutional racism and a cynicism about African American patriotism, black women, especially black southern women, found their own ways through the complex structures of federally organized war work programs. Working steadily throughout the war, if not without confusion and racial tension, they strove to satisfy their communities' immediate needs and to fulfill the longtime promise of racial equality.

NOTES

1. Alice Dunbar-Nelson, personal memorandum, January 1918. Alice Dunbar-Nelson Papers, Special Collections Library, University of Delaware, Newark, Delaware (hereafter ADN).

2. Ibid.

3. Ibid.

4. William J. Breen, "Black Women and the Great War: Mobilization and Reform in the South," in *Our American Sisters: Women in American Life and Thought,* ed. Jean E. Friedman (Lexington, MA: Heath, 1982), 411.

5. Alice Dunbar-Nelson's two sets of diaries, July 29 to December 1921, and November 1926 to December 1931, offer remarkable insight into a thriving African American feminist community, one that interwove sexuality, class, race, and gender into a rich, multilayered consciousness of African American womanhood. Gloria T. Hull has edited these diaries as *Give Us Each Day: The Diary of Alice Dunbar-Nelson* (New York: Norton, 1984).

6. The Circle for Negro War Relief, Inc., Pamphlet and Subscription Cards, January 1918, document, ADN.

7. Caroline S. Bond (New York City) to Alice Dunbar-Nelson, Wilmington, Delaware, January 18, 1918, typed signed letter, ADN.

8. *New York Age,* January 5, 1918, 1.

9. "The Horizon," *Crisis* (June 1918): 83.

10. Dunbar-Nelson's best-known war poems, "I Sit and Sew" and "Let Me Live," were published in the *A.M.E. Church Review* in July 1918. "I Sit and Sew" is reprinted in Dunbar-Nelson's *Dunbar Speaker and Entertainer: The Poet and His Song,* with an introduction by Akasha (Gloria) Hull (1920; repr. New York: G. K. Hall, 1996), 145. "Let Me Live" is found in the *A.M.E. Church Review* (July 1918): 8.

11. Committee on Women's Defense Work of the Council of National Defense, July 8, 1918, Minutes, box 570, Records of the Committee on Women's Defense Work, Records of the Council of National Defense, record Group 62, National Archives Record Administration II, College Park, MD (hereafter cited as WC Minutes with date and box number).

12. Darlene Clark Hine, "The Call That Never Came: Black Women Nurses and World War I, an Historical Note," *Indiana Military History Journal* 8 (1983): 23–27.

13. Committee on Women's Defense Work, July 18, 1918. WC Minutes, Box 570.

14. Hannah Patterson, Washington, D.C., to Alice Dunbar-Nelson, Wilmington, Delaware, July 5, 1918, typed signed letter, ADN.

15. Ibid.

16. Hannah J. Patterson, Resident Director of the Committee on Women's Defense Work, Washington, D.C., to Alice Dunbar-Nelson, Wilmington, Delaware. July 5, 1918, typed signed letter, ADN; Patterson to Dunbar-Nelson, August 12, 1918, typed signed letter, ADN.

17. Mary B. Talbert, Fort Smith, Arkansas, to Anna Howard Shaw, Washington, D.C., October 25, 1918, typed signed letter; Hannah Patterson, Washington, D.C., to Mary B. Talbert, Buffalo, New York, October 29, 1918, typed letter, Box 512, Folder 131, Woman's Committee Central Correspondence. Records of the Committee of Women's Defense Work, Records of the Council of National Defense, Record Group 62A (National Archives and Records Administration II).

18. Alice Dunbar-Nelson, New Orleans, to Hannah Patterson, Washington, D.C., August 14, 1918, autograph letter signed, WC Central Correspondence.

19. Ibid.

20. Hannah Patterson, Washington, D.C., to Alice Dunbar-Nelson, New Orleans, August 19, 1918, typed signed letter, ADN.

21. Alice Dunbar-Nelson, Como, Mississippi, to Hannah Patterson, Washington, D.C., August 19, 1918, WC Central Correspondence.

22. Alice Dunbar-Nelson, Sardis, Mississippi, to Hannah Patterson, Washington, D.C., August 20, 1918, autograph signed letter, WC Central Correspondence.

23. Alice Dunbar-Nelson, Sardis, Mississippi, to Hannah Patterson, Washington, D.C., August 21, 1918, autograph signed letter, WC Central Correspondence.

24. *Vicksburg Evening Post,* July 31, 1918, 24–27, 29; Paula Giddings, *When and Where I Enter: The Impact of Black Women on Race and Sex in America* (New York: Bantam Books, 1988), 141.

25. Alice Dunbar-Nelson, Jackson, Mississippi, to Hannah Patterson, Washington, D.C., August 23, 1918, autograph signed letter, WC Central Correspondence.

26. Alice Dunbar-Nelson, Selma, Alabama, to Hannah Patterson, Washington, D.C., August 25, 1918, typed signed letter, WC Central Correspondence.

27. Ibid.

28. Dunbar-Nelson, "Things that have to be explained to Colored audiences and Committees," September 1918, typed document, ADN.

29. Alice Dunbar-Nelson, Birmingham, Alabama, to Hannah Patterson, Washington, D.C., August 26, 1918, autograph signed letter, WC Central Correspondence.

30. Alice Dunbar-Nelson, Birmingham, Alabama, to Hannah Patterson, Washington, D.C., August 28, 1918, autograph signed letter, WC Central Correspondence.

31. Ibid.

32. Ibid.

33. Alice Dunbar-Nelson, Mobile, Alabama, to Hannah Patterson, Washington, D.C., August 29, 1918, autograph signed letter, WC Central Correspondence.

34. Council of National Defense, State Council Section, News Bulletin and Press Release, September 18, 1918, document, ADN; Emily N. Blair, *The Woman's Committee: United States Council of Defense, An Interpretive Report: April 21, 1917 to February 27, 1919* (Washington, DC: U.S. Government Printing Office, 1920), 125–26.

35. Hannah Patterson, Washington, D.C., to Alice Dunbar-Nelson, Wilmington, Delaware, October 11, 1918, typed signed letter, ADN.

36. Ibid.

37. Alice Dunbar-Nelson, "Negro Women in War Work," in *Scott's Official History of the American Negro in the World War,* ed. Emmett J. Scott (1919; repr. New York: Arno Press and the New York Times, 1969), 376.

38. Ibid.

Chapter 13

Antilynching Plays

Angelina Weld Grimké, Alice Dunbar-Nelson, and the
Evolution of African American Drama

Koritha A. Mitchell

During the post-bellum–pre-Harlem era, drama and lynching became inextricably linked, and African Americans could not afford to ignore either phenomenon. In 1906, Thomas Dixon Jr. established production companies to bring his historical romance *The Clansman* (1905) to life. The actors traveled throughout the United States performing a play version of the novel, which featured proud Ku Klux Klansmen and burning crosses.[1] Impressed with Dixon's dramatic renditions of white supremacist ideology, D. W. Griffith recruited him to write the screenplay for 1915's *Birth of a Nation.* The movie portrays black men as brutes who must be violently controlled, and its message was well received. It ran for eleven months and was the first film screened at the White House. After seeing it, President Woodrow Wilson remarked, "It is like writing history with lightning. And my only regret is that it is all so terribly true."[2] As literary historian Sandra Gunning explains, the film was so influential that "its opening in Atlanta marked the reorganization of the Ku Klux Klan in the twentieth century."[3]

Never underestimating the power of drama to promote racial violence, many African Americans protested when *Birth* was scheduled to arrive in their town.[4] However, blacks did not simply oppose Dixon's scripts: they wrote their own. As early as 1914, Angelina Weld Grimké had written her antilynching play *Rachel*, thereby using drama to address racial violence before *Birth* debuted in theatres.[5] Still, because the film was so widely endorsed, black intellectuals knew that their community needed more playwrights. In 1915, the same year as Dixon's success, W. E. B. Du Bois called for black-authored plays and created a Drama Committee within the NAACP. The committee sponsored a production of Grimké's *Rachel* in March 1916, and after this production, African Americans began consistently writing—not just performing—serious, nonmusical scripts.[6]

Nevertheless, many theatre histories underestimate Grimké's significance and locate the origin of black drama in the mid-1920s.[7] Willis Richardson's *Chip Woman's Fortune* became the first black-authored play to reach Broadway in 1923, and Langston Hughes's *Mulatto* began an unprecedented two-year run on Broadway in 1935. As a result, these men are often seen as the fathers of black drama. However, African American playwrights made important contributions long before Broadway audiences took note. Years earlier, Grimké rejuvenated black drama by establishing an antilynching tradition within it.

Performed in 1916, Grimké's *Rachel* transformed African American theatre.[8] Though she was not the first to write serious drama, hers was the first black-authored, nonmusical script to enjoy stage success outside of black-only community theatre.[9] More importantly, Grimké's text marks the emergence of the African American playwright because, unlike its predecessors, it inspired a number of writers to become dramatists.[10] At the turn of the century, there were many professional black actors, but they generally performed scripts written by whites. Shortly after the appearance of Grimké's *Rachel*, however, a number of African Americans tried playwriting for the first time. Whether impressed or disappointed with Grimké's work, black writers suddenly turned to drama and worked to develop conventions, cultivate themes, and generally perfect the craft.[11]

Individual writers may have entered drama for different reasons, but their debt to Grimké is undeniable, because she inspired the intellectuals who created opportunities for new playwrights. *Rachel* was written before Du Bois formed the Drama Committee. Therefore, it was not a response to his call for black-authored plays, but an inspiration for it.[12] Grimké similarly motivated Howard University professors Alain Locke and Montgomery Gregory. When the NAACP used the production of *Rachel* to advance a "propagandist platform," Locke's and Gregory's were the only dissenting votes. They argued their case in Drama Committee meetings, but realized that they could promote their "purely artistic approach" only if they created their own organization. They established Howard University's theatre department in 1920.[13] Thus, Grimké's *Rachel* motivated the founders of both the NAACP Drama Committee and Howard University's theatre department—institutions that would encourage and train black playwrights throughout the 1920s. Not incidentally, dramatists who were groomed by these organizations often won the contests that *Crisis* and *Opportunity* began sponsoring in 1924 to fuel black literary production.[14]

Yet Grimké's central importance to the development of black drama, and that of black female playwrights generally, has too often been ignored. Locke and Gregory began the trend of discounting Grimké, because their 1927 anthology *Plays of Negro Life* elevated white dramatist Ridgely Torrence as the first significant playwright to capture black experience. Since Torrence used African American actors to bring his script to life on Broadway in 1917, he was said to have inspired black dramatists.[15]

However, it was Grimké's *Rachel* that significantly advanced African American drama in general, and its power to do so lay in its antilynching protest. As much as lynching spurred African Americans to migrate from South to North in 1915,[16] it encouraged their shift from prose and poetry to drama. Blacks simply could not ignore the escalating brutality of the mob or the undeniable power of the stage.

The combination of lynching and theatre in *Rachel* was enough to turn prose writers and poets into committed dramatists,[17] and many of their texts contained trends now recognized as literary conventions. Of course, African American writers had always protested racial violence. In fact, the first black-authored drama published in the United States—William Wells Brown's *The Escape; or, A Leap for Freedom: A Drama in Five Acts* (1858)—features a lynching threat. However, mob violence had not taken center stage as it would after *Rachel*. As theatre scholar Judith Stephens explains, the genre developed "when playwrights moved beyond brief references and focused on a specific lynching incident."[18] Accordingly, "a lynching drama is *a play in which the threat or occurrence of a lynching, past or present, has major impact on the dramatic action.*"[19]

Many of the plays in *Rachel*'s wake document lynching's centrality to early black drama and confirm women's involvement in the antilynching movement. Between 1916 and 1935, at least fourteen antilynching plays were written, and ten of them are by women.[20] Such plays are still written today, but the earliest ones reveal how blacks who lived while racial violence was virtually sanctioned by law dealt with this violent phenomenon.

Antilynching Activism

Those who opposed mob violence in the post-bellum–pre-Harlem years used every tool available. Activism ranged from bold advertising campaigns to silent marches; from investigative reporting to praying; from congressional lobbying to creative writing. As activists added playwriting to their arsenal, lynching drama emerged as a genre with Grimké's *Rachel* and Alice Dunbar-Nelson's *Mine Eyes Have Seen* (1918). These plays provide a blueprint for the genre and reveal the values and assumptions that inspired its development.[21] For instance, despite many scholars' tendency to see literature and politics as separate spheres, post-bellum–pre-Harlem activists used drama as a political tool, not unlike legislative lobbying.

Still, of the hundreds who participated in the antilynching campaign, Ida B. Wells is most prominent because her efforts spanned more than four decades. She wrote bold editorials and lectured internationally in the 1890s, and led demonstrations against racial injustice in the 1920s. Wells often stood alone, but she also created organizations that would effect change without her direct participation. She was great not only because she was fearless but also because she inspired others to join the fight.[22]

Wells helped found the NAACP, which began as the National Negro Committee. Leaders formed the committee in direct response to an Illinois race riot during which two blacks were lynched and two thousand more, forced to flee.[23] In the summer of 1909, the Committee sponsored an interracial political conference to discuss strategies for racial uplift, and when Wells addressed the assembly, she suggested that the organization push for antilynching legislation.[24] At the end of the conference, the National Negro Committee faded, and the NAACP emerged as an organization determined to use publicity to end racial violence. Du Bois became its first "Director of Publications and Research" and editor of its magazine, *The Crisis*. The NAACP aimed to fight physical force with "exposure, public education, judicial remedy, and legislation."[25] In essence, the organization would join in Wells's investigative reporting, but leaders also planned to add formal lobbying to their repertoire, as Wells had urged.

It was not long before the nascent organization faced an injustice that demanded action, and the incident that claimed its attention epitomized the convergence of mob violence and American theatre. In 1911, Will Porter was tied to an opera house stage in Livermore, Kentucky. As historian Robert Zangrando reports, "[H]is body [was] riddled with one hundred bullets by mob members who *purchased tickets* to participate."[26] Fifty men paid to occupy either orchestra seats, from which six shots would be allowed, or balcony seats, from which they were asked to limit themselves to one shot.[27]

Immediately, the NAACP appealed to President Taft. When he labeled the incident a state issue and refused support, the NAACP used the press to expose the federal government's indifference.[28] Leaders increasingly aimed for federal legislation and began supporting Leonidas Dyer (R-Missouri). Dyer first presented antilynching legislation to Congress in 1918, and NAACP officials James Weldon Johnson and Walter White worked for five years to get the bill passed, beginning in 1919.[29] Despite tireless efforts, the bill never became law.

Fortunately, antilynching activism never depended solely on any one forum. Wells used newspaper editorials and pamphlets to debunk the mob's justifications, and she delivered speeches around the world to expose American barbarism. But other activists put Wells's message in dramatic form because theatre and lynching were increasingly intertwined. After all, Dixon and Griffith used drama to praise the Ku Klux Klan and to portray black men as rapists who deserved extermination more than voting rights. In addition, lynching had evolved into a theatrical event, as mobs increasingly wanted (and had) an audience. Beginning in the 1890s, as Leon Litwack explains, "[N]ewspapers . . . announced in advance the time and place of a lynching, special 'excursion' trains transported spectators to the scene, employers sometimes released their workers to attend, [and] parents sent notes to school asking teachers to excuse their children for the event."[30] Furthermore, mob violence followed a script and often attracted large audiences.[31]

Given the undeniable links between mob violence and early American theatre, activists viewed playwriting as a political necessity. When NAACP leaders protested *Birth of a Nation,* they also called for black-authored plays with positive images. If negative portrayals warranted boycotts, picketing, and national letter-writing campaigns, then leaders placed a premium on scripts that favorably depicted African Americans. Therefore, they did not see antilynching drama as separate from their political activism. These plays were not creative accessories to the movement; they were very much a part of it.[32]

All forms of antilynching activism complemented each other to make a national campaign, but interesting patterns formed within the movement.

Specifically, black women dominated playwriting, while black men often concentrated on more traditional tactics such as lobbying. If the NAACP seemed the national forum for civil rights activism at the turn of the century, black women found it to be both invigorating and stifling.[33] Though Wells helped found the NAACP and set its antilynching agenda, she soon felt alienated from it. Remembering the inaugural meeting, Wells wrote in her diary that it was Du Bois's "deliberate intention . . . to ignore me and my work."[34] Upon her death, his comments in *The Crisis* seemed to confirm her suspicion: "[Her] work has easily been forgotten because it was afterward taken up on a much larger scale by the N.A.A.C.P. and carried to greater success."[35]

Though these words now seem harsh and inaccurate given Wells's forty years of activism, modern histories lead readers to similar conclusions about many women. For example, most accounts of Dyer Anti-Lynching Bill activity center on the NAACP, but Mary Talbert worked with Dyer long before NAACP leaders joined forces with him.[36] In fact, though she was not a national officer, it was Talbert who secured Dyer a place on the national convention platform so that he could solicit the group's support. Because leaders considered Talbert's opinion, the partnership between Dyer and NAACP officers James Weldon Johnson and Walter White was born. Just as importantly, Talbert later organized the "Anti-lynching Crusaders" to raise money to promote the bill. Using the network she had developed as a club woman in the 1890s, she mobilized activists in forty states. Though they did not reach their one-million-dollar goal, the group was much more than an "ad hoc committee that the [NAACP] would occasionally utilize"—as many histories would have us believe.[37] Without the Crusaders, the NAACP's famous "Shame of America" advertising campaign would not have been possible. Also, when the NAACP began lobbying again in the 1930s for federal antilynching legislation, the effort was financed by the fund that the Crusaders had created.[38]

Because women played a larger role in political movements than some histories imply, feminist scholars expand accepted historical narratives. Though we can never document all that women endured at the turn of the century, revisionist histories illuminate at least one truth: when women activists faced obstacles, they continued their work by developing new tools.

Antilynching Drama

When black women created new spaces for their activism by writing anti-lynching plays, they continued a tradition established by their foremothers. Viewing writing as a political act, nineteenth-century African American women saw themselves as "doers of the word." For them, as for playwrights who followed, "speaking and writing constituted a form of doing, of social action continuous with their social, political, and cultural work."[39] Therefore, when black women developed antilynching drama, the obstacles that they faced in political organizations became less debilitating.

This genre also appealed to black women because they believed that their unique perspective on mob violence deserved dramatic delivery. The ten antilynching plays that they wrote before 1935 suggest that they understood mob violence as no one else could. The dramatists routinely set the action in a harmonious black home, where women beautifully maintain what male family members have worked to establish.[40] Soon, the mob kills the man of the house, and his family is emotionally and financially devastated. The action in antilynching plays typically revolves around women who remain in the home before, during, and after the lynching.[41] From this vantage point, the woman of the house does not witness physical violence.[42] While others may see the brutalized body hanging from a tree, she is privy to a less physical, but more enduring, torture.

By focusing on the survivors' devastation, the dramatists document the mob's ability to terrorize long after the original bloody event has ended. The playwrights need not portray physical violence because, if the mob targets a black man, his family deteriorates along with his mutilated remains. Making reference to a hanging corpse becomes unnecessary, because the victim's home *is* a lynched body. When a father, brother, or son is torn from the family, the household is castrated and its head removed.

Rachel by Angelina Weld Grimké

Rachel inaugurates antilynching drama by fixing the reader's gaze on the home and emphasizing the importance of men within it. The text also adds a dramatic dimension to the migration narrative, portraying a fatherless family in search of "safe spaces."[43] As in the later *Mine Eyes Have*

Seen, the father has been murdered before the action begins, and the play is set in a new northern home. The family unit now consists of sixteen-year-old Rachel, her older brother Tom, and Mrs. Loving, their mother. Though Rachel and her brother are well educated, they cannot secure suitable jobs. However, the family's poverty does not prevent domestic success. The rooms are "scrupulously neat and clean" and filled with books, inexpensive paintings, and black women who happily sew, cook, and nurture neighborhood children.[44]

Their peaceful home is a testament to the mother's strength, but Grimké does not allow that serenity to overshadow the damage that lynching causes. The play begins the genre's tradition of documenting what I call "de-generation," or generation removal and prevention.[45] With its particular vengeance toward men, the mob alters the structure of the family and eliminates the generation that would otherwise guarantee the black community's healthy survival. The plays usually feature a grandmother and grandchildren, but no mother-father pairing in the middle. The mob accomplishes de-generation in one of two ways: either the mother and father are missing altogether, or lynching keeps the husband-wife unit from functioning. In *Rachel,* the mother is still alive, but the marriage unit does not function because her husband was killed when he refused to remove a controversial article from his newspaper.[46] In response, white neighbors "broke down the front door and made their way to our bedroom."[47] As the men dragged her husband down the hall, her oldest son tried to rescue him. Mrs. Loving explains, "it ended in [the mob] dragging them both out."[48] Thus, lynching has already claimed her husband and her first son.

Though they now live in the North, the family does not escape the mob's power. Unfortunately, generation removal leads to generation prevention. After hearing her mother's story, Rachel realizes that all black males are potential targets. She agonizes, "Why—it would be more merciful—to strangle the little things at birth."[49] Later, Rachel rages, "And so this nation—this white Christian nation—has deliberately set its curse upon the most beautiful—the most holy thing in life—motherhood!"[50] Soon, Rachel rejects her suitor's proposal because she believes she hears children begging not to be born. She loves Mr. Strong and he has prepared a home for her, but she refuses to have children.[51] With one attack, the mob destroys an existing home and prevents the construction of a new one. Lynching disrupts two generations of marriage and destroys countless generations of children.

Mob violence keeps Rachel's suitor, Mr. Strong, from becoming the head of a household, but the racism that sustains it targets black males long before they contemplate marriage and family life. With Rachel's brother Tom, Grimké suggests that black manhood is always under attack. When Tom realizes that his friend no longer visits because she has been criticized for associating with blacks, he vows never to speak to her again. His mother says she understands how he feels, but "I wish my son to always be a gentleman." Tom quickly responds, "If being a gentleman means not being a man—I don't wish to be one."[52] Clearly, Tom questions the standards by which his behavior should be judged. His mother implies that a "gentleman" would be courteous in spite of the slight against him. However, for Tom, accepting the insult would make him a coward and a disgrace to his courageous father's memory.

In this debate, the issue is whether the code of conduct for a "gentleman" applies to situations involving the kind of disrespect that black men endure. To fulfill his mother's expectations, Tom would argue, is to deny his specific experience as a black man. Understanding turn-of-the-century conceptions of manhood helps us appreciate Tom's argument. As historian Gail Bederman explains, manhood could be expressed as either "manliness" or "masculinity." Rooted in Victorian values, "manliness" demanded high-minded morality and good judgment: to be "manly" was to control one's passions.[53] "Masculinity" referred to one's capacity to be instinctively aggressive and protective.[54] With the debate between Tom and his mother, Grimké acknowledges the difficulties a black man faces in fulfilling gender expectations. He cannot apply either of society's conceptions without pause. The manliness that would bring honor to white men only brings him shame.[55]

Still, given her portrayal of Mr. Strong as the most admirable man in the play, Grimké seems to support manliness rather than masculinity. He works hard and refuses to react passionately to the injustices he suffers, particularly the fact that he is well educated but must be a waiter. When Rachel says that their plight makes her pessimistic and morbid, he says that he refuses to feel that way.[56] Though he knows he deserves better employment, he is content because his priorities are in manly order. His job allows him to care for his mother and prospective wife, and that is enough for him to do his duty.[57] Clearly, Grimké would have black men think of their families before reacting to social inequities. After all, masculine pride often results in a lynching that leaves the black family devastated. Though she is proud of her late husband, Mrs. Loving says that she "used to plead with him to be more careful. I was always afraid for him."[58] In making Mr. Strong a role model, Grimké criticizes black men who assert their manhood at their family's expense. Meanwhile, with the debate between Tom and his mother, Grimké also criticizes those who would simply graft Victorian values onto blacks—even in the North.

Ultimately, white definitions of manhood are not the answer; neither manliness nor masculinity will do. African American men must define manhood for themselves—keeping the black family the priority. Grimké shows that society forces black men to make decisions others never face. Often denied the right to defend themselves, they must constantly choose between personal dignity and staying alive to be with their families. By exposing the injustice of having to make such decisions, Grimké honors black men—including those who die trying to strike a balance.

Mine Eyes Have Seen *by Alice Dunbar-Nelson*

Like *Rachel*, *Mine Eyes Have Seen* (1918) is set in the North because the successful father was lynched in the South. In this new home, eighteen-year-old Chris prematurely becomes head of household. Soon, he is called to serve in World War I, and arguments about whether he should fight dominate the text. Insisting that America has committed too many crimes against African Americans to win his loyalty, Chris passionately and consistently rejects patriotic rhetoric. At the end of the play, though, he suddenly changes his mind and seems to forget the injustices he has cited. Nevertheless, his words haunt the reader, as it becomes clear that his impending absence will devastate his family, just as his father's has. Ultimately, *Mine Eyes Have Seen* demonstrates that both lynching and war unfairly claim black men's lives.

Early in the play, Dunbar-Nelson equates the mob and the military by giving them similar weapons. The father was lynched because he owned a nice house and educated his children.[59] We are told that, when local whites grew tired of his success, they posted notices that the family should "leave town because niggers had no business having such a decent home."[60] The mob set the house on fire and, when the father tried to save it, they shot him. Thus, when her brother is drafted, Lucy proclaims, "Oh, it can't be! They won't take you from us! And shoot you down, too?"[61]

Just as Lucy predicts Chris's fate, the reader can predict the family's. The black man's absence means sorrow and poverty for his loved ones, whether he is victimized by a mob or drafted by the army. When the father is taken from the home, his progeny move into a squalid tenement that is soon filled with painful memories. Shortly after arriving in the North, the mother dies because she is not accustomed to the bleak climate. Then, the oldest son Dan is maimed because the northern economy forces him into factory work. In short, a successful generation is missing from this new household, and those who remain struggle to reclaim their dignity, although surrounded by reminders of everything they have lost. With the primary wage earner lynched and his successor crippled, they must "eat and live in the kitchen."[62] Surely, the family's descent will be complete when the war claims its newest breadwinner.

If the family's original prosperity enraged their white neighbors, then their financial problems in the North represent a victory for the mob. However, the family's devastation is best demonstrated not by the small space they occupy but by the dissension that flourishes within it. Unlike the genre's other homes, this one accommodates a number of characters whose intentions are questionable. The visitors include an Irish neighbor, a Jewish boy, and a settlement worker. Each of them advises Chris to join the army and dismisses his reasons for resisting.

Throughout the debate, it is clear that the visitors are not concerned about Chris or his family. For example, when Lucy tells the Irish neighbor that her brother has been drafted, the woman answers, "An' ef he has, what of it? . . . [T]hey took me man from me . . . an' it's a widder I am wid me five kiddies, an' I've niver a word [of complaint] to say."[63] Mrs. O'Neill feels that if her husband has been sacrificed, why should her neighbor be spared? Chris protests that her husband died for "his own," while he would be dying for a country that has only mistreated African Americans.[64] At this point, the Jewish boy Jake dismisses Chris, saying, "There isn't a wrong you can name that your race has endured that mine has not suffered, too."[65] As Jake challenges Chris's grievances with his own, he does not care that Chris speaks of American crimes on American soil. Essentially, these visitors create dissension with their "advice," and their ability to do so proves how damaged the family is.

Embarrassed that these immigrants are more patriotic than he is, Chris's girlfriend Julia agrees with the visitors. She encourages him to serve because "Chris—it IS our country."[66] As she speaks, the father's death hovers over the household, and his spirit seems to beg the reader to remember Chris's original objection: "Must I go and fight for the nation that let my father's murder go unpunished?"[67] The text leaves this question unanswered, but its significance increases at the end of the play, when the settlement worker compares soldiers to Jesus. She says, "As He died to make men holy, let us die to make them free!" Though Chris has agreed to fight at this point, Dunbar-Nelson would have the reader question what freedom means for African Americans. After all, the family had been living the American dream and enjoying freedom when they were, in Chris's words, "driven like dogs from our home."[68]

In spite of his legitimate reasons for resisting, Chris agrees to enlist because he cannot stand to have his manhood questioned. He remains resolved to avoid the draft until his brother Dan calls him a slacker and a weakling. Dan says that black soldiers are real men who brought honor to the race in American wars.[69] He is ashamed that Chris does not want to continue that legacy, and he wishes that he could go in his place. Dan declares, "Oh God! If I were but whole and strong! If I could only prove to a doubting world of what stuff my people are made!" As Dan speaks, he "half tears himself from the chair, the upper part of his body writhing while the lower part is inert, dead."[70] Sadly, he cannot embody the manhood that he praises because he is crippled, and it is interesting that his condition does not kill his patriotism. After all, he might not have been paralyzed if the mob had not forced him to relocate and take up hazardous factory work.

By highlighting Dan's desire to serve, Dunbar-Nelson marks an important contradiction in prowar rhetoric. Dan wants to prove to the world that black men are honorable and brave. However, he has just explained that blacks fought in four wars "and saved the day, too, many a time."[71] One wonders why the world still questions black manhood. Will dying in one more war convince this doubting world? When Dan persuades Chris to enlist and "The Battle Hymn of the Republic" plays in the background, the irony is striking. Like so many before him, Chris will prove his manhood by fighting for the country that allowed his father's murderers to go unpunished.

Many scholars see *Mine Eyes Have Seen* as a prowar text. Gloria T. Hull represents what many critics have asserted when she says, "[The play's] blatant intent is to persuade black people to support the war."[72] While Dunbar-Nelson's war work may have led scholars to conclude that the play is yet another piece of propaganda, a close reading of *Mine Eyes*, in light of new research, suggests that her stance was not static but evolving. Appearing when the war was ending, her play dramatizes the price that African American families pay when black men leave to serve Uncle Sam.

Prowar interpretations assume that Chris's conversion accurately represents Dunbar-Nelson's stance, but such readings overlook the importance antilynching dramatists placed on domesticity. As clubwomen, Grimké and Dunbar-Nelson committed themselves to racial uplift, which they believed could be achieved only by constructing solid black homes.[73] Because they valued domestic success, depictions of the home within their texts are always important. If critics treat domesticity as seriously as these authors do, the argumentative guests in the play gain significance. Otherwise, the visitors' presence seems arbitrary—simply a way of including diverse perspectives on the war. But, if this were their only purpose, we might easily accuse Dunbar-Nelson of using weak dramatic devices. Instead, we recognize that the suspicious characters illuminate the black woman's perspective. Those who would encourage the black man to fight do not respect his authority within his own home. Furthermore, they do not care if he dies serving a nation that allows lynching.

Mine Eyes ends as it began. Readers see the damage that the father's murder has caused and know that Chris's death will complete the family's descent. Lucy has already prophesied that Chris will die just as his father did. In this text, the mob and the military use the same weapons, and both claim black men's lives, with no regard for the family they leave behind. Chris's death and his father's murder are not part of the plot, but they create a frame for the action. This strategy allows the text to tell many more truths than the playwright could record.

Dunbar-Nelson does not depict the men's murders, but she presents the family's devastation in detail. When forced from their home, mother soon dies, Dan is crippled, and Lucy walks with a limp. In Chris's words, Lucy's "soul [has] shriveled with fear," Dan has become "a shell of a man," and "me, with a fragment of an education and no chance—only half a man."[74]

Grimké and Dunbar-Nelson cannot represent the torture that each lynch victim experienced, but the genre they initiate faithfully documents the black family's devastation. Not all victims were shot or burned or hanged, but all of their families were diminished. To tell the truth about lynching, the dramatists focus on the home, not the body. Post-bellum–pre-Harlem black women playwrights refuse to give gruesome details of physical mutilation, but their antilynching dramas nevertheless tell a painful truth. When a father, brother, or son is removed, the black home is castrated, as, we might guess, they are.

NOTES

1. Sandra Gunning, *Race, Rape, and Lynching: The Red Record of American Literature, 1890–1912* (New York: Oxford University Press, 1996), 28–29.

2. Thomas Cripps, *Slow Fade to Black: The Negro in American Film, 1900–1940* (New York: Oxford University Press, 1977), 52.

3. Gunning, *Race*, 29.

4. African American leaders worked to limit the film's impact on American minds. NAACP headquarters supplied branch offices with model protest letters and newspaper clippings documenting the violence that the movie inspired in formerly peaceful cities. Also, there were physical protests. In April 1915, black Bostonians gathered in the streets and in the lobby of a (segregated) theatre that was showing the film. William Monroe Trotter cut short his speaking tour to join the demonstration and was assaulted by police while speaking against the film in the theatre lobby. For more information, see Cripps, *Slow Fade*, 59–60, 63.

5. Gloria T. Hull, *Color, Sex, and Poetry: Three Women of the Harlem Renaissance* (Bloomington: Indiana University Press, 1987), 117–23.

6. "Nonmusical" is significant here. Important progress in developing serious dramatic content had already been made by performers like the Hyers Sisters, whose musicals *Out of Bondage* (1876) and *Peculiar Sam; or, The Underground Railroad* (1879) enjoyed success in the nineteenth century despite containing political messages. But, these shows add to a musical tradition that diverges from the more realistic drama that African Americans felt was necessary at the turn of the century. For more on performers like the Hyers Sisters, see Thomas Riis, *Just before Jazz: Black Musical Theater in New York, 1890–1915* (Washington, DC: Smithsonian Institution Press, 1989).

7. The term "drama" often refers to written plays, whereas "theatre" is a more general term and includes both text and performance. When referring to playwrights' achievements, scholars often overlook works written before the 1920s, even as they acknowledge what black performers accomplished. Perhaps the trend began with the assumption that blacks did not enter the "legitimate" American stage until white dramatist Ridgely Torrence used black actors to portray black characters in his *Plays for a Negro Theater* (New York: Macmillan, 1917). This moment did not rely on black playwrights, so many deemed African American dramatists irrelevant, a sentiment solidified with Alain Locke and Montgomery Gregory's 1927 drama anthology *Plays of Negro Life: A Source-Book of Native American Drama* (1927; repr. Westport, CT: Negro Universities Press, 1970). Locke credits white playwrights Torrence, Eugene O'Neill, and Paul Green with the "pioneering genius" that made 1917 to 1927 an "experimental and groundbreaking decade" (i). Similarly, Gregory says that the production of Torrence's plays "marks the first important movement in the development of an authentic drama of Negro life and the establishment of Negro Theatre" (410). Though modern scholars also

routinely minimize early black playwrights' work, exceptions include James Hatch. For examples of his approach, see his *Black Theatre, U.S.A.: Forty-five Plays by Black Americans, 1847–1974* (New York: Free Press, 1974) and *The Roots of African American Drama: An Anthology of Early Plays, 1858–1938* (Detroit: Wayne State University Press, 1991).

8. As my task here is to provide historical and theoretical context for works that are readily available but often misunderstood, I focus on published, black-authored, nonmusical plays. Serious black-authored scripts that precede *Rachel* were executed on the amateur stage. Between 1901 and 1910, Katherine Davis Chapman Tillman published four dramas for production in elementary and Sunday schools through the A.M.E. Book Concern and the *A.M.E. Church Review*. See *The Works of Katherine Davis Chapman Tillman* (New York: Oxford University Press, 1991) and Claudia Tate's thorough introduction for more information.

Two plays for a more general audience were written before 1916: William Wells Brown's *The Escape; or, A Leap for Freedom: A Drama in Five Acts* (1858) and *Caleb, the Degenerate: A Play in Four Acts* (1901) by Joseph Seamon Cotter. Some may also think of Du Bois's 1913 *Star of Ethiopia* as an underappreciated early dramatic text. However, it is a pageant, not a play, as his *Crisis* writings attest. Ira Aldridge and Victor Séjour also wrote significant dramas during the 1800s. However, to the extent that they are not written for African American actors or for American audiences, their plays do not help shape an African American theatre tradition.

9. I argue that *Rachel* actually revived amateur theatre within the black community. However, it would not have inspired that revival if it had not reached a large audience via the semiprofessional stage.

10. Georgia Douglas Johnson, who hosted a literary salon in her Washington, D.C., home, became an important conduit for Grimké's influence. These weekly sessions began in 1921, and Grimké regularly attended: see Elizabeth McHenry, *Forgotten Readers: Recovering the Lost History of African American Literary Societies* (Durham, NC: Duke University Press, 2002), 274. By this time, *Rachel* had been on stage in Washington, D.C., Massachusetts, and New York. Surely, as she participated in the salon, she shared her ideas on racial violence and on aesthetics. Regular attendees included Johnson as host, Alice Dunbar-Nelson, Mary Burrill, and May Miller—all of whom became antilynching dramatists.

Even before these regular meetings began in 1921, Grimké interacted with Johnson as a friend and with Mary Burrill as a fellow teacher at M Street High School. As Johnson and Burrill developed playwriting skills, they constantly revised what Grimké had presented in *Rachel*. See Grimké, " 'Rachel,' The Play of the Month: Reason and Synopsis by the Author," in *Lost Plays of the Harlem Renaissance*, ed. James V. Hatch and Leo Hamalian (1920; repr. Detroit, MI: Wayne State University Press, 1996), 424–26. Such revisions demonstrate the degree to which they felt that the work Grimké started was important but needed to be supplemented. For more on the playwrights' interaction, see Hull's *Color, Sex, and Poetry* and McHenry's *Forgotten Readers*.

11. Grimké jumpstarted the genre partly because her play disturbed many, motivating intellectuals and writers such as Du Bois, Locke, and Gregory to become more involved with black theatre and create their own dramas. With nine more lynching plays by black women in the decade that followed *Rachel,* we can see that black writers wanted to dramatize the story of lynching in ways that *Rachel* had not.

12. Most assume that Du Bois motivated Grimké. For example, theatre historian William B. Branch calls *Rachel* "the first produced play to result from Dr. Du Bois's call" (*Black Thunder: An Anthology of Contemporary African American Drama* [New York: Penguin, 1992], xv). However, the script was available to Du Bois by the time he founded the NAACP Drama Committee because it had already been written. Grimké shared drafts as early as January of 1915 with NAACP officials, including Du Bois's confidant Mary White Ovington (Hull, *Color, Sex, and Poetry,* 117–23).

13. Gregory, in Locke and Gregory, *Plays,* 414.

14. These magazines published most extant antilynching plays. The *Crisis,* for example, conferred short story prizes as early as 1923, but in 1924 offered awards of seventy-five, forty, and ten dollars specifically for plays. See David Levering Lewis's *When Harlem Was in Vogue* (New York: Knopf, 1981), 102, and Jennifer Burton's introduction to *Zora Neale Hurston, Eulalie Spence, Marita Bonner, and Others: The Prize Plays and Other One-Acts Published in Periodicals* (New York: G. K. Hall; London: Prentice-Hall, 1996), xix–lx.

15. No doubt, Torrence changed American theatre by using African American actors to portray black characters in his *Three Plays for a Negro Theatre* in 1917. But it seems to me that Locke and Gregory went too far when they claimed that it was this bold move on Torrence's part that inspired blacks to become playwrights.

16. The years 1915 to 1930 constitute acceptable parameters for what has been termed the "Great Migration." If 1915 is an important year in blacks' movement from the South to the North, then Grimké's text marks the intersection not only of lynching and theatre but also of lynching and migration. Notably, Grimké's immediate successor, Dunbar-Nelson, also writes about an uprooted family. See Farah Jasmine Griffin's *"Who Set You Flowin'?": The African American Migration Narrative* (New York: Oxford University Press, 1995).

17. Johnson exemplifies this commitment. Though she gained much more notoriety as a poet, she wrote drama until her death, and persevered despite vehement rejections from the Federal Theatre Project, as detailed in Winona Fletcher's essay "From Genteel Poet to Revolutionary Playwright: Georgia Douglas Johnson," *Theatre Annual* 40 (1985): 40–64.

18. Judith Stephens, introduction to *Strange Fruit: Plays on Lynching by Ameri-*

can Women, ed. Judith Stephens and Kathy Perkins (Bloomington: Indiana University Press, 1998), 4.

19. Ibid., 4. Stephens identifies Ridgely Torrence's *Granny Maumee* (1914) as the first antilynching play. I will use "antilynching drama" and "lynching drama" interchangeably. As Stephens explains, some scholars believe that the "anti-" is redundant for black-authored plays because none of them advocate lynching. Nevertheless, I find both terms useful.

20. I say "at least" because future research may provide other examples. Also, scholars may not immediately recognize all of the plays that fit Stephens's definition. In fact, I categorize Johnson's *Blue Blood* (1926) as a lynching play, though Stephens has not included it in her listings. Currently known and published lynching plays written by blacks before 1935 are *Rachel* (1916) by Angelina Grimké; *Mine Eyes Have Seen* (1918) by Alice Dunbar-Nelson; *Aftermath* (1919) by Mary Burrill; *For Unborn Children* (1926) by Myrtle Smith Livingston; *A Sunday Morning in the South* (1925), *Blue Blood* (1926), *Safe* (1929), and *Blue-Eyed Black Boy* (1930) by Georgia Douglas Johnson; *Climbing Jacob's Ladder* (1931) by Regina Andrews; and *Nails and Thorns* (1933) by May Miller. Black men published far fewer plays during this period: *Frances* (1925) by G. Lipscomb, *Son-Boy* (1926) by Joseph Mitchell, *Scottsboro Limited* (1931) by Langston Hughes, and *Bad Man* (1934) by Randolph Edmunds. *A Sign* (1934) by George Streator is often included as an antilynching play. It is much less than one act long, however, with a total of about ten lines.

21. For more on antilynching activities, see Robert Zangrando's *The NAACP Crusade against Lynching, 1909–1950* (Philadelphia: Temple University Press, 1990); Jacquelyn Dowd Hall's *Revolt against Chivalry: Jessie Daniel Ames and the Women's Campaign against Lynching* (New York: Columbia University Press, 1993) and Wells's biographies (see note 22 below).

22. Biographies on Wells include Linda O. McMurry's *To Keep the Waters Troubled: The Life of Ida B. Wells* (New York: Oxford University Press, 1998), Dorothy Sterling's *Black Foremothers: Three Lives* (1979; repr. Old Westbury, NY: Feminist Press, 1988), and Wells's autobiography, *Crusader for Justice* (Chicago: University of Chicago Press, 1970).

23. Zangrando, *NAACP Crusade*, 22.

24. Ibid., 23.

25. Ibid., 24.

26. Ibid., 26.

27. Philip Dray, *At the Hands of Persons Unknown: The Lynching of Black America* (New York: Random House, 2002), 178.

28. Zangrando, *NAACP Crusade*, 27.

29. It was similar to a bill drafted in 1901 by Bostonian Albert Pillsbury.

30. See *Without Sanctuary: Lynching Photography in America,* ed. James Allen et al. (Santa Fe, NM: Twin Palms, 2000), 12–13.

31. Trudier Harris's seminal study *Exorcising Blackness: Historical and Literary*

Lynching and Burning Rituals (Bloomington: Indiana University Press, 1984) explains that lynching evolved into ritual violence that contained predictable elements: an accusation, an obligatory confession, and a lengthy torture for the crowd's benefit. Often, the crowd took body parts as souvenirs and this too became part of the ritual.

32. Leaders valued creative scripts because the NAACP wanted to produce a public response to *Birth of a Nation* (1915). Du Bois offered his pageant *Star of Ethiopia* (1913) but others were not interested in using it. The executive committee therefore entertained offers from Universal Pictures to make a film called *Lincoln's Dream*. For details on the NAACP response to *Birth of a Nation,* see David Levering Lewis, *W. E. B. Du Bois: Biography of a Race, 1868–1919* (New York: Henry Holt, 1993), 506–9; and Cripps, *Slow Fade to Black,* 41–69.

33. I distinguish between black and white women here because the executive board did not contain black women. In fact, Mary White Ovington showed considerable power over the black women activists in the Anti-lynching Crusaders and used her NAACP position to pressure the Crusaders to fund an advertising campaign. See Kate Masur's unpublished essay "'The Work at This End Is *Tremendous*': The Anti-Lynching Crusade of 1922," based on research for her prize-winning *Reconstructing the Nation's Capital: The Politics of Race and Citizenship in the District of Columbia, 1862–1878* (Ph.D. diss., University of Michigan, 2002).

34. Wells, *Crusader for Justice,* 326–28.

35. W. E. B. Du Bois, "Postscript," *Crisis* 40.6 (June 1931): 207.

36. Masur, "'Work,'" 10.

37. See Zangrando, *NAACP Crusade,* 78.

38. Masur, "'Work,'" 49.

39. Carla L. Peterson, *"Doers of the Word": Black Women Speakers and Writers in the North, 1830–1880* (New York: Oxford University Press, 1995), 3.

40. The plays privilege traditional, heterosexual coupling patterns, even in the last two, which are not set in black homes. The playwrights primarily present lynching as an attack on black men; the mob wants to rob black men of their lives and/or their right to protect and govern their own homes. Rather than criticizing the dramatists' traditional values, I find taking their perspective the best way to understand the cultural work they hoped to perform. I am influenced by Hazel V. Carby's *Reconstructing Womanhood: The Emergence of the Afro-American Novelist* (New York: Oxford University Press, 1987); Claudia Tate's *Domestic Allegories of Political Desire: The Black Heroine's Text at the Turn of the Century* (New York: Oxford University Press, 1992); and Ann duCille's *Coupling Convention: Sex, Text, and Tradition in Black Women's Fiction* (New York: Oxford University Press, 1993).

41. None of the plays by black women before 1935 mentions women lynch victims. As this essay demonstrates, women dramatists had particular reasons for focusing on male victimization, even though they knew that women became victims too. In addition, because the myth of the black male rapist relied on black

women being whores, these women defended themselves at the same time that they defended black men. Nevertheless, the image of an always male lynch victim has had a tremendous impact on America's conception of racial injustice. For an exploration of these implications, see Elsa Barkley Brown's "Imaging Lynching: African American Women, Communities of Struggle, and Collective Memory," in *African American Women Speak Out on Anita Hill-Clarence Thomas,* ed. Geneva Smitherman (Detroit, MI: Wayne State University Press, 1995), 100–124.

42. Trudier Harris sees the playwrights' refusal to portray violence as a flaw. She says that "African American women playwrights could almost be accused of disguising the horrors that serve as the impetus to their work" (32). Harris's assessment is particularly disturbing to me because she sees that these women are "more interested in the effect of lynching upon hearth, home, and mind instead of the body" (30), but she does not appreciate the profundity of that concern. For Harris's assessment, see "Before the Strength, the Pain: Portraits of Elderly Black Women in Early Twentieth-Century Anti-Lynching Plays," in *Black Women Playwrights: Visions on the American Stage,* ed. Carol P. Marsh-Lockett (New York: Garland Publishing, 1999), 25–42.

43. I mean this in Griffin's sense. She borrows the term from Patricia Hill Collins but complicates it in order to understand the migration narrative. For Griffin, safe spaces are "either the locus for producing and maintaining the negative effects of urbanization . . . or safe havens from these negative effects. See Griffin, *"Who Set You Flowin'?"* 8.

44. Angelina Weld Grimké, *Rachel,* in Stephens and Perkins, *Strange Fruit,* 27.

45. The earliest lynching dramas written by black women document the mob's power to lynch generations—not just bodies—because it attacks the most productive men of the race. It is men who are always missing. In *Mine Eyes Have Seen, Aftermath, A Sunday Morning in the South,* and *For Unborn Children,* there is no middle generation at all: grandmothers replace mothers so that the household can function. However, the grandmothers are widows, so there is no substitute for the missing father. Furthermore, when dramas include a middle generation, the mother is often its only representative. In *Rachel* and *Blue Blood,* only women survive, but their presence simply allows them to tell the children about their father and to mourn a marriage that has been destroyed.

46. Grimké, *Rachel,* 40.

47. Ibid., 41.

48. Ibid., 42.

49. Some thought that Grimké was promoting race suicide. She addresses these concerns in "'Rachel,' The Play of the Month" (see note 10).

50. The protagonist is named after the biblical Rachel, as described in Matthew 2:18: "In Rama was there a voice heard, lamentation, and weeping, and great mourning, Rachel weeping for her children, and would not be comforted, because they are not" (Hull, *Color, Sex,* 118).

51. Grimké, *Rachel*, 75–78.

52. Ibid., 38.

53. Gail Bederman, *Manliness and Civilization: A Cultural History of Gender and Race in the United States, 1880–1917* (Chicago: University of Chicago Press, 1995), 11–12.

54. Ibid., 17–18.

55. Bederman explains how manhood could exist in two very different forms and how those forms relate to race and civilization. The white man exemplified manliness, while "The Negro" was the ultimate primitive. However, Bederman does not take the next step to examine the ways in which a man's race virtually determined how he could express his manhood. I use her two-pronged conception of manhood to examine how race necessarily influenced behavior. Middle-class white men could adopt either manliness or masculinity, depending upon the situation, because their civilization was rarely questioned, even if they behaved barbarously. Accordingly, a post-bellum–pre-Harlem white newspaper reporter reasoned that "civilized man . . . had evolved the capacity to suppress the unmanly passions, but when they joined lynch mobs, they allowed the savage within themselves free reign" (Bederman, *Manliness*, 72). Black men did not enjoy such flexibility.

56. Grimké, *Rachel*, 54.

57. Ibid., 51.

58. Ibid., 40.

59. Alice Dunbar-Nelson, *Mine Eyes Have Seen, The Crisis* (1918): 271–75.

60. Ibid., 271.

61. Ibid., 272.

62. Ibid., 271.

63. Ibid., 272.

64. Dunbar-Nelson's visitors represent what David R. Roediger calls the "not-yet-white ethnic" immigrants. Poorly treated upon arrival, these groups often needed to find ways to assert their whiteness in order to avoid oppression. I do not want to suggest that only African Americans have been mistreated in the United States. However, even those who explore the complexities of ethnic oppression concede that European immigrants and racial minorities have not experienced the same injustices on American soil. Roediger explains that while African Americans experience oppression because of their race, immigrants often *choose* to race themselves as white. See "Whiteness and Ethnicity in the History of 'White Ethnics' in the United States" in his *Towards the Abolition of Whiteness: Essays on Race, Politics, and Working-Class History* (London: Verso, 1994), 181–98.

65. Dunbar-Nelson, *Mine Eyes Have Seen*, 273.

66. Ibid., 274.

67. Ibid., 272.

68. Ibid., 272.

69. Ibid., 273.

70. Ibid., 274.

71. Ibid., 273.

72. Hull, *Color, Sex,* 71.

73. For more on the black women's club movement, see Paula Giddings's *When and Where I Enter: The Impact of Black Women on Race and Sex in America* (New York: Bantam, 1988), especially 95–118; Gerda Lerner's *Black Women in White America: A Documentary History* (1972; repr. New York: Vintage Books, 1992); Hazel V. Carby, *Reconstructing Womanhood: The Emergence of the Afro-American Woman Novelist* (New York: Oxford University Press, 1987), 96–97; and Angela Y. Davis, *Women, Race, and Class* (New York: Random House, 1981), 127–36, among others.

74. Dunbar-Nelson, *Mine Eyes Have Seen,* 271–72.

Chapter 14

Henry Ossawa Tanner and W. E. B. Du Bois
African American Art and "High Culture" at the Turn into the Twentieth Century

Margaret Crumpton Winter and Rhonda Reymond

The discourse upon African American art that began in the nineteenth century still influences the way this tradition is approached today. Some forms of black art were labeled as "primitive" because they were not viewed as the product of the same skill and training needed to produce the "high art" of Western civilization.[1] Another point of demarcation has been subject matter: Can works be considered African American if the artist does not depict black subjects? Both of these critical areas of contention are addressed in the works of the writer, sociologist, and philosopher W. E. B. Du Bois and the painter Henry Ossawa Tanner.[2] Yet these conventional ways of framing discussions of African American art have too often neglected its spiritual dimension, one that Du Bois early on recognized as seminal. In his book *The Souls of Black Folk* (1903), he suggests a unifying theory of black arts by revealing that the African American artistic experience had its foundation in, and continues to evolve out of, the rich and creative religion developed by blacks during slavery. At the turn of the twentieth century, both Tanner and Du Bois were able to draw from this religious tradition to make creations that met the standards of the prevailing Western "high art" yet were indelibly rooted in a tradition exclusive to black Americans.

Tanner's paintings are highly spiritual creations, and their religious nature links them at a profound level to the tradition of African American artistic expression. On the other hand, Du Bois most often used the tenets and tropes of African American religion to advance the cause of black uplift, a cause to which he dedicated his life. Yet connecting Tanner and Du Bois, above all, are the persistent undercurrents of beauty and spiritual thriving in their works, the ways that both use the forms and teachings of the black church to reach the hearts of their audience. They are also allied by a certain sensibility—born of education, personality, and historical circumstance—that compelled them to make their mark as men of culture in a world where culture was defined for them by Western European standards. They succeeded in this realm; nevertheless, in their success they did not "lose" their blackness nor compromise their allegiance to their race. On the contrary, both men in all their works advanced through international discourse the idea of freedom, the great metaphor and common trope of African American history, experience, and art.

The tremendous significance of their success at inserting African American works into the cultural discourse of their day can only be understood in light of the oppressive racial atmosphere at the turn into the twentieth century. The historian Rayford W. Logan labeled this period the "nadir of African American life and thought," calling the year 1901 the "lowest point in the quest for equal rights."[3] By that year virtually every southern state in the nation had rewritten its constitution to disfranchise black citizens. With the *Plessy v. Ferguson* decision of 1896, the highest court in the land had upheld an American system of apartheid, and lynchings were claiming the lives of about one hundred black persons a year. The fact that state and nation upheld the dehumanizing system of Jim Crow only served to validate the most racist beliefs of the American public. Disturbing images of African Americans appeared regularly in periodicals and other popular publications, including covers for sheet music. The most common depictions of blacks to be found in the contemporary literature were the child-like, docile slaves in the works of white southerners like Thomas Nelson Page or the violent defilers of white womanhood in the works of Thomas Dixon. Practitioners of science and sociology also played a role in the diminishing public opinion of black people by publishing such "scientific" works as Dixon's *Mystery Solved: The Negro a Beast* (1900). Through the new evolutionary theories of Charles Darwin, many "researchers" of the day were attempting to prove the validity of the antiquated idea that there was a hierarchy of creation (with white males, of course, at the top). Their argument was that people of African descent were lower down on the evolutionary scale than whites, and therefore inferior to them.

This, then, is the social and political climate in which Henry Ossawa Tanner and W. E. B. Du Bois came of age. In his ninety-five years, Du Bois would prove himself to be an important American voice and figure, but at the turn into the twentieth century he was beginning his career. Raised by a single mother among the working-class New England poor, but educated at Fisk, Harvard, and the University of Berlin, Du Bois was a man of exquisite intellect and purpose who had a profound understanding of Europe and America, of the South and the North, and of black and white life. Yet as he completed his Harvard Ph.D. and began his career as an academic in the 1890s, one of the most educated men in the United States, Du Bois faced a nation that was still questioning the very humanity of black people.

Henry Ossawa Tanner's beginnings were more auspicious than those of Du Bois. Tanner's father, Benjamin Tucker Tanner, was a bishop, scholar, author, teacher, and activist in the service of the African Methodist Episcopal (A.M.E.) Church. "The Preacher" was, according to Du Bois, "a leader, a politician, an orator," and "the most unique personality developed by the Negro on American soil," and he was the center of the church, which was itself the heart of African American religious, social, and political life.[4] Although quite the antithesis of his forceful father—timid, of ill health and artistic temperament—young Henry nonetheless would be affected by this spiritual home environment. Rather than succeed his father into the clergy, Henry followed his own artistic inclinations and by the age of thirteen knew that he was destined to become an artist: "no ordinary one" but, indeed, a "great artist."[5] With this goal in mind, Tanner earned a place in the Pennsylvania Academy of Fine Arts, arguably one of America's premier art institutes. Despite the racism directed at him from some of his classmates, he persevered in his training. In the 1890s, a serious student seeking to become a professional was obliged to study in Paris to refine his skills, and, being as serious as any, Tanner chose to attend the celebrated Académie Julian. It was in Paris that he finally found his work judged on its artistic merit alone, his race no longer an issue.

Notwithstanding his physical removal from America's racist atmosphere, Tanner remained aware of white America's ethnocentric notion of "civilization" in which black culture was stuck in some former or "primitive" age of development, the evidence being that African Americans had never created "high art." Rebuttal of this assumption was Tanner's express purpose in presenting the paper "The American Negro in Art" at the 1893 World's Congress on Africa, held in conjunction with the World's Colombian Exposition.[6] He proclaimed that African American artists had already proven that they had the talent and ability to compete with white artists.

The Exposition reified the cultural hegemony of whites by making explicit the grand achievement of "civilized" society, represented by the ordered, classical Court of Honor in the White City. This was in direct contrast to the adjacent Midway Plaisance, which included a jumble of carnival attractions, including the world's first ferris wheel, and pseudo-scientifically presented "exotic" cultures, coordinated to highlight their picturesque, quaint, and so-called primitive qualities, even at the expense of anthropological correctness. The "high art" of the White City and the "low art" of the Midway were mutually exclusive.

Tanner could very well have been trying to repudiate this assumption pictorially with his series of black genre images, the first to be painted by an African American artist. He married contemporary French "high art" techniques, such as loose brushwork, impressionistic colorism, and a tilted ground plane, with a sympathetic desire to reveal both the warm heart and "serious and pathetic" side of black life.[7] In *The Banjo Lesson* (1893), Tanner takes a normally stereotypical theme, the happy minstrel, and subverts it, avoiding the aspect of public entertainment and emphasizing instead the transmission of knowledge through the tender gestures. Among others, the classicist William Sanders Scarborough, future president of Wilberforce University, the nation's oldest private black college, believed that in Tanner, African Americans had found a champion who would depict the race with dignity and grace.[8]

Tanner, however, opted to develop his career in quite a different direction. Upon returning to France he discontinued making his black genre paintings. His refusal to continue in this vein might very well be attributed to the limitations of the traditional Dutch genre image and its current connotations in Europe, where the type was used almost exclusively in connection with so-called quaint or picturesque cultures, such as those of the country Dutch or French Bretons. Powerful, educated, or forward-thinking people were not depicted in genre paintings. Perhaps the artist began to chafe at the idea of sophisticated audiences making similar assumptions about African Americans based on his portrayals of them in the genre mode. Furthermore, at Le Salon de la Societe des Artistes Français, the official body granting artistic recognition, genre painting was not ranked as highly as history painting, with its grand traditions of depicting lofty mythological, religious, or historical subjects. Tanner passionately strove for official recognition of his talents in a highly competitive field, and any artist associated with genre painting would never be ranked among history painters and, in consequence, would never be con-

Henry Ossawa Tanner. *The Banjo Lesson,* 1893. Oil on canvas. 49 x 35 1/2 inches. Hampton University Museum. Hampton, Virginia.

sidered a truly great painter. For Tanner this was the true challenge: to make a success of his life and to be a concrete example, an African American who competed and shone at an international level with the best artists of his generation.

Back in the United States, as a black American writer, W. E. B. Du Bois faced similar challenges. Despite evidence to the contrary, including the talent and success of Henry Ossawa Tanner, America still adhered to the idea that black culture and "high culture" were by definition mutually exclusive. Du Bois's razor-sharp book *The Souls of Black Folk* cut through this racist miasma with intelligence, logic, style, and emotion. Though other African Americans were writing important sociology, fiction, and poetry at this time, there is no other single text that can match its varied content or impact. The book can be examined on many levels, including its artistic implications. It was clear to most at the time, and is abundantly so to all now, that *The Souls of Black Folk* is a major work of literary art. Du Bois wrote in the time-honored tradition of the essay, a genre revered in Europe and America as the right form for men of intellect and reason. His use of epigraphs from European and American poetry is a familiar technique that further aligns him with Western literary tradition. In fact, the very language of Du Bois's prose, its elevated tone and educated— even classical—diction, met, if not exceeded, every standard of "good writing" for his day.

In short, *The Souls of Black Folk* shattered every myth about African American capability and potential that was circulating at the time. Through his style and the depth and breadth of his knowledge, Du Bois demonstrated that a black writer was able to meet any criteria of "high culture" set by Anglo America. Yet his text was not merely imitative of Western forms. In fact, its innovations marked this book as something new and important on the literary landscape. It transformed the genre of the essay by combining sociology, fiction, and autobiography into a text that quickens both the mind and the heart. In fact, not only is *The Souls of Black Folk* important to American literature, but it also has shaped our understanding of the African American literary tradition, and continues to do so. The book, then, is both a part of what is known as the "Western canon" and profoundly African American.[9]

While some "experts" at the time maintained that black Americans lacked a documented artistic tradition, and therefore a coherent culture, *The Souls of Black Folk* demonstrated that the nexus of black American culture and the location of its most developed artistic forms could be found in its religion, which developed, against all odds, during slavery. Du Bois believed that the most important form of African American art to come out of this religion, and indeed, one of the most important American art forms in general, was the spiritual, or what he terms the "Sorrow Songs." He states, without equivocation, that "the Negro folk song—the rhythmic cry of the slave—stands today not simply as the sole American music, but as the most beautiful expression of human experience born this side the seas."[10] For all its alleged sophistication, Du Bois implies, the West is unable to recognize preliterary forms of expression—oral traditions and music—as art. He demonstrates this deficiency in Western thinking in the second epigraph of each chapter. In an innovative move, a line from a spiritual follows each passage of formal poetry. The lines are in musical notation only—they are not accompanied by the lyrics that would help his audience identify the songs. The notes, then, variously speak to or confound the reader, depending on his or her level of initiation into this African American art form. Du Bois shows how spirituals, as well as the other methods of expression to come out of the religion (including its stories and sermons), were highly developed, with their own codes and styles that could be analyzed by those educated within the tradition. In this tradition, emphasis was placed on improvisation, and the stories that were shared and the songs that were sung are invariably about exile, redemption, and a humanity that had never been lost.

What Du Bois finally develops in *Souls of Black Folk* is the beginning of an insightful and important theory of African American arts. He posits that African Americans had arrived in the twentieth century already endowed with a whole culture, a culture that had survived slavery and Reconstruction, a culture that was preserved by and found its deepest artistic expression in its religion. His theory would prove prophetic in the twentieth century, as many writers, musicians, and artists would be influenced by these preliterate traditions and would use them in their art. Just as Du Bois maintained that the slave found in religion the "expression of his higher life," future African American artists, including Tanner, would draw from this wealth of material to represent their personal and communal struggles and triumphs.

The moniker appropriately bestowed upon Tanner, "poet-painter of Palestine," attests to the important role religious themes played in his art.[11] Tanner's religious affinity is evident even in his early genre paintings. In its depiction of two humble souls saying grace, *The Thankful Poor* (1893–1894) makes manifestly clear the importance of religion in the

Henry Ossawa Tanner. *And He Vanished Out of Their Sight,* 1901. The Pennsylvania Academy of the Fine Arts, Philadelphia. Archives.

daily life of an African American family. Through his composition, and the displacement of the child's plate from in front of the child to the front of the table, Tanner draws a parallel to traditional images of the Last Supper at Emmaus. This underlying religious theme is made even more explicit when *The Thankful Poor* is compared to Tanner's own version of the Last Supper, entitled *And He Vanished Out of Their Sight* (1901), which exhibits the same empty plate at the front of the table. Even *The Banjo Lesson,* through its use of gesture, composition, and lighting, is invested with a warmth and humanity worthy of the most tender depictions of the Madonna and Child. While the formal elements call to mind this traditional religious imagery, the subject and title, which both emphasize teaching, prefigure Tanner's later explicitly religious scene, *Christ and His Mother Studying the Scriptures* or *Christ Learning to Read* (c. 1909), which discloses the artist's imaginings of the simple domestic side of the Holy Family. (Incidentally, the artist used his wife and son for the models in this painting.) Moreover, Tanner's choice of Christ's instruction in reading—a noncanonical topic—connects him to the trope of literacy in African American iconography that reaches back into generations.[12]

Henry Ossawa Tanner. *Christ and His Mother Studying the Scriptures,* c. 1909. Oil on canvas. Overall: 48 3/4 x 40 inches (123.82 cm x 101.6 cm.). Dallas Museum of Art, Deaccession Funds.

Henry Ossawa Tanner. *Daniel in the Lion's Den,* 1895. The Pennsylvania Academy of the Fine Arts, Pennsylvania. Archives.

While Du Bois's writing at the turn into the twentieth century was wholly dedicated to representing and promoting blacks in America, the relation of Tanner's biblical paintings to African American life is much more subtle.[13] For example, many viewers might miss the connection between his *Christ Learning to Read* and the trope of literacy that has long been central to African American arts. In Tanner's religious paintings, moreover, as in the spirituals described by Du Bois, "there breathes a hope —a faith in the ultimate justice of things. The minor cadences of despair change often to triumph and calm confidence."[14] This "calm confidence" can be seen in *Daniel in the Lion's Den* (1895), Tanner's first painting to win official recognition, in the form of a *Mention,* at the Salon. Within a darkened chamber the lonely figure of Daniel stands, head bowed and wrists bound, his lower half illuminated by a bright shaft of light that pierces his prison. Walking forward out of an amorphous darkness to share this spotlight is a majestic lion that ignores his lone human companion. For the initiated viewer, this exquisite scene of exile is illuminated by the hope of delivery, another important trope in African American religion, spirituals, and history. According to Albert J. Raboteau, Daniel was a favorite biblical character in the early black church, one of "the models, the analogues, reminding the slaves to hold on to their faith despite grief, doubt, and fear."[15] The messages of fidelity and hope that Tanner's painting evokes echo the ideas expressed in a powerful spiritual that voices the assurance of people of faith by asking, "Didn't my Lord deliver Daniel? Then why not every man?"

Many of Tanner's religious paintings also reflect the theme of the desolate journey, one that Du Bois also identifies in African American spirituals. The Sorrow Songs, he writes, "tell of death and suffering and unvoiced longing toward a truer world, of misty wanderings and hidden ways . . . mother and child are sung . . . fugitive and weary wanderer . . . rocks and mountains are known, but home is unknown."[16] Du Bois's haunting details are repeatedly evoked in Tanner's approximately fifteen different versions of *Flight into Egypt.* The fact that he painted this subject multiple times surely signifies the cultural and personal resonance of the image of wandering and release.[17] The tale of the Holy Family fleeing into Egypt is one of the biblical stories that for the slaves "gave form, and, thus, assurance to their anticipation of deliverance."[18] It was not, however, as privileged a text as the exodus of Israel from slavery to the Promised Land, which evokes a communal vision of freedom. Instead, Tanner's treatment of the themes of flight and redemption most often strikes a personal note, as the isolated individual or family awaits God's mercy. Paintings such as *Flight into Egypt* or *Daniel in the Lion's Den* reveal humanity in its darkest hour, just before the moment of glory.

Du Bois's description of the Sorrow Songs finds a visual analogue in the final version of *Flight into Egypt* (1935), with its three diminished travelers trudging across a desolate landscape that includes only a few spindly

Henry Ossawa Tanner. *Flight into Egypt,* 1935. Oil on canvas. 29 x 26 in. (73.7 x 66 cm). The Metropolitan Museum of Art, Marguerite and Frank A. Cosgrove Jr. Fund, 2001. (2001. 402a) Photograph, all rights reserved, The Metropolitan Museum of Art.

trees. The vast and eerie grotto-green sky casts its odd glow over the scene, which is relieved only by the hope of the half-risen moon and the glow emanating from the isolated family. Tanner's paintings of weary wandering are reminiscent of spirituals that advise "my brudder, you want to git religion, / Go down in the lonesome valley" or "Go in de wilderness / To wait upon the Lord."[19] *Flight into Egypt* can variously signify the weary wanderers of the Sorrow Songs, or the exilic condition of Tanner himself, who found peace and freedom only as an expatriate.

While Tanner's many versions of the *Flight* signify an undeniable link with his black religious heritage, they also attest to his desire to inscribe himself into the longstanding traditions of Western art by painting a scene with a history dating back to the fifth century. Tanner's biblical paintings filled a void in American artistic traditions. Since America had, for the most part, no strong tradition of religious visual imagery, it relied upon the word—be it written, spoken, or sung—to convey spiritual messages. However, over the previous fifteen hundred years, Europe had created in the service of religion countless examples of some of the most powerful visual art ever. Tanner, then, could allude to this lengthy Western canon and yet make something innovative and reflective of himself, his race, and his country.

It is significant that Tanner the artist was the son of an A.M.E. minister. Doubtless, many of the biblical scenes that he painted, which gave him comfort and manifested his richest talents, were part of the very same stories that, as a youth, he had heard his father lecture on and read. From his father and other black ministers Tanner seemed to imbibe another lesson: The Bible was only a point of departure for a sermon. Cognizant of preliterate traditions, including slave's spirituals, an effective African American preacher would elaborate on biblical stories and create parables that would resonate within his audience. This, too, was Tanner's way. His goal was not to illustrate specific biblical narratives with literary exactitude, but to suggest the inner lives of the men and women of the Bible, as he did in *Christ Learning to Read* and *Daniel in the Lion's Den*. In fact, when his painting *Two Disciples at the Tomb* (1905) was to be exhibited at a religious service dedicated to improving race relations, Tanner instructed the clergyman to use it "in any flight of the imagination that might add power to the subject in hand."[20] He hoped that his paintings might strike a harmonious chord of empathy within his fellow men and women, regardless of race, prompting thoughts and actions in accordance with Christ's teachings and revealing that every soul carried "a little of God" within it.[21]

Even as he acknowledged the importance of spiritual feeling in religious pictures, Tanner believed that mastery of artistic technique had to be present as well. His conviction of the importance of "color harmonies" makes clear his knowledge of fellow American expatriate James Abbott McNeill Whistler's theories of subjective visual poetry, musical analogy, and suggestive veils of color in the creation of art.[22] While this signals Tanner's alliance to the late-nineteenth-century Tonalist mode, it may owe something to his African American heritage as well. Spiritual melodies, Du Bois's "Sorrow Songs," were often in coded metaphor, creating oral pictures. The caller or soloist was expected to improvise his response freely, as the spirit moved him. Songs were never the same twice, and this was one of the few areas in life where an African American's subjective individual response and freedom of expression were validated. Thus, these two aesthetic strains, one European, one African American, reinforced each other in authorizing Tanner's own intensely personal poetic response to religion. As European as Tanner's paintings may be with respect to technique and religious visual traditions, when we view them through "an African American cultural poetics"[23] created by Du Bois, we can identify them as located squarely within a tradition of black American art.

When African American artistic forms attracted serious critical attention at the end of the twentieth century, the works of Tanner—and even, to some degree, Du Bois—were set aside in favor of those of later artists, who moved farther away from European influences. By conceiving and articulating a theory of African American cultural derivation, Du Bois has provided us the means to understand how Tanner's internationally acclaimed biblical paintings are connected to and informed by African American religious forms. Indeed, the productions of both men are deeply rooted in African American religious expression. Through Du Bois, we come to understand how both his and Tanner's art spring from the same cultural source.

A *Crisis* cover from 1925 highlights the linkage between Du Bois and Tanner and their aspirations to be international artists. This drawing depicts a young black man standing in the fields of the South, with a plow and a bale of cotton beside him.[24] He is dressed, incongruously, in a suit, and his gaze is directed up and to the left, to images of great black cultural figures. There are Tanner and Du Bois, as well as Frederick Douglass (1818–1895), the renowned abolitionist and author of *My Bondage and My Freedom* (1855), one of the most celebrated autobiographies in the English language. Next to Douglass is a man who is very likely Alexandre Dumas, *père*

Cover illustration by Albert Alex Smith of *The Crisis* (August 1925). Ilah Dunlap Little Memorial Library. The University of Georgia.

(1802–1870), the noted mixed-race French novelist and playwright (not to be confused with his famous namesake and son Alexandre Dumas, *fils* [1824–1895], also an author), and Paul Laurence Dunbar (1872–1906), the famed American poet; and on the far right there is Samuel Coleridge-Taylor (1875–1912), the talented British composer who, coincidentally, came to America and used the spirituals as the basis for some of his greatest works. This image grasps the importance of these men as sources of inspiration for the younger generation of African Americans. Du Bois, Tanner, and the others signify the possibility and potential of the black artist.

Women are notably absent in this vision of black artistic achievement. A likely candidate to be included among these luminaries would have been Francis Ellen Watkins Harper (1825–1911), whose 1893 novel *Iola Leroy* was the best-selling work of fiction by an African American writer in the nineteenth century. Another preeminent African American artist whose work ranked among those of the best American sculptors working in Rome in the third quarter of the nineteenth century was Edmonia Lewis (1854–?). Two more women sculptors who both studied in Paris merited inclusion: Meta Warrick Fuller (1877–1968) and Augusta Savage (1882–1961). This omission of female predecessors is ironic, considering the fact that Jessie Redmon Fauset (1882–1961), as literature editor of the *Crisis,* helped shape the Harlem Renaissance by nurturing and publishing the works of talented men and women, including poet and painter Gwendolyn Bennett (1902–1981). As an additional irony, Fauset's own novel *Plum Bun* (1928) features a black woman artist struggling for visibility and voice in an all-male, all-white art world.

Nevertheless, a complete picture of African American cultural production must include the recognition that Du Bois and Tanner were among the pioneering artists who blurred the artificial distinction between "high" art and black art at the turn into the twentieth century. When Du Bois makes the correspondence in *The Souls of Black Folk* between creations of "high art" and the preliterate art forms of the African American religious experience, he powerfully reveals this division to be as arbitrary and false as the color line. In this context, it is clear that, although Tanner turned from black genre paintings to biblical subjects, he never abandoned the topics and tropes long sacred to African American thought and art. Like the black preachers, who were instrumental to the formation of an African American sensibility, Tanner with his brush and Du Bois with his pen served as skilled cultural emissaries and stirring moral guides to send a redemptive message of self-worth, communal love, and trust.[25]

NOTES

1. This trope held sway as late as 1940 when Alain Locke addressed it in *The Negro in Art: A Pictorial Record of the Negro Artist and of the Negro Theme in Art* (Washington, DC: Associates in Negro Folk Education, 1940).

2. Locke was especially critical of Tanner, who, he thought, had "handicapped racially representative art." Ibid., 9.

3. Rayford Whittingham Logan, *The Negro in American Life and Thought: The Nadir, 1877–1901* (1954; repr. New York: Dial Press, 1997), xxi.

4. See chapter 10, entitled "Of the Faith of the Fathers," in W. E. B. Du Bois, *The Souls of Black Folk*, ed. Henry Louis Gates Jr. and Terri Hume (1903; repr. New York: Norton, 1999), 120. Du Bois first began to articulate the history of the African American church and its leaders in *The Philadelphia Negro: A Social Study* (1899), which Dan S. Green and Edwin D. Driver describe as "the earliest large-scale empirical study in the history of sociology" (*W. E. B. Du Bois on Sociology and the Black Community* [Chicago: University of Chicago Press, 1978], 113). The theories touched on in this study were expanded in "The Negro Church" (1903), also considered to be a groundbreaking work as "not only the first extensive, in-depth sociological study of African-American religion specifically, but . . . the first book-length sociological study of religion in general undertaken in the United States." See Phil Zuckerman, ed., *Du Bois on Religion* (Walnut Creek, CA: AltaMira, 2000), 109.

Du Bois considered contemporary black preachers to be descendents of the African spiritual leader transplanted in the American slave system who "found his function as the interpreter of the supernatural, the comforter of the sorrowing, and the one who expressed . . . the longing and disappointment and resentment of a stolen people." Ibid., 113.

5. Henry O[ssawa]. Tanner, "The Story of an Artist's Life, II," *The World's Work* 18.3 (1909): 11,662.

6. There are no known copies of Tanner's address, but a summary was published in a report on the Congress by Frederick Perry Noble, who wrote that "Professor Tanner (American) spoke of negro painters and sculptors, and claimed that actual achievement proved negroes to possess ability and talent for successful competition with white artists." Frederick Perry Noble, "The Chicago Congress on Africa," *Our Day* 12 (1895): 116.

7. Dewey F. Mosby, *Henry Ossawa Tanner* (Philadelphia: Philadelphia Museum of Art, 1991), 116.

8. W. S. Scarborough, "Henry Ossian [sic] Tanner," *The Southern Workman* 31.12 (1902): 665–66.

9. For a detailed discussion of these innovations, see chapter 5, entitled "Swing Low: *The Souls of Black Folk*," in Eric J. Sundquist, *To Wake the Nations: Race in the Making of American Literature* (Cambridge, MA: Harvard University Press, 1993), 457–539.

10. Du Bois, *Souls of Black Folk,* 155.

11. The sobriquet is from Clara T. MacChesney, "Poet-Painter of Palestine," *International Studio* 50.199 (1913): xi–xiv. Our essay takes the critical conversation on Tanner's religious themes in a new direction by situating him in a cross-disciplinary context with Du Bois that demonstrates how both artists partook of the "high culture" tenets of the day while retaining their own African American culture, which derives from religious expression. Besides Mosby, other contemporary art historians have examined Tanner's religious paintings in light of his personal beliefs, familial connections, and cultural milieu. See, for example, Sharon F. Patton, *African-American Art* (New York: Oxford University Press, 1988), 100–101; Jennifer J. Harper, "The Early Religious Paintings of Henry Ossawa Tanner: A Study of the Influences of Church, Family, and Era," *American Art* 6.4 (Autumn 1992): 68–85; Marcus Bruce, *Henry Ossawa Tanner: A Spiritual Biography* (New York: Crossroads Publishing Company, 2002); Alan C. Braddock, "Painting the World's Christ: Tanner, Hybridity, and the Blood of the Holy Land," *Nineteenth-Century Art Worldwide: A Journal of Nineteenth-Century Visual Culture* 3.2 (Autumn 2004), http://www.19thc-artworldwide.org/autum_04/articles/brad_print.html (accessed November 5, 2004). Tanner's work was often alluded to as poetic. See, for example, F. J. Campbell, "Henry O. Tanner," *Fine Arts Journal* (March 1911): 163–66.

12. The iconography of literacy—images of figures with books or pen in hand, faces in profile, and looking not down but outwards, as if in a moment of deep contemplation—served as visual representation of individual black accomplishment. Such images can be seen on frontispieces of books by African American authors dating back to Phillis Wheatley's *Poems on Various Subjects, Religious and Moral* (1773). Late-nineteenth-century photographs depicting two or more people with faces looking down towards a text seem to translate earlier iconography to capture a sense of African American group achievement. The narratives and fictions of numerous authors, from Frederick Douglass to Frances E. W. Harper to Richard Wright, include the motif of literacy as a means to truth and freedom. The theme of literacy is not as prevalent in painting, yet it continues to be a subject of interest to African American artists. See, for example, Jacob Lawrence's "The Library" (1960).

13. It was, however, discernable to a sensitive viewer like Booker T. Washington, who saw in them a resonance with the spirituals: "[H]e paints . . . with something of the spirit in which these same incidents are pictured in the old plantation hymns." Booker T. Washington, *The Story of the Negro: The Rise of the Race from Slavery,* vol. 2 (New York: Doubleday, 1909), 296.

14. Du Bois, *Souls of Black Folk,* 162.

15. Albert J. Raboteau, *Slave Religion: The "Invisible Institution" in the Antebellum South* (New York: Oxford University Press, 1978), 250.

16. Du Bois, *Souls of Black Folk,* 157, 160.

17. Note that flight is a major theme in both the secular and religious tradi-

tions in African American culture. Tales of the flying Africans, the history of the Underground Railroad, the migration of African Americans northward after Reconstruction, and the Old Testament story of the exodus of Israel out of the land of slavery that was a favorite text in the antebellum South—all these stories and histories resound with the message of escape and freedom. The isolated nature of the travelers in his multiple *Flights* also points to Tanner's own self-imposed exile in Europe.

18. Raboteau, *Slave Religion*, 312.

19. Ibid., 254.

20. Marcia M. Mathews, *Henry Ossawa Tanner: American Artist* (Chicago: University of Chicago Press, 1969), 239.

21. Ibid., xiii. See Jesse Ossawa Tanner's description here of his father's belief in the interdependence of man and God.

22. Tanner explicitly addresses these ideas by taking Whistler's most famous work, *Arrangement in Black and Grey: The Artist's Mother* (1871), commonly known as *Whistler's Mother*, as the basis for his own *Portrait of the Artist's Mother* (1897).

23. Sundquist, *To Wake the Nations*, 485.

24. For over twenty years Du Bois edited the highly influential *Crisis*, the journal of the NAACP and one of the major cultural vehicles for the Harlem Renaissance. This cover perhaps references depictions in antiquity of Cincinnatus, a Roman statesman who gained fame after being called from the plough and his farm in 458 B.C.E. to aid the Roman army, which was under siege. He assembled an army within fifteen days and in a single day, it was said, defeated the enemy. He then abandoned the reins of power to return to his land, and to earn a reputation for moral purity, selfless patriotism, and devotion to country. In the eighteenth century, American revolutionaries appropriated the iconography of Cincinnatus to associate Enlightenment ideals of citizenship, honor, service, nationalism, and moral behavior with General George Washington, who educated many of his slaves and liberated them in his will. It is possible that, inspired by the scholarship of early black classicists such as William Sanders Scarborough, Edward Wilmot Blyden, and William Henry Crogman, the 1925 *Crisis* cover intends similar connotations in reference to post-bellum–pre-Harlem African Americans. For more on George Washington as Cincinnatus, see Garry Wills, *Cincinnatus: George Washington and the Enlightenment* (New York: Doubleday, 1984), 36, 228, 234.

25. Eugene D. Genovese presents an in-depth discussion of the black preacher's leadership in his *Roll, Jordan, Roll: The World the Slaves Made* (New York: Pantheon, 1974). See also Dolan Hubbard, who writes of "the preacher-as-creator" in his study entitled *The Sermon and the African American Literary Imagination* (Columbia: University of Missouri Press, 1994), 12.

Chapter 15

The Folk, the School, and the Marketplace
Locations of Culture in The Souls of Black Folk

Andrew J. Scheiber

Historian, sociologist, novelist, political activist—W. E. B. Du Bois has worn many hats as a culture worker in the American and African American intellectual tradition. What is not widely acknowledged, however, is his formulation in his early writings of a theory of the relationship between culture and capital that in some ways anticipates more recent insights in cultural theory and cultural studies. This essay will attempt to elucidate this relationship, paying attention to the various spheres of ideological influence that intersect in it. While not entirely separable from one another, in Du Bois's analysis there are mainly three spheres of influence: (1) vernacular beliefs and practices, transmitted mainly through the habitus of a particularistic cultural community; (2) "high" or "learned" culture, preserved and communicated mainly through prestige institutions like the college; and (3) the values and practices that characterized American market capitalism at the century's turn and beyond.

Du Bois's image of the "wheel within a wheel" suggests both the simultaneity of these ideological spheres and the seeming hierarchy within which they exist with respect to one another. It also suggests that the points of contact between these spheres are sites of tension and conflict. Seen in this way, Du Bois's famous formulation of the black American's "double consciousness" is but the most trenchant symptom of a conflict in aims and values that lies unacknowledged at the root of American life. This conflict is best understood not in terms of race per se, or even in terms of differing zones of cultural production (such as that between vernacular and elite culture). Rather, in Du Bois's analysis, the curse of conflicting aims arises from the animus between the culture of particularistic communities and the practices of market capitalism itself.

The Culture of the Folk

The "double consciousness" explored in chapter 1 of *The Souls of Black Folk* (1903) is customarily interpreted as a consequence of the asymmetry of value accorded African and European cultural expression in the American context. Du Bois describes the African American cultural aspirant as doubly alienated,

> confronted by the paradox that the knowledge his people needed was a twice-told tale to his white neighbors, while the knowledge which would teach the white world was Greek to his own flesh and blood. The innate love of harmony and beauty that set the ruder souls of his people a-dancing and a-singing raised but confusion and doubt in the soul of the black artist; for the beauty revealed to him was the soul-beauty of a race which his larger audience despised, and he could not articulate the message of another people. This waste of double aims, this seeking to satisfy two unreconciled ideals, has wrought sad havoc with the courage and faith and deeds of ten thousand people.[1]

These ideals are irreconcilable not because they represent contradictory values but rather because they are themselves *valued in contradictory ways,* and because the social power flowing from these valuations is distributed asymmetrically. What black folk know *as black folk* is considered worthless by the "white world"—and what the white world knows, though valuable, is off limits to black folk, a cultural property maintained within a preserve of community privilege and power.

Du Bois emphasizes the role of racial ideology in generating these barriers and the divided consciousness they impose upon American blacks. His remedy for this affliction of double consciousness appears at first glance to be the recognition of cultural parity between black and white: "This, then, is the end of his [the black person's] striving: to be a co-worker in the kingdom of culture, to escape both death and isolation, to husband and use his best powers and his latent genius." Moreover,

The history of the American Negro is the history of this strife,—this longing to attain self-conscious manhood, to merge his double self into a better
and truer self. In this merging he wishes neither of the older selves to be
lost. He would not Africanize America, for America has too much to teach
the world and Africa. He would not bleach his Negro soul in a flood of
white Americanism, for he knows that Negro blood has a message for the
world.[2]

But what are the elements of this "double self" that are to be merged, and
what might this have to do with the "latency" (as opposed to the fruition)
of black genius? And how are we to understand the opposition of such
terms as "white Americanism" with "Negro blood," especially in the context of an argument whose goal is to argue for the centrality of blacks to
American life? It seems clear that the terminology of race, though inextricably implicated in the psychic complex Du Bois analyzes here, ultimately
obscures rather than clarifies the issue.

I will stipulate at the outset that a phrase such as "Negro blood" is best
understood metaphorically rather than biologically. Though Du Bois's
views on the biological component of racial identity have been intensely
contested, the definition he puts forward in his 1897 essay "The Conservation
of Races" still probably makes the best reference point for this discussion.
There he defines a race as "a vast family of human beings, *generally* of common blood and language, *always* of common history, traditions, and
impulses, who are both voluntarily and involuntarily struggling together for
the accomplishment of certain more or less vividly conceived ideals of life."[3]

But this definition does not resolve all terminological problems. Even if
such terms as "black" and "white" (or their seeming correlatives "African"
and "American") are understood as cultural rather than biological mark-
ers, the question remains as to how one is to comprehend the significance
of the distinctions they mark. Are they parallel terms, to be understood as
separate but equal? Or is one enveloped within the other, as suggested by
Du Bois's metaphor of "the wheel within the wheel"? It seems clear that
even when invidious biological implications are removed, such terms as
"black" and "white" are highly unstable, concealing within themselves a
host of unacknowledged variables.

We may begin to clarify matters if we recognize that the "black folk"
whose soul-life Du Bois elucidates are specifically *southern* blacks, and, in
particular, the recently emancipated slaves and their offspring. If a "race" is
to be defined in terms of a common culture and condition, it is significant

that Du Bois has so little to say in *Souls of Black Folk* regarding the culture and condition of blacks of long tenure in the North—a species of experience he was more than familiar with. For rhetorical purposes that I hope will shortly become apparent, Du Bois chooses to treat the southern black, recently emancipated from slavery to peasantry, as a synecdoche of the larger and more varied cohort of Americans of African descent.

As a highly educated, northern, light-skinned black man, for whom the South comprised something like a foreign country, Du Bois's location of his own soul's voice in the collective expression of these southern "black folk" is a conundrum that vexes the very term "black." It is certainly true that Du Bois's immersion in this milieu, through his work with the post-bellum–pre-Harlem literacy corps, was for him a major personal and intellectual epiphany. The biographer David Levering Lewis recounts the transformative effects of "the voices of the dark submerged and unheard —those voices heard by [Du Bois] for the first time in the Tennessee back-country."[4] For both Du Bois and the nation, these southern black voices represent the return of the repressed (or at least the oppressed). The historical silencing and devaluation of these voices betokens a national psychic illness, born of historical amnesia and bad faith.

Du Bois's strategy for addressing this repression, and for correcting the disparity in cultural valuation that accompanies it, is to insist upon the centrality of black contributions to the culture of the nation as a whole. *Souls* is a veritable catalogue of the gifts and resources the southern freedmen and women bring to the table of national life: historical patience and forbearance; religiosity and reverence; storytelling and musical performance; and, perhaps most of all, a love and understanding of freedom, honed by the long period of captivity and slavery. Though the cultural property of a marginalized people, these ideals of life are fundamentally American:

> [T]here are to-day no truer exponents of the pure human spirit of the Declaration of Independence than the American Negroes; there is no true American music but the wild sweet melodies of the Negro slave; the American fairy tales and folklore are Indian and African; and, all in all, we black men seem the sole oasis of simple faith and reverence in a dusty desert of dollars and smartness.[5]

Du Bois's choice of adjectives here is telling: his emphasis on the "wildness," the "simple," and the folkloric suggests the *vernacular* or unlettered quality of the culture he is valorizing. As Shamoon Zamir has noted, Du Bois's rhetorical strategy in such passages cannily evokes his age's linkage of racial and national identities, even as he works to undo that linkage. By tapping into the then popular Herderian thesis that the culture of *der Volk* represents a "basis for national self-definition," Du Bois's citation of the Sorrow Songs suggests that "black experience, as it is embodied and voiced in the spirituals, must stand at the very center of any American national self-fashioning."[6]

The point, then, is not that the Sorrow Songs are *black* (which of course they are), but rather that they are *vernacular* in this honorific sense; they spring from a community whose culture is prior to and independent of the "modern" technological, economic, and political armature of the nation-state. Regardless of the personal journey that brought Du Bois, a highly educated northern black, to his embrace of the Sorrow Songs, it is clear that he is rhetorically positioning the culture of the southern freedman and woman in terms of the broader culture's habit of searching in "folk culture"—however ideally or romantically imagined—for "a set of values to place in opposition to the materialism and technological rationality the folklorists took to be the dominant spirit of their age."[7]

That Du Bois shared such dim views of the "dominant spirit of his age" is manifestly evident in other sections of *Souls*, as I shall subsequently discuss. And that he embraced black vernacular culture as at least a partial antidote to this soul-killing spirit is also clear. As suggested in "The Conservation of Races," the oppositional values that would confront the age's vulgarity and materialism are necessarily the indigenous products of a *community* (call it a "race" if one will) united not only in "common blood" but also by "similar habits of thought and a conscious striving together for certain ideals of life."[8] Key chapters in *Souls*—not just the introductory "Of Our Spiritual Strivings" but also those dealing with black religion and with the Sorrow Songs—develop this thesis, demonstrating not just the distinctive "ideals of life" particular to the African American experience but also the vernacular and indigenous origins of those ideals.

The problem, of course, is the seemingly essentialist equation of *black* with *vernacular* culture—a formula that, at least at first glance, appears to cede to the "white world" the properties of high or elite culture. This problem is perhaps most symptomatically encoded in the opening epigraphs Du Bois chooses for most of the chapters in *Souls*. Lewis suggests that the epigraphs, with their alternation of the Sorrow Songs with verses from canonical European poets like Browning, Byron, and others, illustrate the basic principle of equivalence between white and black, and that Du Bois "twinned them in this manner in order to advance the then-unprecedented notion of creative parity and complementarity of white folk and black folk alike."[9]

But culturally or historically speaking, a poem by Byron does not stand in the same relation to the "souls of white folk" as the Sorrow Songs, with their collective and anonymous authorship, do to the "souls of black folk." If the point is simply to argue for the "creative parity of white and black *folk* alike" (my italics), the appropriate complements to the Sorrow Songs would be drawn from a source all but unacknowledged in *Souls*—that is, the *vernacular* traditions of story, song, and worship particular to the *white* community, perhaps even that community of poor southern whites that exists alongside, and in frequent communication with, the world of southern blacks.

Thus the primary axis implied here is not one of race as such, but of differing orders of cultural production; the epigraphs do not "twin" the cultural heritage of southern peasant blacks with *white* culture, but rather with *lettered* or *learned* culture—something like the Arnoldian formula of "the best that has been thought and written."

The aforementioned curse of "double aims" afflicting the black artisan results from the enforced segregation of these different orders of cultural consciousness, just as much as from the social and civic discrimination between the races. Both are linked in Du Bois's analysis as tragic and unnecessary effects of an American racism that instantiates a cleavage between black and white on cultural grounds, stigmatizing vernacular or folk culture as the expression of allegedly "inferior" races and identifying lettered or learned culture with the white and the European. The integrated psyche that will resolve the accursed double consciousness, then, is not a marriage of white and black, but a marriage of vernacular and learned cultures that this racist cultural anatomy has made to appear as an improbable—if not impossible—miscegenation.

The Culture of the (Black) School

In implying a "parity" not only between white and black but also between vernacular and learned forms of cultural expression, Du Bois anticipates the critiques of "high-culture" hegemony that would characterize the coming century. But unlike the authors of such latter-day critiques, Du

Bois is far from convinced of the bankruptcy of the existing canons of learning and culture. For him there is no *necessary* contradiction between the ideals of life as conceived behind the Veil and as expressed in the learned cultural knowledge from which blacks have historically been barred. As I have argued above, this apparent contradiction is produced by a racist society's asymmetrical treatment of differing forms and locations of cultural production. And one of the effects of this asymmetry is a cleavage between vernacular and learned culture that impoverishes both.

In the case of the black artisan this impoverishment produces a conundrum of absence, of silence. As Du Bois puts it in "The Conservation of Races," "Manifestly some of the great races of today—particularly the Negro race—have not as yet given to civilization the full spiritual message which they are capable of giving."[10] But this failure is not for the lack of a message; elsewhere Du Bois insists that "Negro blood has a message for the world"[11] and implies that such spiritual messages are the gifts of the "folk." So why has that message not yet been fully expressed on the stage of world civilization and history?

The answer to this question lies in blacks' lack of access to higher learning. For Du Bois, vernacular culture represents a necessary but insufficient basis for the worldly existence of a people. Just as a community must recognize and value its own intrinsic resources (and, more to the point, the wider world must recognize and value them), that community must also engage with and participate in a broader human cultural heritage.

This idea is metaphorically underscored by Du Bois's use of the biblical image of the "wheel within the wheel," derived from the Old Testament prophet's vision of another nation-within-a-nation, that of the Babylonian captivity. In the Babylon of the American South, the ability of blacks to participate in this larger process of human civilization has been frustrated by "the social separation of the races."[12] This separation has a compound aspect, involving both the undervaluation of black culture by whites and the disbarment of blacks from access to the "learned culture" that has itself become encrypted in "the cabalistic letters of the white man."[13]

So while Du Bois acknowledges the *internal* effectiveness of such vernacular forms as the black church and musical performance to maintain cultural coherence and continuity, for him one of the most destructive effects of the Veil of Race is the way in which it denies black Americans the necessary resources to project their collective consciousness beyond their own circle. The problem for black Americans is one of claiming a more general civic and human identity without sacrificing the particular attributes imparted by their shared cultural and historical experience, since both are necessary for authentic participation in the "ideal of human brotherhood," "in large conformity to the greater ideals of the American Republic."[14]

For Du Bois the forum for addressing this twin problem is education—specifically, the black university, with its mission of pursuing and transmitting the common cultural resources of humanity, and of developing in African Americans a sense of their place in the world "beyond the veil" which does not at the same time deny their own cultural and historical experience:

> Above our modern socialism, and out of the worship of the mass, must persist and evolve that higher individualism which the centres of culture must protect: there must come a loftier respect for the sovereign human soul that seeks to know itself and the world about it. . . . Herein the longing of black men must have respect: the rich and bitter depth of their experience, the unknown treasures of their inner life, the strange rendings of nature they have seen, may give the world new points of view and make their loving, living, and doing precious to all human hearts.[15]

Most discussion of Du Bois's notion of the university has focused on its internal role within the black community, its responsibility "to furnish the black world with adequate standards of human culture and lofty ideals of life."[16] But equally important is its external mission of fully articulating what remains "naturally veiled and half articulate" in the form of the Sorrow Songs—the "great message we have for humanity."[17] The full expression of this message depends upon an integration of the lived and the learned, the vernacular and the lettered, which have been alienated from one another by the interposition of the Veil of Race. The black university is where this integration is to take place: it is the organ by which the shared life of a people finds its expression in the larger heritage of human thought and creativity, and which enables the African American artisan to become a "co-worker in the kingdom of culture."[18]

There are some difficulties with Du Bois's vision that must be acknowledged and, to the extent possible, countered. First among these is his apparent representation of learned or lettered culture in essentially classical and Western terms; he suggests, for instance, that "the riddle of existence" is to be found in "the college curriculum that was laid before the

Pharaohs, that was taught in the groves by Plato, that formed the *trivium* and *quadrivium*."[19] While such statements appear at first glance to identify a "universal" cultural heritage with European civilization, the implicit equivalence of "white" with learned culture is for Du Bois both as rhetorically convenient and as analytically vexed as the equivalence between "black" and vernacular culture discussed earlier.

Indeed, there is the question of how the products of ancient Greece and Egypt became assimilated as "white" (or, even more specifically, Anglo-Saxon) intellectual property to begin with—a question that Du Bois found himself returning to with some regularity. Six years before the publication of *Souls* he noted that "it is still a mooted question among scientists as to just how far Egyptian civilization was Negro in its origin; if it was not wholly Negro, it was certainly very closely allied."[20] And *Darkwater,* published in 1920, offers the observation that "the discovery of personal whiteness among the world's peoples is a very modern thing" and opines that "the ancient world would have laughed at such a distinction."[21] Furthermore, Caucasian Europe's claims of "greatness" as a civilization rest upon "the foundations which the mighty past have furnished her to build upon"—foundations which include "the iron trade of ancient, black Africa."[22]

It may be a stretch to argue that such comments fully anticipate Martin Bernal, whose 1987 book *Black Athena* ignited controversy for its hypothesis that the Western classical heritage is significantly black African in origin. But while *Souls* does not explicitly address the question of the African contributions to ancient Mediterranean culture, it insists (as Du Bois would continue to do in later works) that at the very least this heritage is not "white" in any exclusive or proprietary way; it cannot be construed as the birthright of *any* particular *race,* however the term might be understood. The learning of the ages, classical or otherwise, belongs as much to "the freedmen's sons [and, one presumes, the daughters] of Atlanta university" as to anyone. As he rhapsodizes in his conclusion to "Of the Training of Black Men," "I sit with Shakespeare and he winces not. Across the color line I move arm in arm with Balzac and Dumas, where smiling men and welcoming women glide in gilded halls. . . . So, wed with Truth, I dwell above the Veil."[23]

However utopian his evocation of this cultural fraternity might be, Du Bois theorizes its relationship to the vernacular culture of southern blacks neither as hierarchical nor simply egalitarian but, rather, dialectical. Although this is racial heresy for 1903, it is in other ways very much in keeping with his and his era's Hegelian habits of historiography. Even conservative race theorists like Count Arthur de Gobineau argued that great civilizations evolved out of the contact and interchange between differing peoples (though for de Gobineau the mingling of white and black suggested a degenerate miscegenation). When in "The Conservation of Races" Du Bois asserts that black Americans as a people are "the first fruits of this new nation, the harbinger of that black tomorrow which is yet destined to soften the whiteness of the Teutonic today,"[24] he is evoking this paradigm of dialectical progression and development. And in this paradigm learned culture is itself the fruit of contact and interchange between groups, each with its own distinctive ideals of life—a process that allows for "that transference and sifting and accumulation of the elements of human culture which makes for wider civilization and higher development."[25]

Thus Du Bois's valorization of black vernacular culture must be understood as dialectically intertwined with his belief that it must be brought into dialogue with the wider zone of cultural production embodied in the university, the better to develop and project its own particular message to the world. It is the integration of these two dimensions of cultural consciousness, even more than the integration of white and black, that stands in *Souls* as the basis for blacks' full entry into "the ideal of human brotherhood, gained through the unifying ideal of Race."[26]

In light of much of recent culture theory, Du Bois's rhapsodic vision of the fraternity of human civilization to be found "above the Veil" might appear at first glance as a sentimental extravagance. For instance, one could argue that the ancient syllabus of *trivium* and *quadrivium* so positively evoked by Du Bois is (and perhaps always has been) the property, if not of particular peoples or races, at least of particular social elites distinguished by their enjoyment of a wide variety of exclusive privileges, including educational ones. Rather than achieving its mission of uplifting others in the black community, the black university's production of a "Talented Tenth" might well in fact have the opposite effect, as such high-achieving individuals become, in John Guillory's words, "assimilated to the 'caste' of all those with an interest in preserving the rights and privileges of their acquired capital."[27]

However, Du Bois sees a distinction between the *contents and character* of the cultural capital conveyed in institutions of "higher learning" and the strategies and priorities of human investment that are implicit in the way such capital is transmitted and distributed through the educational apparatus. In his view the university is not destined to reproduce the inequalities of existing social relations; neither is it fated to reproduce the existing contradiction in the valuation of vernacular and learned cultures. But he does acknowledge that the university will betray its higher and proper aims so long as its mission is defined as the education of particulate *individuals*, without regard to their identities as members of a *people*.

Indeed, as I shall shortly discuss, the idea that the end of education is merely to endow the individual with competitive advantage in the marketplace is one that Du Bois regards as a peculiar aberration of modern capitalism. For the moment, though, it is important to note that Du Bois's vision of the university in *Souls* is not generic, but specific to the needs of a particular people. He is not talking about scholarships to Harvard for the children of the southern freedmen and women, a practice that surely is susceptible to the criticisms alluded to above. Rather, he is speaking of specifically *black* institutions of higher learning, whose blackness consists less in the Africanicity of their curricula than in their organic relationship to the larger life and interests of the group.

The black university, and its relationship to the larger cultural and political processes within which it is to operate, must be developed in cognizance of a proper understanding of the body politic not as an aggregation of *individuals* but rather as a dynamic interaction of *cultures* or *peoples*. Whether we are speaking in terms of the nation or of humankind in general, the fundamental *unit*, as the imagining and realization of "vividly conceived ideals of life" is concerned, is not the individual but the collective. This is a "patent fact of human history," Du Bois says, that those "reared and trained under the individualistic philosophy of the Declaration of Independence and the laissez-faire philosophy of Adam Smith are loath to see and loath to acknowledge."[28]

This mission of the university itself must be conceived in light of this "patent fact": "We are training not isolated men but a living group of men, —nay, a group within a group. And the final product of our training must be neither a psychologist nor a brickmason, but a man. And to make men, we must have ideals, broad, pure, and inspiring ends of living,—not sordid money-getting."[29] The goal of the university is not the horizontal integration of a *caste*, composed of high-achieving individuals united in their distinction above their fellows, but the vertical integration of a *community*, whose total culture embraces the lived and the learned—a goal to be achieved "by founding the common school on the university, and the industrial school on the common school; and weaving thus a system, not a distortion, and bringing a birth, not an abortion."[30]

The Market as Culture

I think it is clear from my discussion thus far that Du Bois does not regard the animus between vernacular and elite culture as necessary. It is in his view an historically produced phenomenon, a consequence of the particular character of a society that confuses civic and economic value, whose ethical and political evolution have been distorted by practices that put a price on human gifts and human bodies, especially (but not exclusively) black ones. It is thus for him not simply not a matter of what Raymond Williams once characterized as the "centralized cultural dominance" that instantiates an invidious "distinction of areas and kinds of life" between the outlands and the metropolis, the primitive and the modern, the local and the national.[31] As is implied in the twinned epigrams that head his chapters, Du Bois is attempting to dissolve such invidious distinctions, even as he employs the rhetorical frameworks that enable them. The point is not that agrarian or vernacular culture is primary to metropolitan or learned culture (or the other way around), but rather that both are increasingly in thrall to the regime of values defined by market capitalism.

Williams himself defines this regime as "an amalgam of financial and political power which is pursuing different ends from those of any local community but which has its own and specific internal rationale"[32]—a characterization that aptly captures the gist of Du Bois's position in *Souls*. As I have been parsing it, in this work he is ultimately concerned not with a conflict between races or regions but with what he sees as a contradiction between the "vividly conceived ideals" of particular human collectivities and the "internal rationale" of the capitalist enterprise to which those collectivities are increasingly subjected. And this subjection does not only threaten the local and the vernacular; for Du Bois there is also an antagonism between the aims of the capitalist regime and the heritage of *learned culture*.

The trick is in capitalism's ability to make these two zones of culture see one another as rivals rather than as complements to one another. In fact, a fully integrated human and national personality, valuing both vernacular and learned sources of experience and wisdom, might serve as a source of effective resistance to this new market hegemony; but this integration is frustrated by the alienation of the lived from the learned—an alienation encoded, reinforced, and perpetuated by the racial alienation of black from white, of the inner world from the outer.

As we have seen, Du Bois's analysis of the relationship between these inner and outer worlds is both expressed and obscured by the problematical racial terms in which he necessarily formulates it. In particular there are differing, even contradictory, connotations that attach to the "white" world beyond the Veil. Sometimes it is associated with the culture of higher learning, of which Du Bois clearly approves; yet at others it looms as a sinister force, threatening to destroy whatever of value is to be found within the "little world" of the black community. Such contradictions point to the inadequacy and instability of Manichean racial categories in illuminating Du Bois's analysis and obscure what I believe to be the principal object of his critique in *Souls*: not the "white world" as such, but the set of beliefs and practices associated with market capitalism, the "dusty desert of dollars and smartness" that looms as the true threat to the health of black souls. Even while acknowledging the centrality of the racial problematic, chapters such as "The Wings of Atalanta" and "The Meaning of Progress" ultimately confront a vision of society in which racial and cultural identity are subordinated to a new, allegedly unifying set of norms derived from exchange values in a market society. Lewis notes that, for Du Bois, "The true spelling of this progress . . . was Mammon, the commercialization of ideas and institutions by *white and black people* [my emphasis] who knew only how to fix prices but nothing about values."[33]

It would appear then that the fundamental problem marking the dawn of the twentieth century is not between the races, or even between the cultures of the folk and the school. It is rather the situation of culture *as such* as it is rendered captive to the absolute horizon of market capitalism. For the Israelites of African descent, the face of Babylon is not white, but green and gold. As Du Bois remarks in the first chapter of *Souls*, "To be a poor man is hard, but to be a poor race in a land of dollars is the very bottom of hardships."[34] It is not simply poverty that he laments here, but the tension between the denomination of value assigned by a market society and alternative, nonmaterialistic denominations of value found in *both* vernacular and elite cultures—a problem that not even the advancement of material prosperity will ameliorate: "as the black third of the land grows in thirst and skill, unless skilfully guided in its larger philosophy, it must more and more brood over the red past and the creeping, crooked present, until it grasps a gospel of revolt and revenge."[35]

Most disturbing to Du Bois is the supplanting of former custodians of cultural value by those who embody mere economic achievement:

Neither the black preacher nor the black teacher leads as he did two decades ago, into their places are pushing the farmers and gardeners, the well-paid porters and artisans, the businessmen,—all those with property and money; to-day the danger is that these ideals [those embodied in the preacher and the teacher], with their simple beauty and weird inspiration, will suddenly sink to a question of cash and a lust for gold."[36]

It is significant that he introduces one of his major tropes for the black community—the "wheel within the wheel"—in the context not of racial politics but of economics, in the chapter "The Wings of Atalanta." In this section of *Souls* Du Bois argues that wealth is not an end in itself, complains that public schooling has degenerated into lessons on how to make money, and laments that the outer world of what he calls "Mammonism" is invading the "the World Beyond the Veil"; even here, he notes, "the habit is forming of interpreting the world in dollars."[37]

The white world beyond the Veil is undergoing a similar degrading transformation, as white and black southerner alike experience the obsolescence of any value regime other than hard currency. The "dream of material prosperity as the touchstone of all success" is already "replacing the finer type of Southerner with vulgar money-getters; it is burying the sweeter beauties of Southern life beneath pretence and ostentation." In place of "the old ideal of the Southern gentleman,—that new-world heir of the grace and courtliness of patrician, knight, and noble," the South now "stooped to apples of gold,—to men busier and sharper, thriftier and more unscrupulous."[38]

This valorization of the southern planter, whose regime Du Bois himself later admits was "show and tinsel built upon a groan,"[39] seems striking in a book whose ostensible purpose is to examine and affirm the spiritual gifts of black freedmen and women. Similarly, his implicit endorsement of the feudal figures of "patrician, knight, and noble" seems a false note in a work that argues so strenuously for honoring the political rights of the former slaves through universal male suffrage. But in contrast to "the money-makers," who wish only to use the black person "as a laborer" and to reduce him to "semi-slavery," among "sons of the masters" there is at least a vestigial sense of honor that impels some to assist the black man in attaining his place as a civic and cultural equal.[40]

Du Bois's implicit pooling of the interests of freedmen and women with those of "the sons of the masters" seems shocking and counterintuitive, unless we grasp what I believe to be his central point: that "the souls of black folk" are not endangered by the "souls of white folk" per se. The fact is, all souls, black, white, and otherwise, are endangered by the way in which economic regimes of value—specifically those associated with market and finance capitalism—threaten to eradicate all other denominations of human value, whether they find their expressions in the Sorrow Songs or in the *trivium* and *quadrivium*.

For Du Bois the putative "freedoms" of capitalism have supplanted the bondage of southern feudalism with a tragic result: the apotheosis of a purely economic understanding of human activity and progress, one that paradoxically eviscerates the political and philosophical principles of Emancipation even as it claims to set them in action. This is the basis of his criticism of Booker T. Washington, who "so thoroughly did . . . learn the speech and thought of triumphant commercialism, and the ideals of material prosperity, that the picture of a lone black boy poring over a French grammar amid the weeds and dirt of a neglected home soon seemed to him the acme of absurdities."[41]

Du Bois does not object to the values preached by Washington: thrift, hard work, self-control—in sum, the classical ethos of continence that underlies the teachings of the *trivium* and *quadrivium*. What he does reject is Washington's representation of the human person so exclusively in terms of his or her existence as *homo economicus,* which ignores the "higher aims and ideals of life" expressed only through the collective consciousness of a shared culture. Such a definition of the human person is barely a step beyond the peculiar institution's definition of the human being as a material asset: if the plantation represents the enslavement of the body, commercialism represents the enslavement of the intellect and the spirit.

Thus, the fundamental problem is not American racism, but an instrumental attitude toward people, derived from the practices of a capitalist society, of which racism is a correlative and consequence. As "The Wings of Atalanta" suggests, this instrumental attitude is displacing not only the spiritual orientation embodied in the Sorrow Songs and other black vernacular resources; it is—and has been—destructive of the social, ethical, and intellectual resources embodied in the traditions of learned culture as well. The "ancient university foundations" of the Old South may already "have dwindled and withered under the foul breath of slavery"; but of more immediate concern is the desiccation they have suffered under the purported "freedoms" of a laissez-faire economy, as they fight "a failing fight for life in the tainted air of social unrest and commercial selfishness."[42]

Du Bois's critique of market capitalism is the key to understanding the cultural dynamic that inflicts a "double consciousness" upon the black artisan—and perhaps upon others who struggle to come to terms with the vernacular sources of their own identities and sensibilities. Capitalism devalues vernacular culture—in particular, black vernacular culture—because, in contrast to learned culture, it is not privileged *as a form of capital.* And learned culture is privileged not because its sentiments are superior but because its acquisition is by and large a product of the paid or expropriated labor of others—which is to say, it is capable of taking on the spectral character of a *commodity.*

But Du Bois stubbornly refuses to accept this complex as inevitable; he insists that defining the benefits of higher learning in terms of increased earning power or social status is a perversion rather than a fulfillment of the mission of the school: "The function of the university is not simply to teach bread-winning, or to furnish teachers for the public schools, or to be a centre of polite society; it is, above all, to be the organ of that fine adjustment which forms the secret of civilization."[43]

In the end, though, Du Bois's greatest fear is not the commodification of culture, but the configuring of commodity relations and practices *as a culture,* as a medium of universal value that trumps all other values, whether conveyed through the everyday culture of a people or through the learned culture of the school. The pursuit of financial security, necessary as it might be in instrumental terms, is not the same as the pursuit of the "higher aims of life," however those aims might be variously defined by various cultural communities. *The Souls of Black Folk* makes most complete and consistent sense when read in this context, as a plea for the preservation of human collectivities whose notions of value are not simply derivatives of prevailing economic processes.

The Souls of Black Folk, then, is as timely at the dawn of the twenty-first century as it was at the dawn of the twentieth. In our contemporary historical moment, in which economics has replaced civics as the primary description of our shared social life, his critique has lost little of its relevance. His description of an American culture increasingly in thrall to the regime of market ideology sounds more like a prophetic warning than the melancholy ranting of a displaced patrician intellectual.

Most salient in this critique is his insistence that, while culture may be a diverse, multilayered, and many-splendored thing, *capitalism is not a cul-*

ture: it will not raise our children or impart dignity and purpose to our labor. This is an insight that, of late, has ideologically united agents of high culture (artists, intellectuals, and their fellow travelers in the professoriate) with peoples whose local cultures are being threatened with absorption by the still-rising tides of a globalized economic rationalism. Perhaps, ironically, what Du Bois envisions in *The Souls of Black Folk* is coming true: the cleavages of double consciousness—between white and black, vernacular and learned culture—may well find mending in the process of resisting the very reign of capital that is at its root. A utopian scenario, perhaps— but certainly a more viable one than the capitalist utopia it, like *The Souls of Black Folk,* so bravely and hopefully confronts.

NOTES

1. W. E. B. Du Bois, *The Souls of Black Folk,* in *The Oxford W. E. B. Du Bois Reader,* ed. Eric Sundquist (1903; repr. New York: Oxford, 1997), 103.

2. Ibid., 102.

3. Du Bois, "The Conservation of Races" (1896), in Sundquist, *Du Bois Reader,* 40. Italics are mine.

4. David Levering Lewis, *W. E. B. Du Bois: Biography of a Race, 1868–1919* (New York: Henry Holt, 1993), 278.

5. Du Bois, *Souls,* in Sundquist, *Du Bois Reader,* 106.

6. Shamoon Zamir, *Dark Voices: W. E. B. Du Bois and American Thought, 1888– 1903* (Chicago: University of Chicago Press, 1995), 175.

7. Ibid., 173.

8. Du Bois, "Conservation," 41.

9. Lewis, *Du Bois,* 278.

10. Du Bois, "Conservation," 42.

11. Du Bois, *Souls,* in Sundquist, *Du Bois Reader,* 102.

12. Ibid., 150.

13. Ibid., 104.

14. Ibid., 106.

15. Ibid., 156.

16. Ibid., 151.

17. Ibid., 234; Du Bois, "Conservation," 42.

18. Du Bois, *Souls,* in Sundquist, *Du Bois Reader,* 102.

19. Ibid., 43.

20. Du Bois, "Conservation," 42.

21. Du Bois, *Darkwater,* in Sundquist, *Du Bois Reader,* 497–98.

22. Ibid., 503.

23. Du Bois, *Souls,* in Sundquist, *Du Bois Reader,* 157.

24. Du Bois, "Conservation," 44.

25. W. E. B. Du Bois, "The Development of a People," in *The Souls of Black Folk,* ed. David W. Blight and Robert Gooding-Williams (Boston: Bedford Books, 1997), 295.

26. Du Bois, *Souls,* in Sundquist, *Du Bois Reader,* 106.

27. John Guillory, *Cultural Capital: The Problem of Literary Canon Formation* (Chicago: University of Chicago Press, 1993), 47.

28. Du Bois, "Conservation," 40.

29. Du Bois, *Souls,* in Sundquist, *Du Bois Reader,* 145.

30. Ibid., 145.

31. Raymond Williams, *Writing in Society* (London: Verso, 1983), 230.

32. Raymond Williams, *Country and City* (New York: Oxford University Press, 1973), 292.

33. Lewis, *Du Bois,* 290.

34. Du Bois, *Souls,* in Sundquist, *Du Bois Reader,* 105.

35. Ibid., 100.

36. Ibid., 142.

37. Ibid., 141–42.

38. Ibid., 141.

39. Ibid., 164.

40. Ibid., 130.

41. Ibid., 123.

42. Ibid., 144.

43. Ibid., 144.

Topical List of Selected Works

Print Resources

Art and Photography

Edward Mitchell Bannister, 1828–1901. New York: Kenkeleba House, 1992; Stamford, CT: Whitney Museum of American Art at Champion; New York: distributed by Harry N. Abrams, 1992. An exhibition catalog.

Edward M. Bannister: A Centennial Retrospective. New York: Kenkeleba House, 2001. An exhibition catalog.

Library of Congress. *A Small Nation of People: W. E. B. Du Bois and African American Portraits of Progress.* With essays by David Levering Lewis and Deborah Willis. New York: Amistad/HarperCollins, 2003.

Mathews, Marcia M. *Henry Ossawa Tanner: American Artist.* Chicago: University of Chicago Press, 1969.

Mosby, Dewey F. *Henry Ossawa Tanner.* Philadelphia: Philadelphia Museum of Art, 1991.

Smith, Shawn Michelle. *American Archives: Gender, Race, and Class in Visual Culture.* Princeton, NJ: Princeton University Press, 1999.

———. *Photography on the Color Line: W. E. B. Du Bois, Race, and Visual Culture.* Durham, NC: Duke University Press, 2004.

Education

Anderson, James D. *The Education of Blacks in the South.* Chapel Hill: University of North Carolina Press, 1988.

Crummell, Alexander. "The Need of New Ideas and New Aims for a New Era." In *Civilization and Progress: Selected Writings of Alexander Crummell on the South,* ed. J. R. Oldfield. Charlottesville: University of Virginia Press, 1995. 120–33.

Jones, Jacqueline. *Soldiers of Light and Love: Northern Teachers of Blacks, 1865–1873.* Chapel Hill: University of North Carolina Press, 1980.

Laney, Lucy Craft. Vertical File. Georgia Historical Society. Savannah, Georgia.

———. Vertical File. Library of Congress. Manuscript Division.

———. Vertical File. Moorland-Spingarn Research Center. Washington, DC: Howard University.

McCluskey, Audrey Thomas. "We Specialize in the Wholly Impossible: Black Women School Founders and Their Mission." *Signs: Journal of Women in Culture and Society* 22.2 (1997): 403–26.

Murdy, Elizabeth-Anne. *Teach the Nation: Pedagogies of Racial Uplift in U.S. Women's Writing of the 1890s.* New York: Routledge, 2002.

Ronnick, Michele Valerie. *The Autobiography of William Sanders Scarborough: An American Journey from Slavery to Scholarship.* Detroit, MI: Wayne State University Press, 2005.

Gender and Sexuality

Giddings, Paula. *When and Where I Enter: The Impact of Black Women on Race and Sex in America.* 1st ed. New York: William Morrow, 1984.

Guy-Sheftall, Beverly. *Daughters of Sorrow: Attitudes toward Black Women, 1880–1920.* Brooklyn, NY: Carlson Publishers, 1990.

Hunter, Teresa W. *To 'Joy My Freedom: Southern Black Women's Lives and Labors after the Civil War.* Cambridge, MA: Harvard University Press, 1997.

Jenkins, Earnestine, and Darlene Clark Hine, eds. *A Question of Manhood: A Reader in U.S. Black Men's History and Masculinity.* Vol. 2, *The Nineteenth Century: From Emancipation to Jim Crow.* Bloomington: Indiana University Press, 2001.

Somerville, Siobhan B. *Queering the Color Line: Race and the Invention of Homosexuality in American Culture.* Durham, NC: Duke University Press, 2000.

Wallace, Maurice O. *Constructing the Black Masculine: Identity and Ideality in African American Men's Literature and Culture, 1775–1995.* Durham, NC: Duke University Press, 2002.

History

Conyers, James L., Jr. *Carter G. Woodson: An Historical Reader.* New York: Garland Publishing, 2000.

Foner, Eric. *Reconstruction: America's Unfinished Revolution, 1863–1877.* New York: Harper and Row, 1988.

Hine, Darlene Clark, Elsa Barkley Brown, and Rosalyn Terborg-Penn, eds. *Black Women in America: An Historical Encyclopedia.* 2 vols. Brooklyn, NY: Carlson Publishers, 1993.

Litwack, Leon F. *Trouble in Mind: Black Southerners in the Age of Jim Crow.* New York: Knopf, 1988.

Mossell, Mrs. N. F. [Gertrude]. *The Work of the Afro-American Woman.* Introduction by Joanne Braxton. 1894. Reprint New York: Oxford University Press, 1988.

Painter, Nell Irvin. *Exodusters: Black Migration to Kansas after Reconstruction.* New York: Knopf, 1977.

Sterling, Dorothy. *Black Foremothers: Three Lives*. 2nd ed. New York: Feminist Press, 1988.

Journalism

Bullock, Penelope L. *The Afro-American Periodical Press,* Baton Rouge: Louisiana State University Press, 1981.

Corrothers, James David. *The Black Cat Club: Negro Humor and Folk-Lore*. New York: Funk & Wagnalls, 1902.

Gilbert, Peter, ed. *The Selected Writings of John Edward Bruce, Militant Black Journalist*. New York: Arno Press, 1971.

Penn, I[rvine]. Garland. *The Afro-American Press and Its Editors*. Springfield, MA: Willey, 1891.

Vogel, Todd, ed. *The Black Press: New Literary and Historical Essays*. New Brunswick, NJ: Rutgers University Press, 2001.

Literary Criticism and Theory

Andrews, William L. *The Literary Career of Charles W. Chesnutt*. Baton Rouge: Louisiana State University Press, 1980.

Baker, Houston A., Jr. *Blues, Ideology, and African American Literature: A Vernacular Theory*. Chicago: University of Chicago Press, 1984.

Bruce, Dickson D., Jr. *Black American Writing from the Nadir: The Evolution of a Literary Tradition, 1877–1915*. Baton Rouge: Louisiana State University Press, 1989.

Carby, Hazel V. *Reconstructing Womanhood: The Emergence of the Afro-American Woman Novelist*. New York: Oxford University Press, 1987.

Christian, Barbara. *Black Women Novelists: The Development of a Tradition, 1892–1976*. Westport, CT: Greenwood Press, 1980.

duCille, Anne. *The Coupling Convention: Sex, Text, and Tradition in Black Women's Fiction*. New York: Oxford University Press, 1993.

Fabi, M. Giulia. *Passing and the Rise of the African American Novel*. Urbana: University of Illinois Press, 2001.

Foster, Frances Smith. *Written by Herself: Literary Production by African American Women, 1746–1892*. Indianapolis: Indiana University Press, 1993.

Goldsby, Jacqueline. "Keeping the Secret of Authorship: A Critical Look at the 1912 Edition of James Weldon Johnson's *Autobiography of an Ex-Colored Man*." In *Print Culture in a Diverse America*, ed. James P. Danky and Wayne A. Wiegand. Urbana: University of Illinois Press, 1998. 244–71.

Griffin, Farah Jasmine. *"Who Set You Flowin'?": The African-American Migration Narrative*. New York: Oxford University Press, 1995.

Hull, Gloria T. *Color, Sex, and Poetry: Three Women of the Harlem Renaissance.* Bloomington: Indiana University Press, 1987.

Jackson, Blyden. *A History of Afro-American Literature (1746–1895).* Vol. 1. Baton Rouge: Louisiana State University Press, 1989.

Kilcup, Karen, ed. *Nineteenth-Century American Women Writers: A Critical Reader.* Oxford, England: Blackwell, 1998.

McDowell, Deborah E. *The "Changing Same": Black Women's Literature, Criticism, and Theory.* Bloomington: Indiana University Press, 1995.

McHenry, Elizabeth. *Forgotten Readers: Recovering the Lost History of African American Literary Societies.* Durham, NC: Duke University Press, 2002.

Peterson, Carla L. *"Doers of the Word": Black Women Speakers and Writers in the North, 1830–1880.* New York: Oxford University Press, 1995.

Pryse, Marjorie, and Hortense J. Spillers, eds. *Conjuring: Black Women, Fiction, and Literary Tradition.* Bloomington: Indiana University Press, 1995.

Stepto, Robert B. *From behind the Veil: A Study of Afro-American Narrative.* 2nd ed. Urbana: University of Illinois Press, 1991.

Sundquist, Eric J. *To Wake the Nations: Race in the Making of American Literature.* Cambridge, MA: Belknap Press of Harvard University Press, 1993.

Tate, Claudia. *Domestic Allegories of Political Desire: The Black Heroine's Text at the Turn of the Century.* New York: Oxford University Press, 1992.

Literature

Andrews, William L., Frances Smith Foster, and Trudier Harris, eds. *The Oxford Companion to African American Literature.* New York: Oxford University Press, 1997.

Bennett, Paula Bernat, ed. *Nineteenth-Century American Women Poets: An Anthology.* Oxford: Blackwell, 1998.

Butcher, Philip, ed. *The William Stanley Braithwaite Reader.* Ann Arbor: University of Michigan Press, 1972.

Chesnutt, Charles Waddell. "Aunt Mimy's Son" and "The Dumb Witness." In *The Short Fiction of Charles W. Chesnutt,* ed. Sylvia Lyons Render. Washington, DC: Howard University Press, 1974. 153–63, 202–8.

———. *The Colonel's Dream.* New York: Doubleday, Page, 1905.

———. *The Conjure Woman and Other Conjure Tales.* Introduction by Richard H. Brodhead. 1899. Reprint Durham, NC: Duke University Press, 1993. 1–21.

———. *The Conjure Woman and Other Conjure Tales.* Ed. Robert M. Farnsworth. 1899. Reprint Ann Arbor: University of Michigan Press, 1969.

———. "The Future American: A Complete Race Amalgamation Likely to Occur." In *Charles W. Chesnutt: Essays and Speeches,* ed. Joseph McElrath Jr. et al. Stanford, CA: Stanford University Press, 1999. 131–36.

————. *The House behind the Cedars*. 1901. Reprint Athens: University of Georgia Press, 1970.

————. *The Journals of Charles W. Chesnutt*. Ed. Richard H. Brodhead. Durham, NC: Duke University Press, 1993.

————. *The Marrow of Tradition*. Ed. Robert M. Farnsworth. 1901. Reprint Ann Arbor: University of Michigan Press, 1969.

————. "Post-Bellum–Pre-Harlem." In *Breaking into Print: Being a Compilation of Papers Wherein Each of a Select Group of Authors Tells of the Difficulties of Authorship and How Such Trials Are Met, together with Biographical Notes and Comment by an Editor of the* Colophon, ed. Elmer Adler. 1931. Reprint New York: Simon and Schuster, 1937. 47–56.

————. *Stories, Novels, and Essays*. Compiled by Werner Sollors. New York: Literary Classics of the United States, 2002.

————. "*To Be an Author*": *Letters of Charles W. Chesnutt, 1889–1905*. Ed. Joseph R. McElrath Jr. and Robert C. Leitz III. Princeton, NJ: Princeton University Press, 1997.

————. "Tobe's Tribulations." *The Southern Workman* 29 (November 1900): 656–63.

Dunbar, Paul Laurence. *The Collected Poetry of Paul Laurence Dunbar*. Ed. Joanne M. Braxton. Charlottesville: University Press of Virginia, 1993.

————. *The Complete Poems of Paul Laurence Dunbar*. Introduction by William Dean Howells. New York: Dodd, Mead, 1944.

————. *The Fanatics*. New York: Dodd, Mead, 1901.

————. *In His Own Voice: The Dramatic and Other Uncollected Works of Paul Laurence Dunbar*. Ed. Herbert Woodward Martin and Ronald Primeau. Athens: Ohio University Press, 2002.

————. *The Love of Landry*. New York: Dodd, Mead, 1900.

————. Papers. Ohio Historical Society. Columbus, Ohio.

————. *The Sport of the Gods*. Introduction by William L. Andrews. 1902. Reprint New York: Signet Classics, 1999.

————. *The Uncalled, a Novel*. New York: International Association of Newspapers and Authors, 1901.

[Dunbar-Nelson] Moore, Alice Ruth. *Give Us Each Day: The Diary of Alice Dunbar-Nelson*. Ed. Gloria T. Hull. New York: Norton, 1984.

————. *Mine Eyes Have Seen. The Crisis* (1918): 271–75.

————. Papers. Special Collections. Morris Library. Newark: University of Delaware.

————. *The Works of Alice Dunbar-Nelson*. Ed. Gloria T. Hull. 3 vols. New York: Oxford University Press, 1988.

Dunbar-Nelson Moore, Alice Ruth, ed. *The Dunbar Speaker and Entertainer: The Poet and His Song*. Introduction by Akasha (Gloria) Hull. 1920. Reprint New York: G. K. Hall, 1996.

Gates, Henry Louis, Jr., Nellie Y. McKay, Frances Smith Foster, Richard A. Yarborough, et al., eds. *The Norton Anthology of African American Literature.* 2nd ed.
New York: Norton, 2004.

Griggs, Sutton E. *The Hindered Hand; or, The Reign of the Repressionist.* Nashville,
TN: Published by the author, 1905.

Harper, Frances E. W. *Iola Leroy; or, Shadows Uplifted.* 1892. Reprint Boston: Beacon Press, 1987.

Hopkins, Pauline E. *Contending Forces: A Romance Illustrative of Negro Life North
and South.* 1900. Reprint New York: Oxford University Press, 1988.

———. *The Magazine Novels of Pauline Hopkins.* New York: Oxford University
Press, 1988.

Johnson, James Weldon. *Along This Way: The Autobiography of James Weldon Johnson.* 1933. Reprint New York: Viking, 1973.

———. *The Autobiography of an Ex-Colored Man.* 1912. Reprint New York: Penguin, 1990.

———. *Black Manhattan.* Introduction by Sondra Kathryn Wilson. 1930. Reprint
New York: Da Capo Press, 1991.

———. *God's Trombones: Seven Negro Sermons in Verse.* 1927. Reprint New York:
Penguin, 1976.

———. *The Selected Writings of James Weldon Johnson: Social, Political, and Literary Essays.* Ed. Sondra Kathryn Wilson. 2 vols. New York: Oxford University
Press, 1995.

Johnson, Maggie Pogue. *Virginia Dreams: Lyrics for the Idle Hour, Tales of the Time
Told in Rhyme.* N.p.: John M. Leonard, 1910. New York Public Library. Digital
Schomburg: African American Women Writers of the Nineteenth Century.
http://digilib.nypl.org/dynaweb/digs/wwm9712/@Generic__BookView.

Kelley-Hawkins, Emma Dunham. *Megda.* Introduction by Molly Hite. 1891.
Reprint New York: Oxford University Press, 1988.

Moorer, Lizelia Augusta Jenkins. *Prejudice Unveiled: And Other Poems.* 1907.
Reprint Boston: Roxburgh, 2004. American Verse Project. University of Michigan. http://www.Hti.Umich.Edu/cgi/t/text/text-idx?

Sherman, Joan R., ed. *African-American Poetry of the Nineteenth Century: An
Anthology.* Urbana: University of Illinois Press, 1992.

Thompson, Clara Ann. *Songs from the Wayside.* In *Collected Black Women's Poetry,*
ed. Joan R. Sherman. Vol. 2. 1908. Reprint New York: Oxford University Press,
1988.

Thompson, Priscilla Jane. *Gleanings of Quiet Hours.* In *Collected Black Women's
Poetry,* ed. Joan R. Sherman. Vol. 2. 1907. Reprint New York: Oxford University
Press, 1988.

Washington, Mary Helen, ed. *Invented Lives: Narratives of Black Women, 1860–
1960.* 1st ed. Garden City, NY: Doubleday, 1987.

Lynching and Racial Violence

Allen, James, et al. *Without Sanctuary: Lynching Photography in America.* Santa Fe, NM: Twin Palms, 2000.

Dixon, Thomas. *The Clansman, an Historical Romance of the Ku Klux Klan.* New York: Grosset and Dunlap, 1905.

———. *The Leopard's Spots: A Romance of the White Man's Burden, 1865–1900.* New York: Grosset and Dunlap, 1902.

Dray, Philip. *At the Hands of Persons Unknown: The Lynching of Black America.* New York: Random House, 2002.

Goldsby, Jacqueline. *A Spectacular Secret: Lynching in American Life and Literature.* Chicago: University of Chicago Press, 2005.

Gunning, Sandra. *Race, Rape, and Lynching: The Red Record of American Literature, 1890—1912.* New York: Oxford University Press, 1996.

Page, Thomas Nelson. *Red Rock: A Chronicle of Reconstruction.* 1898. Reprint Boston: Gregg Press, 1967.

Stephens, Judith, and Kathy Perkins, eds. *Strange Fruit: Plays on Lynching by American Women.* Bloomington: Indiana University Press, 1998.

Wells-Barnett, Ida B. *Crusader for Justice: The Autobiography of Ida B. Wells.* Chicago: University of Chicago Press, 1970.

———. *Southern Horrors and Other Writings: The Anti-Lynching Campaign of Ida B. Wells, 1892–1900,* ed. Jacqueline Jones Royster. 1892–1900. Reprint Boston: Bedford Books, 1997.

Zangrando, Robert. *The NAACP Crusade against Lynching, 1909–1950.* Philadelphia: Temple University Press, 1990.

Music

Berlin, Edward A. *Ragtime: A Musical and Cultural History.* Berkeley: University of California Press, 1980.

Murray, Albert. *Stomping the Blues.* New York: Da Capo Press, 1976.

O'Meally, Robert G., ed. *The Jazz Cadence of American Culture.* New York: Columbia University Press, 1998.

———. *The Norton Anthology of African American Literature Audio Companion.* 2nd ed. New York: Norton, 2004.

Southern, Eileen. *The Music of Black Americans: A History.* 3rd ed. New York: Norton, 1997.

Politics, Culture, and Intellectual Thought

Baker, Houston A., Jr. *Turning South Again: Re-Thinking Modernism/Re-Reading Booker T.* Durham, NC: Duke University Press, 2001.

Cooper, Anna Julia. *A Voice from the South.* 1892. Reprint New York: Oxford University Press, 1988.

———. *The Voice of Anna Julia Cooper, 1858–1964.* Ed. Charles Lemert and Esme Bahn. Lanham, MD: Rowman and Littlefield, 1998.

Du Bois, W. E. B. *Black Reconstruction in America: An Essay Toward a History of the Part Which Black Folk Played in the Attempt to Reconstruct Democracy in America, 1860–1880.* New York: Russell and Russell, 1935.

———. *The Oxford W. E. B. Du Bois Reader.* Ed. Eric J. Sundquist. New York: Oxford University Press, 1996.

———. *The Philadelphia Negro.* Philadelphia: Published for the University of Pennsylvania, 1899.

———. *The Souls of Black Folk.* Ed. Henry Louis Gates Jr. and Terri Hume. 1903. Reprint New York: Norton, 1999.

Fabre, Geneviève, and Klaus Benesch, eds. *African Diasporas in the New and Old Worlds: Consciousness and Imagination.* Amsterdam: Rodopi, 2004.

Gaines, Kevin K. *Uplifting the Race: Black Leadership, Politics, and Culture in the Twentieth Century.* Chapel Hill: University of North Carolina Press, 1996.

Gates, Henry Louis, Jr. "The Trope of a New Negro and the Reconstruction of the Image of the Black." In "America Reconstructed: 1840–1940." Special issue, *Representations* 24 (Fall 1988): 129–55. Reprinted in *The New American Studies: Essays from Representations,* ed. Philip Fisher. Berkeley: University of California Press, 1991. 319–45.

Gatewood, Willard B. *Aristocrats of Color: The Black Elite, 1880–1920.* Bloomington: Indiana University Press, 1993.

Lewis, David Levering. *W. E. B. Du Bois: Biography of a Race, 1868–1919.* New York: Henry Holt, 1993.

Locke, Alain. *The New Negro.* New York: Albert and Charles Boni, 1925. Reprint New York: Atheneum, 1968.

Logan, Rayford Whittingham. *The Negro in American Life and Thought: The Nadir, 1877–1901.* New York: Dial Press, 1954. Reprinted as *The Betrayal of the Negro from Rutherford B. Hayes to Woodrow Wilson.* Introduction by Eric Foner. New York: Da Capo Press, 1997.

Mitchell, Michele. *Righteous Propagation: African Americans and the Politics of Racial Destiny after Reconstruction.* Chapel Hill: University of North Carolina Press, 2004.

Rampersad, Arnold. *The Art and Imagination of W. E. B. Du Bois.* New York: Schocken Books, 1990.

Smith, Susan Harris, and Melanie Dawson, eds. *The American 1890s: A Cultural Reader.* Durham, NC: Duke University Press, 2000.

Stansell, Christine. *American Moderns: Bohemian New York and the Creation of a New Century.* New York: Metropolitan, 2000.

Terrell, Mary Church. *A Colored Woman in a White World.* 1940. Reprint New York: Arno Press, 1980.

Washington, Booker T. *The Booker T. Washington Papers.* Ed. Louis Harlan et al. 14 vols. Urbana: University of Illinois Press, 1972–1989.

———. *Up from Slavery: An Autobiography.* Ed. William L. Andrews. 1901. Reprint New York: Norton, 1996.

Washington, Booker T., N. B. Wood, and Fannie Barrier Williams. *A New Negro for a New Century.* With an introduction by J. E. MacBrady. 1900. Reprint New York: Arno Press, 1969.

Zamir, Shamoon. *Dark Voices: W. E. B. Du Bois and American Thought, 1888–1903.* Chicago: University of Chicago Press, 1995.

Religion

Billingsley, Andrew. *Mighty Like a River: The Black Church and Social Reform.* New York: Oxford University Press, 1999.

Montgomery, William E. *Under Their Own Vine and Fig Tree: The African-American Church in the South, 1865–1900.* Baton Rouge: Louisiana State University Press, 1993.

Raboteau, Albert J. *Canaan-Land: A Religious History of African Americans.* Oxford: Oxford University Press, 2001.

Wheeler, Edward L. *Uplifting the Race: The Black Minister in the New South, 1865–1902.* Lanham, MD: University Press of America, 1986.

Woodson, Carter Godwin. *The History of the Negro Church.* Reprint Washington, DC: Associated Publishers, 1972.

Theater and Drama

Cotter, Joseph Seamon. *Caleb, the Degenerate: A Play in Four Acts: A Study of the Types, Castes, and Needs of the American Negro.* Louisville, KY: Bradley and Gilbert, 1903.

Hatch, James V., ed. *The Roots of African American Drama: An Anthology of Early Plays, 1858–1938.* Foreword by George C. Wolfe. Detroit, MI: Wayne State University Press, 1991.

Hatch, James V., and Leo Hamalian, eds. *Lost Plays of the Harlem Renaissance, 1920–1940.* Detroit, MI: Wayne State University Press, 1996.

Riis, Thomas. *Just before Jazz: Black Musical Theater in New York, 1890–1915.* Washington, DC: Smithsonian Institution Press, 1989.

Sotiropoulos, Karen. *Staging Race: Black Performers in Turn-of-the-Century America.* Cambridge, MA: Harvard University Press, 2005.

Electronic Resources (Databases, Web Sites, and CD-ROMs)

African American Biographical Database. Edited by Randall K. Burkett, Nancy Hall Burkett, and Henry Louis Gates Jr. Ann Arbor, MI: ProQuest Information and Learning.

African American Perspectives: Pamphlets from the Daniel A. P. Murray Collection, 1818–1907. Library of Congress American Memory. Washington, DC: Rare Book and Special Collections Division, Library of Congress. http://memory.loc .gov/ammem/aap/aapcoll.html/.

African American Poetry, 1750–1990. Ann Arbor, MI: ProQuest Information and Learning. CD-ROM.

African American Women Writers of the Nineteenth Century. The Digital Schomburg Collection. New York: New York Public Library/Schomburg Center for Research in Black Culture. http://digital.nypl.org/schomburg/writers_aa19/.

Black Literature, 1827–1940. Edited by Henry Louis Gates Jr. Ann Arbor, MI: ProQuest Information and Learning. CD-ROM.

The Church in the Southern Black Community. Documenting the American South. The University Library at the University of North Carolina at Chapel Hill. http://docsouth.unc.edu/church/.

The Digital Library of Georgia. Athens: University of Georgia. http://dlg/Galileo/ usg/edu.

Electronic Text Center. Charlottesville: University of Virginia Library. http://etext.lib.virginia.edu/collections/languages/.

First-Person Narratives of the American South, 1860–1920. Library of Congress American Memory. Washington, DC: Rare Book and Special Collections Division, Library of Congress. http://memory.loc.gov/ammem/award97/ncuhtml/ caption.html.

From Slavery to Freedom: The African American Pamphlet Collection, 1822–1909. Library of Congress American Memory. Washington, DC: Rare Book and Special Collections Division, Library of Congress. http://memory.loc.gov/ammem/ aapchtml/aapccap.html.

Images of African Americans from the Nineteenth Century. The Digital Schomburg Collection. New York: New York Public Library/Schomburg Center for Research in Black Culture. http://digital.nypl.org/schomburg/images_aa19/.

The New Georgia Encyclopedia. Athens: Georgia Humanities Council and University of Georgia Press. http://www.georgiaencyclopedia.org.

Films

The Black Press: Soldiers without Swords. Produced and directed by Stanley Nelson. San Francisco: California Newsreel, 1998.

Ida B. Wells: A Passion for Justice. Produced and directed by William Greaves. San Francisco: California Newsreel, 1989.

Jubilee Singers: Sacrifice and Glory. Directed by Llewellyn Smith. The American Experience Series. Boston: WGBH Educational Foundation, 2000.

The Rise and Fall of Jim Crow. Produced by Richard Wormser. San Francisco: California Newsreel, 2002.

This Far by Faith. Produced by June Cross. San Francisco: California Newsreel, 2003.

W. E. B. Du Bois: A Biography in Four Voices. Produced and directed by Louis Massiah. San Francisco: California Newsreel, 1995.

Wild Women Don't Have the Blues. Produced and directed by Christine Dall. San Francisco: California Newsreel, 1989.

About the Contributors

Barbara A. Baker is Associate Professor of English at Tuskegee University. She is the author of *The Blues Aesthetic and the Making of American Identity* and articles exploring African American musical manifestations in American literature. A participant in Tuskegee University's National Center for Bioethics and Research, she has received two grants from the NEH.

Paula Bernat Bennett is Professor Emerita, Southern Illinois University–Carbondale. She is the author of *Emily Dickinson: Woman Poet* and *Poets in the Public Sphere: The Emancipatory Project of American Women's Poetry, 1800–1900*. With Karen L. Kilcup, she is presently coediting a volume of essays on nineteenth-century American poetry for the MLA's *Options for Teaching* series.

Nikki L. Brown teaches at Kent State University. Her interests include U.S. women's history, twentieth-century African American women, and warfare and society. Her book, tentatively titled *The Clubwoman and the Doughboy: African American Women and World War I*, is forthcoming. She has earned a Woodrow Wilson National Foundation Fellowship and a Fulbright Junior Lecturing Award.

Robert M. Dowling is Assistant Professor of English at Central Connecticut State University. He has published essays on nineteenth- and early twentieth-century authorship. His book, *Slumming in New York: From the Waterfront to Mythic Harlem*, is forthcoming, and he is working on a book entitled *Critical Companion to Eugene O'Neill*.

Frances Smith Foster is the Charles Howard Candler Professor of English and Women's Studies at Emory University. Her numerous publications include *Written by Herself: Literary Production of African American Women*

Writers, 1746–1892, and *The Norton Anthology of African American Literature,* with Henry Louis Gates Jr., Nellie Y. McKay, et al. She is researching the way the early African American press defined and disciplined attitudes towards family, marriage, and morality.

Caroline Gebhard is Associate Professor of English at Tuskegee University. She has published essays on nineteenth-century American women writers and is working on a book on Paul Laurence Dunbar, for which she earned a 2002 NEH Faculty Research Grant. She is also coauthor with Gwendolyn S. Jones and Vivian L. Carter of a book in progress, *Invisible Legacy: The Women of Tuskegee, 1881–1981.* She was awarded an Alabama State Council on the Arts Grant to curate the exhibition, "African Visions/American Spirit: Edward L. Pryce," with Amy Bryan and Teresa Valencia.

Philip J. Kowalski is a Senior Fellow in the Department of English at the University of North Carolina–Chapel Hill. His research interests lie primarily in the areas of nineteenth-century American literature and American Studies. He is completing his dissertation on hereditarian rhetoric and home influence in the works of Horace Bushnell, Nathaniel Hawthorne, Harriet Beecher Stowe, and Edith Wharton.

Barbara McCaskill is General Sandy Beaver Teaching Professor (2005–2008) and Associate Professor of English at the University of Georgia. She was a 2004–2005 Augustus Anson Whitney Fellow at the Radcliffe Institute for Advanced Study, and a Fall 1999 Fellow at Harvard University's Du Bois Institute. She has coedited, with Suzanne M. Miller, *Multicultural Literature and Literacies: Making Space for Difference,* and edited *Running One Thousand Miles for Freedom; or, The Escape of William and Ellen Craft from Slavery.* She is writing a book about William and Ellen Craft and co-directs the Civil Rights Digital Library Initiative with Timothy B. Powell and P. Toby Graham.

Audrey Thomas McCluskey is Associate Professor and Director of the Black Film Center/Archive in Indiana University–Bloomington's Department of African American and African Diaspora Studies. She has published many journal articles on black women educators, and with Elaine M. Smith, she edited *Mary McLeod Bethune: Building a Better World—Essays and Selected Documents.* Her forthcoming works include *Frame by Frame III: A Filmography of the African Diasporan Image* and a collection on South African filmmakers. She is completing a manuscript on black women school founders, in which Lucy Craft Laney is the central focus.

Koritha A. Mitchell is Assistant Professor of English at the Ohio State University. Utilizing black feminist criticism, she centers her work on African American literature at the turn of the twentieth century. Mitchell is revising a manuscript on lynching drama written before 1935.

Carla L. Peterson is Professor of English at the University of Maryland and affiliate faculty of the Departments of Women's Studies, American Studies, and African American Studies. She has published *"Doers of the Word": African-American Women Speakers and Writers in the North, 1830–1880.* She is writing a social and cultural history of African Americans in nineteenth-century New York City, as seen through the lens of family history.

Rhonda L. Reymond is a Ph.D. candidate in art history at the University of Georgia, specializing in American art. Her dissertation is "A Religion of Beauty: Richard Morris Hunt, George W. Vanderbilt, and All Souls' Church." She won a Dean's Award, a Freeman Research Grant, and a University of Georgia Humanities and Arts Grant to support her research, as well as a fellowship to the Erasmus Institute.

Barbara Ryan is a member of the Scholars Programme at the National University of Singapore. With Amy M. Thomas, she coedited *Reading Acts: U.S. Readers' Interactions with Literature, 1800–1950.* Her book *Love, Wages, Slavery: The Literature of Domestic Servitude* covers the period 1810 to 1900.

Andrew J. Scheiber is Professor of English at the University of St. Thomas, Saint Paul, Minnesota, where he teaches nineteenth-century American literature, literary theory, and twentieth-century African American literature. His articles on nineteenth-century American writers have appeared in such journals as *Legacy, American Transcendental Quarterly,* the *Henry James Review,* and *Literature and Medicine.*

Gwendolyn DuBois Shaw is Associate Professor of the History of Art at the University of Pennsylvania. She was a 2003–2004 Fellow at the Radcliffe Institute for Advanced Study and is a Ford Foundation Postdoctoral Fellow. She has written *Seeing the Unspeakable: The Art of Kara Walker.*

Margaret Crumpton Winter is Assistant Professor of English at the California State University at Stanislaus. She has completed a manuscript entitled *American Narratives: Citizenship and Literature in the Age of Realism.* With Lorraine López, she is coediting a volume of essays on the works of Judith Ortiz Cofer.

Index

Addams, Jane, 185–186, 194

Africa, 23, 49, 50, 51–52, 53, 73n15, 134, 136, 139, 142, 165

African American culture: and Africa, 23, 49, 50, 51–52, 53, 73n15, 134, 136, 139, 142, 165, 233; and Anglo-European influences, 18; black folk culture, 12, 84, 134, 135, 136, 251, 253; black Bohemia, 117–121, 130; blues aesthetic in, 133–135, 136, 140–141; collaboration in, 9, 17–18, 19, 20, 22–28, 29–31; and conjure, 141, 142, 143; continuity of, 8, 9, 30, 32n21; contributions to American culture, 253; Creolized or hybrid nature of, 18, 50, 53, 134; Francophonic or Creole communities in, 21, 22; humor in, 134–135, 137, 142–144; invented traditions of, 37, 38–39, 40, 51; marriage of secular and sacred in, 106–107, 108, 109, 110; and the Middle Passage, 10, 19, 23, 30, 67; in Muslim communities, 18–21; and white "slumming" in, 118, 122–123, 126–128. *See also* American culture; Art; Education, black; Family, black; Language; Literature; Music; Press, the black; Religion, black

African Americans: activism of, 17, 21, 23, 28, 81, 83, 84, 107–108, 113n31, 207, 212, 213–216; associations of, 18, 26–27, 30–32, 84; black Creoles, 18, 21, 21–22,

173; black Creole clubs (night life), 124–125, 129; black manhood, 218–219, 221, 229n55; black women's club movement, 74, 81, 84, 199, 201, 215, 222, 228n42; blacks in the North, 23, 24, 25–26, 27, 28, 59, 62, 63, 65, 103, 118, 217, 219; blacks in the South, 10, 11, 12, 22, 79, 80, 81, 83–84, 101–103, 107, 133, 134, 135, 136, 139, 144 ; citizenship, 36, 37, 41, 42, 43, 47, 50, 107, 110, 189; colored aristocracy, 84, 103; in interracial marriages/relationships, 45–46, 47, 50, 51, 118, 122–123, 129; middle-class, 11, 63, 65, 74, 181, 182–183, 185, 187, 190, 193; migrations of, 4, 5, 65, 117, 118, 130, 212, 225n16; as "new issue" or post-slavery servants, 89–90, 91–92, 98; stereotypes of, 49, 84, 127, 140, 142–143, 152, 155, 160n6, 169, 174, 232. *See also* African American culture; American culture; Antilynching movement; Family, black; NAACP; "New Negro," the; Racial violence; Uplift; Women, black

Albert, Octavia V. Rogers, 6, 22

Allen, Carol, 85

Allen, Richard, 27, 29

A.M.E. Book Concern, 29. See also *Christian Recorder*; *Christian Review*; Press, the black; Religion, black

American culture: as culturally black, 135–136, 137; as "Creole," fusion of